BURN THE RULES: LEAD FROM WITHIN

BY CHET H RANI

BURN THE RULES

Lead From Within

CHET HIRANI

978-1-968944-00-1   (paperback)

For my wife Romi,
For my daughter Lana

The two who make every challenge worth it
and every success meaningful.

With love, always.

Contents

Introduction

> *"The most powerful leaders aren't those who command, they're those who inspire. And true inspiration begins within."*

This isn't a book about leadership in the traditional sense. You won't find corporate jargon or one-size-fits-all management strategies. Instead, this book is about leading from within, about discovering the energy, resilience, and clarity that already resides within you, and using them to shape your world.

BURN THE RULES

Leadership isn't confined to boardrooms or business titles. It's a mindset, a way of living, that influences how you show up for yourself and others. It's found in how you nav gate tough decisions, respond to setbacks, and inspire those around you, even in the quiet moments when no one is watching. Most people follow the rules they've been given. The ones who claim leadership have one look, one success, one path, and growth in one direction. This book is here to challenge that. You don't need to follow the rules. You need to burn them.

WHY THIS MATTERS

Leadership isn't about titles, authority, or ticking off skills on a resume. It's about how you respond, and how you operate when things get tough.

I've spent over 20 years in the corporate world, leading global test and quality teams in high-pressure environments. From scaling tech delivery at Tesco and Selfridges to heading quality for brands like Ted Baker, DHL and M&S, I wasn't just in the room, I was responsible for making sure what left the room actually worked.

I built teams from scratch, led multi-million-pound programs, and drove transformation across international functions. I worked directly with C-suite and senior stakeholders, often being the one calling out hard truths when delivery or risk was off track.

What I saw again and again: burnout, self-doubt, and the gap between what leaders know they should do and what they actually do under pressure. That gap isn't closed with more knowledge, it's closed by rewiring how you think, decide, and act in real time.

For years, I followed the rules about how leadership should look and how success should be earned. I watched others do the same, only to burn out along the way. Success without internal alignment, leads to frustration and exhaustion. But when you burn the rules and lead from within, everything changes. You build trust, take bold action, and create an impact on your own terms, professionally and personally.

But this book wasn't born in a boardroom. It came to life during the Dulux London Revolution, a 180-mile bike ride over two days.

It started just outside London on a cold, grey morning. No fanfare, just me, the bike, and a quiet discomfort I couldn't explain. I was carrying more than gear, years of pressure, burnout, and a need to prove something to myself. The route looped around the city, cutting through tough country terrain and iconic landmarks, finishing back where it started. Two days. All on my own.

By mid-day, I was already battling steep climbs and gears I barely knew how to use. My legs gave in before my mindset did. I also fell off the bike more than once. I limped into base camp at the end of Day One, physically wrecked. Day Two was survival. The doubt was loud, but quitting wasn't an option. Every mile stripped something back, the roles, the ego, the noise. What was left was one question: *Who am I when there's no one watching?*

That challenge broke me down physically, forcing me to rethink how I push through setbacks. I realised that leadership, whether in business, in life, or on a grueling road with nothing but your own will to keep you going, relies on five key states:

PLANNING, PRODUCTIVITY, PEOPLE, PROSPECT, AND PERFORMANCE

These became the 5 States of Optimisation, a framework I now used to help executives, entrepreneurs, and professionals operate at their peak.

That ride gave me more than pain and distance. It gave me perspective. Real leadership isn't about how loud you speak in a room, it's about what drives you when no one's clapping. When you lead from within, everything changes.

But the real test came off the bike.

A few years earlier, I was sitting across from a doctor who told me I had cancer. At that moment, everything froze. Career, plans, progress, gone. Later, they discovered it was Tuberculosis. Relief, yes, but also reality. I had been on autopilot, measuring success by outcomes. This forced me to look inward. What mattered now wasn't what I could *do*, it was how I could *lead* from within.

At the time, I was also a martial arts instructor. I still showed up for my students, every class, even when I was exhausted, even when my body fought back. Quitting wasn't just a bad option; it wasn't one at all. That's when I made the shift. I stopped listening to the rules: rest, recover, pause your life, and start listening to something else: the part of me that still wanted to lead.

So, what is leadership about?

It's not about waiting until you're ready. It's not about how you perform when things are smooth. Leadership is what happens in the moments no one sees, when your body's failing, when your career is off track, when fear sits across the table from you. It's what you choose to do next. Not reactively, but deliberately.

What happened after that? I didn't have clarity. I didn't have a plan. But I chose to move, not outward, but inward. I rebuilt it. I created Not Your Ordinary Coach. I refined the 5 States and started helping leaders close that gap between intention and action.

This book isn't about theory. It's about the shift, from following the script to leading from within.

That's why this book exists. It's not about theories or feel-good motivation. It's about real-world mental reprogramming. If you're ready to strip away the noise, take control of your energy, and operate at the level you were built for, then this is for you.

THE PURPOSE OF THIS BOOK

This book is your guide to that transformation. It's a roadmap for mastering the 5 States of Optimisation, a framework I designed to help you lead with purpose and achieve extraordinary results in all areas of your life. These five states—Planning, Productivity, People, Prospect, and Performance—are not just tools for professional success. They're the foundation of a balanced, fulfilling, and impactful life.

A QUICK PREVIEW OF THE 5 STATES OF OPTIMISATION

1. Planning State: *"Clarity turns chaos into confidence."*
   The foundation of all success. The Planning State helps you design a roadmap for your goals, align your energy with your priorities, and stop reacting to ife's demands.

2. Productivity State: *"Focus isn't about doing more—it's about doing what matters most."*
   The Productivity State ensures your actions are aligned with your purpose, helping you work smarter, not harder.

3. People State: *"Connection builds trust; trust creates teams."*
   The People State focuses on social awareness and collaboration, enabling you to build relationships that inspire loyalty and foster growth.

4. Prospect State: *"Relationships are the foundation of opportunity."*
   The Prospect State emphasises the importance of cultivating meaningful, trust-based relationships that open doors to new possibilities.

5. Performance State: *"Growth doesn't happen in comfort zones—it happens in the stretch."*

The Performance State is about continuous growth through reflection, learning, and pushing beyond your limits.

These states work together as a dynamic, cyclical framework that evolves with you. They guide you through challenges, support you in seizing opportunities, and help you sustain success over the long term.

WHO THIS BOOK IS FOR

This book isn't for everyone. If you're content with the status quo or comfortable staying in your comfort zone, that's okay—this may not be the book for you.

But if there's a part of you that knows you're meant for more, if you're ready to stop waiting for permission and start taking control, then this book is for you. It's for the leader who refuses to play by someone else's rules. It's for the person who's done following the script and is ready to create their own.

WHAT YOU'LL GAIN

This book is designed to inspire and equip you to:

- Harness your energy and focus: Learn to manage your time, priorities, and emotions effectively.
- Build meaningful relationships: Cultivate trust, empathy, and collaboration with the people around you.
- Navigate uncertainty with confidence: Develop resilience and embrace challenges as opportunities for growth.
- Achieve alignment in all areas of life: Align your actions with your values to create lasting impact and fulfillment.

Each chapter offers practical tools, personal insights, and actionable steps to help you integrate these principles into your daily life.

HOW THIS BOOK WILL TRANSFORM YOU

When you finish this book, you won't just understand the 5 States you'll live them. You'll feel the shift in your mindset, energy, and approach to leadership. You'll lead differently at work, at home, and in your personal relationships. Mostly, you'll stop asking for permission and start making the decisions that matter.

This isn't about quick fixes or motivational fluff. It's about real, grounded transformation. It's about throwing out the outdated playbook and building a new one—your own.

AN INVITATION TO BEGIN

Leadership isn't about having all the answers. It's about having the courage to challenge the ones you've been given.

As you go through this book, reflect deeply. Question old habits. Take bold action. Burn the rules that don't serve you. Because when you lead from within, you don't just change your results, you change your life.

Let's begin.

CHAPTER 1

Breaking the Boundaries of Your Comfort Zone

EXPERIENCING THE THRILL OF STEPPING BEYOND YOUR COMFORT ZONE

> *"True growth begins where your comfort zone ends."*

You're standing at the edge of a decision, staring at the invisible line between what's comfortable and what's possible. Maybe it's a career move, a difficult conversation, or a personal challenge you've been avoiding. You feel the pull to stay where it's safe, where the outcome is predictable. But deep down, you know that staying still won't take you anywhere new.

This chapter is for that exact moment, the hesitation before the leap. Because on the other side of that line isn't just change, it's the version of you that's been waiting to emerge.

True growth happens outside your comfort zone. When you step into the unknown, you discover new opportunities and untapped potential. It's not an easy path, but it's the one that transforms.

Section 1: My Personal Journey

"Every step outside your comfort zone is a step towards discovering who you really are."

Our comfort zones offer security, predictability, and ease, but they rarely offer growth. True transformation happens when we challenge ourselves, accept uncertainty, and step into spaces that test our resilience. For me, this realisation came through both personal and professional experiences, each teaching me the profound value of discomfort as a catalyst for growth.

CYCLING BEYOND LIMITS

When I decided to take on long-distance cycling, I didn't realise it would redefine how I understood resilience.

The 180 miles over two days, cutting through the English countryside, past rolling hills, steep climbs, and long, empty roads. It was beautiful, but it didn't matter how tired you were. It was grueling. Physically, mentally, emotionally.

I remember one stretch, somewhere deep in the Chiltern Hills. No spectators. No music. Just the sound of my breath, the chain grinding, and the hill that didn't seem to end. My legs were gone. My back was seizing up, and my mind? It was asking every question it could to get me to stop. *Why are you doing this? What's the point? No one would blame you for quitting.*

But something held. Not ego. Not pride. Just the decision to keep going. To see what was on the other side of that hill. That ride didn't just push my body, it exposed every excuse I'd been living with.

And that's where the real shift began.

Pushing past that moment of doubt, I found a strength I didn't know existed, the kind that only surfaces when you step beyond what feels safe. That ride taught me a simple but profound truth: the comfort zone may feel secure, but it's also where growth goes to die. Each mile was a testament to the idea that resilience isn't built in easy moments, it's forged in the face of challenges that stretch you to your limits.

RESTLESSNESS IN ROUTINE

For years, I leaned on the predictability of corporate life. The 5 AM early alarm. The packed train 7.30 AM into the city. Back-to-back meetings that filled the calendar but rarely moved the needle. I was good at it, leading teams, delivering results, hitting targets. I climbed fast. On paper, I had everything you're supposed to aim for.

But under all of that, something was off. I'd wake up, go through the motions, close the laptop at the end of the day, and feel like I hadn't really *done* anything that mattered. The wins felt hollow. The pace felt relentless. And the version of success I was living didn't feel like mine.

There was a restlessness I couldn't explain. Not loud. Just a quiet edge that kept saying: *this isn't it*. I didn't know what "it" was, but I knew I wasn't going to find it sitting in another meeting room talking in circles.

That's when I knew I had to break the pattern.

That restlessness became impossible to ignore. It was the same feeling I'd had halfway through that brutal bike ride, legs cramping, lungs burning, every part of me screaming to stop, but something deeper pulling me to keep going. To push through the discomfort. To see what was next.

So, when the news came that my role was being made redundant, and I didn't get a huge payout, I didn't feel panic or even disappointment.

I celebrated.

It was a Thursday morning. A short video call. "Your role is being made redundant." I nodded, closed the laptop, walked into the kitchen, and cracked open a bottle of champagne. Not because I was happy to lose a paycheck, but because I finally had space. Freedom. Permission, in a way, to build something that actually mattered to me.

I'd spent years delivering for someone else's vision. That moment gave me the chance to build my own. And I didn't waste it.

A LEGACY OF COURAGE: LESSONS FROM MY FATHER

Growing up, I watched my father, Manji, embody the courage to step into discomfort. He didn't follow the typical India-to-England story of chasing opportunity with the family's full blessing and support. He went against what was expected. He and my mother, Jaya, chose love over tradition, a love marriage in a culture that demanded arranged ones. And that decision came with a cost.

They left not just their home, but their safety net. It meant starting a new life without the backing of their families, no approval, no blessing, just the two of them choosing to build something their way. In our community, that wasn't just frowned upon, it was seen as a rejection of the rules.

But they did it anyway.

That's where I get my edge from. My no-nonsense approach. My refusal to follow a path just because it's familiar. I watched my parents take that risk, not for attention, not to prove a point, but because they believed in what they were building. That shaped everything for me.

It taught me early that real leadership isn't about fitting in. It's about standing firm in what you believe, even when no one's clapping. Especially then.

When I reflect on my own decisions, from transitioning careers to navigating personal challenges, I often think of my mother and father's resilience. Their courage inspired me to approach discomfort not as something to fear, but as a space for possibility and growth.

NAVIGATING DISCOMFORT IN LEADERSHIP

One of my most vivid memories of corporate life was leading a team through a major restructuring. The brief was clear, I was to streamline operations, make cuts, and realign teams. But nothing about it felt clean. Departments were out of sync. Morale was fragile. Everyone was waiting for answers I didn't yet have.

I felt the weight of it. I remember sitting in my home office late at night, elbows on the desk, head in my hands, asking myself, *Am I out of my depth? What if I get this wrong? What if the trust never comes back?*

There were easier options, delegate more, keep conversations surface-level, tick the boxes and move on. But I knew that wasn't leadership.

So, I leaned in. I had the hard conversations, even when I didn't have all the answers. I made sure people were heard, not just informed. And I followed through on what I said, every time, even if it was uncomfortable.

It didn't shift overnight. But gradually, I saw the alignment come back. The side conversations quieted. The energy lifted. And I began to rebuild trust, not because things were perfect, but because people saw I wasn't hiding.

Looking back, those nights of doubt and discomfort weren't moments of weakness, they were the making of my leadership. They taught me that growth doesn't come from avoiding pressure. It comes from staying in the room with it, and choosing to lead anyway.

LESSONS FROM THE JOURNEY

Each of these experiences reinforced a powerful truth: discomfort is a necessary ingredient for growth. Whether it's a grueling bike ride, a career pivot, or leading through uncertainty, every step outside your comfort zone reveals more of who you are and what you're capable of achieving.

Section 2: Breaking Free from the Familiar

"The hardest step is often the first; but it's the one that sets everything else in motion."

The hardest step in any journey is often the first one, that leap from what feels safe and predictable into the unknown. It's where uncertainty meets fear, and where doubt threatens to hold you back. Yet, it's also where transformation begins. Every meaningful change I've experienced, whether personal or professional, started with a single, daunting step. But what followed was always worth the risk.

WHY THE FAMILIAR FEELS SAFE (AND STIFLING)

The familiar provides comfort. It's predictable, easy to navigate, and free of surprises. But staying within its bounds comes at a cost. The safety of familiarity often limits potential, holding you back from achieving greatness. Breaking free requires courage, but it's in that discomfort that you discover new strengths, perspectives, and possibilities.

MY FIRST LEAP

Deciding to leave the predictability of corporate life to start my own business was one of the hardest decisions I've ever made. The steady income, defined roles, and daily structure, they were comfortable. They were familiar. But there was a pull I couldn't ignore. A restlessness that kept telling me: *You've done this long enough. Now build something of your own.*

I didn't have a roadmap. Just a decision. I stepped out of the system I'd spent over 20 years mastering, and into the unknown. The first steps into entrepreneurship were raw, and unstable. There were no guarantees. However, in that discomfort, I felt something I hadn't felt in years: clarity. Every uncertain step forward revealed possibilities I couldn't have seen from behind a corporate desk.

That decision became the foundation of *Not Your Ordinary Coach*, a business built on everything I'd learned, and everything the corporate playbook left out. I didn't want to just coach on performance. I wanted to challenge how leaders show up, think, and lead under pressure. The goal wasn't to fix people. It was to get them to lead from within.

One of my former clients, Jacqueline, was a senior executive at a multi-million-dollar tech company—transitioning into a completely new industry. She was sharp, accomplished, but rattled. The rules were different. The team culture didn't match what she knew. She worried she wouldn't keep up. It was the same uncertainty I had faced leaving corporate life. So, we got specific. We built strategies around her strengths, mapped what was transferable, and tackled the discomfort head-on. Slowly, things shifted. She adapted, and more than that, she reshaped the team around her. Confidence followed action.

Her transformation mirrored my realisation: the breakthroughs don't come from playing it safe. They come when you leave the script behind and decide to lead on your own terms.

BREAKING FREE: WHY THE FIRST STEP MATTERS

The first step is the catalyst for change. It may feel like the hardest moment, but it sets everything else in motion. Here's why:

- It Builds Momentum: Taking action, no matter how small, shifts you from inertia to progress.
- It Reframes Fear: Once you act, the unknown becomes less daunting, and confidence begins to grow.
- It Opens New Possibilities: You discover opportunities, strengths, and connections that weren't visible from the safety of the familiar.

PRACTICAL STEPS TO BREAK FREE FROM THE FAMILIAR

- Start Small:
  - » Identify one area in your life or work where you've felt stuck. What's one small, actionable step you can take today to move forward?
  - » Example in Action: If public speaking terrifies you, commit to speaking up in one meeting this week.
- Reframe Fear as Growth:
  - » Instead of asking, *"What if I fail?"* ask, *"What could I learn?"* This mindset shift transforms fear into a motivator.
- Celebrate Progress:
  - » Acknowledge each step you take, no matter how small. Progress, not perfection, is the goal.

THE COMFORT ZONE VS. GREATNESS

Greatness doesn't come from playing it safe. It lies in the moments when you risk failure, face discomfort, and stretch beyond your perceived limits. Each time you push past the familiar, you expand what's possible for yourself.

Section 3: Real-Life Challenges and Lessons

"Failure isn't the opposite of success. It's a part of the process."

Every challenge carries with it a lesson, and every failure is an opportunity to grow. My journey has been shaped by moments of discomfort, setbacks, and perseverance. These experiences not only taught me resilience but also reaffirmed that success is rarely a straight line, it's a series of ups and downs that ultimately shape who we are as leaders.

PUBLIC SPEAKING: FROM FEAR TO STRENGTH

It was in 2010 and the thought of speaking in front of an audience of 250 people was paralysing. My first attempt at public speaking was far from perfect: shaky hands, stammering words, a racing heartbeat that drowned out my voice. I stood on stage, eyes locked on the floor, convinced everyone could see straight through me. For a split second, I even thought about walking off mid-sentence and leaving the room entirely.

The fear was real. And for a while, I considered avoiding it altogether, turning down opportunities, keeping quiet in meetings, and staying behind the scenes. But I knew that wouldn't get me where I wanted to go. So, I did what I've always done when something scares me: I leaned in.

But I knew that avoiding discomfort wasn't the answer. I leaned in. I practiced relentlessly, attended workshops, sought feedback from mentors, and invested in a coach. Each time I spoke, I became a little more confident, learning to accept the nerves rather than fight them.

The defining moment didn't come when I stepped onto the stage, it came in 2022 when I was asked to speak.

I hadn't been chasing a TEDx Talk. In fact, it wasn't even on my radar. But someone approached me and said, *"You have an idea worth sharing with the world."* That one sentence stopped me in my tracks. It was unexpected, and honestly, uncomfortable. My instinct was to hesitate. The old fear of public speaking came rushing back. *Why me? What if I'm not ready?*

But I said yes.

That decision forced me to stop playing small. TEDx isn't like any other talk. It's not a slide deck or a casual conversation. Every word is measured. Every idea has to land. The preparation was intense, hours of writing, rewriting, rehearsing, cutting what didn't matter, and holding my nerve through the doubt.

The moment I stepped onto the red dot, everything shifted. I wasn't delivering a performance. I owned my story. And for the first time, I saw that the discomfort I used to avoid was actually the thing that gave the talk its power.

That moment didn't just change how I speak. It changed how I lead. It reminded me that fear isn't the signal to stop, it's the sign you're about to grow. Today, speaking is one of my strengths, whether it's a boardroom, a stage, or anywhere people need to hear the truth.

MARTIAL ARTS TRAINING: LESSONS IN DISCIPLINE AND RESILIENCE

My journey as a martial arts instructor taught me some of the most profound lessons about discipline, perseverance, and growth. Every belt I earned wasn't just a new colour, it was a symbol of breaking through limits I didn't think I could surpass.

The hours spent sparring, failing, and learning weren't glamorous. They were often frustrating and physically exhausting. But those hours mirrored the lessons of life: progress is messy but rewarding. Martial arts taught me that resilience isn't built in a single moment, it's built in the daily practice of showing up, even when it's hard.

One memorable moment was in July 2008, as I was preparing for a black belt grading. The physical demands were intense, and the mental challenge of staying focused during setbacks tested my limits. Going for my first degree was one test, but then I faced a different test, another level of intensity, and the mental and physical challenge raised my game each time when going for the second and then third degree. But crossing that threshold wasn't just a personal achievement, it was a reminder that perseverance pays off, not just in martial arts but in every area of life.

COACHING FAILURES: GROWTH THROUGH REFLECTION

Not every coaching session or business venture has been a success. In fact, one of my early attempts at launching a group coaching program failed to gain traction. I poured time, energy, and resources into it, only to be met with underwhelming results. I was devastated, questioning whether I had what it took to succeed.

But, instead of dwelling on the failure, I reflected on the experience. What went wrong? What could I have done differently? Through honest self-assessment, I realised I had overlooked the importance of understanding my audience's needs and tailoring the program accordingly. That experience became a cornerstone of my growth, teaching me that failure is often the best teacher when paired with reflection and adaptation.

THE COMMON THREAD: LESSONS FROM DISCOMFORT

Each of these experiences, whether public speaking, martial arts, or coaching, taught me that growth lies on the other side of discomfort.

Failure isn't a sign to stop, it's an invitation to reassess, adjust, and try again.

- Resilience: Keep showing up, even when progress feels slow.
- Adaptability: Use setbacks as opportunities to refine your approach.
- Courage: Step into discomfort. It's there where your greatest growth happens.

PRACTICAL TAKEAWAYS

1. Reframe Failure as Feedback: When faced with setbacks, ask yourself:
   - » *What did I learn from this experience?*
   - » *How can I apply this lesson moving forward?*
2. Commit to Consistency: Growth isn't about sporadic effort, it's about showing up consistently, even when the results aren't immediate.
3. Step into Discomfort: Identify one area where fear or doubt is holding you back, and commit to taking one small step toward it this week.

Section 4: Discovering Boundless Possibilities

"Opportunities multiply when you step beyond what you know."

Stepping beyond your comfort zone is not just an act of bravery, it is an invitation to explore new realms of possibility. It's like opening a door to a room you didn't even know existed, filled with opportunities that challenge you, excite you, and transform you. In my own journey, every time I've pushed beyond what felt safe, I've discovered not just professional growth but profound personal transformation.

STEPPING AWAY FROM THE FAMILIAR

When I transitioned from corporate life to coaching full time, I found myself questioning my decision a few months in. A predictable paycheck and clearly defined goals were hard to let go of. But I felt a pull, a belief that there was more waiting for me outside the confines of what I already knew. Taking that leap was terrifying, but it opened doors I didn't even know existed.

I've had the privilege of working with leaders across industries, helping businesses achieve transformative 10x results. These opportunities allowed me to contribute to meaningful change in organisations while refining my own leadership philosophy. Stepping out of the corporate world didn't just expand my professional scope, it redefined my sense of purpose.

PERSONAL GROWTH BEYOND PROFESSIONAL SUCCESS

Beyond professional gains, the personal growth I've experienced has been equally profound. One of my proudest moments was completing a 180-mile cycling challenge for Macmillan Cancer Support. It wasn't just about the physical endurance, though that was no small feat, but about the broader impact that stepping out of my comfort zone could create.

The ride raised significant funds for a cause close to my heart and inspired others to take on their own challenges. That experience reaffirmed a powerful truth: when you stretch your limits, you don't just grow—you create ripples that inspire growth in others.

WHY STEPPING BEYOND CREATES OPPORTUNITIES

1. Breaks Mental Barriers: Pushing yourself into the unknown helps dismantle self-imposed limitations, revealing what you're truly capable of achieving.
2. Expands Your Network: Venturing into new spaces introduces you to people, industries, and ideas that wouldn't have crossed your path otherwise.
3. Builds Confidence: Every challenge you overcome adds to your belief in your ability to handle uncertainty and adapt to change.

Serena Williams, one of the greatest athletes of all time, didn't stop exploring new possibilities after her tennis career. She launched successful ventures in fashion, philanthropy, and venture capital, applying the same resilience and drive that made her a champion. Her journey highlights that stepping beyond the familiar opens doors to boundless opportunities.

PRACTICAL STEPS TO DISCOVER BOUNDLESS POSSIBILITIES

1. Say Yes to the Unknown: Commit to one opportunity or challenge outside your comfort zone, even if it feels intimidating. For example:
   » Volunteer for a project in an unfamiliar area.

» Attend a networking event in an industry you want to explore.

2. Set Stretch Goals: Identify a goal that feels just out of reach, like learning a new skill, running a marathon, or starting a passion project.

3. Reflect on the Impact: After stepping into the unknown, take time to reflect on what you've learned, how you've grown, and the new opportunities that emerged.

THE RIPPLE EFFECT OF BOLD DECISIONS

When you step beyond what you know, you don't just transform yourself—you inspire those around you. Your courage and willingness to explore new possibilities create a ripple effect, showing others that the unknown isn't something to fear, but a space to grow.

Section 5: Practical Steps to Expand Your Comfort Zone

"The discomfort you feel is temporary, the growth it brings is lasting."

Expanding your comfort zone isn't about dramatic leaps, it's about intentional steps that challenge you without overwhelming you. Growth requires discomfort, but that discomfort is temporary. The lessons and strength you gain by stepping outside your comfort zone are lasting. Here's how you can start moving beyond what feels safe and familiar.

1. START SMALL: BUILD MOMENTUM THROUGH MANAGEABLE CHALLENGES

The journey of expanding your comfort zone begins with small, manageable steps. You don't need to tackle a massive challenge right away, start with something that feels slightly outside your comfort zone but still achievable. These minor victories build confidence and momentum for bigger leaps.

- Examples in Action:
  - » Speak up in a meeting where you'd typically stay silent.
  - » Volunteer for a new project at work that requires you to learn a new skill.
  - » Try an activity you've always avoided, like joining a fitness class or networking event.

I remember one of my first public speaking opportunities, instead of jumping straight into a large audience, I started with small, informal settings. Each successful attempt bolstered my confidence, preparing me for larger stages, including the TEDx Talk.

Practical Tip: Create a list of targeted challenges you can tackle in the next month. Check off each one as you complete it to track your progress.

2. REFRAME FEAR: TURN IT INTO FUEL FOR GROWTH

Fear is often seen as a warning to stop, but in reality, it's a signal that you're stretching your limits. Reframing fear as a natural and necessary part of growth helps you lean into it rather than retreat from it.

- Mindset Shift: Instead of asking, *"What if I fail?"* ask, *"What can I learn from this experience?"*
- Examples in Action:
  - » If you're nervous about giving a presentation, view it as a chance to develop your communication skills.
  - » When considering a career change, focus on the opportunities it could bring rather than the risks.

It started with a small lump in my neck. I told myself it was nothing, maybe stress, maybe a swollen gland. But it didn't go away. After a few days of pretending not to notice it, I booked the appointment. I sat in the waiting room, arms folded, trying to stay calm while my mind ran ahead: *What if it's serious? What if it changes everything?*

Fear gripped me the moment I heard the doctor say, "It's cancer." My mind raced. My body tensed. Everything froze.

Then came the whirlwind, scans, second opinions, waiting rooms, vague updates. But in the middle of all that noise, something surprising cut through—clarity. The kind that only shows up when everything else is stripped away.

I realised I had two choices: let the fear take over or use it as fuel. I chose the latter. By reprogramming my mindset, not with false positivity, but through focusing hard on what I could control and dropping what I couldn't.

That moment reframed everything I thought I knew about fear. It wasn't something to avoid. It was something to work with. Now, I see fear not as the signal to stop, but as the starting point for something bigger.

Practical Tip: The next time fear arises, pause. Write down what's triggering it. Then, list one positive outcome that could result from facing it head-on.

3. LEARN FROM OTHERS: DRAW INSPIRATION FROM THEIR JOURNEYS

Surrounding yourself with people who've stepped out of their comfort zones can inspire and guide you. Their stories of perseverance and growth show what's possible and provide valuable lessons for your own journey.

- Examples in Action:
  - » Attend events or join groups where people share their experiences of overcoming challenges, such as leadership seminars or storytelling workshops.
  - » Seek mentorship from someone who's taken bold steps in their career or personal life.
  - » Read biographies or watch documentaries about individuals who've pushed boundaries in their fields.

One of my greatest inspirations has been my parents. Watching them build a life against the wishes of others has taught me the value of courage and resilience. Their journey reminded me that stepping into discomfort often leads to extraordinary opportunities.

4. TAKE CALCULATED RISKS: BOLDNESS WITH PURPOSE

Risk-taking doesn't mean being reckless; it's about evaluating potential outcomes, preparing thoroughly, and then taking action with intention. Calculated risks push you outside your comfort zone while minimising unnecessary exposure to failure.

- Examples in Action:
  - » If you're considering starting a business, research the market, create a solid plan, and start small.
  - » When pursuing a new leadership role, assess your readiness, seek mentorship, and identify areas to develop.

The time that I was unexpectedly made redundant, it could have set me back. Instead, I saw it as an opportunity. Rather than scrambling for another corporate role, I bet on myself and built my coaching business from the ground up. It wasn't a blind risk. I had the experience, the skills, and the drive to make it work. That decision not only reshaped my career but also reinforced a key lesson: calculated risks aren't about playing it safe; they're about backing yourself with the right preparation and taking action despite uncertainty.

Practical Tip: Before taking a risk, ask yourself:
- » *What's the best possible outcome?*
- » *What's the worst probable outcome, and how would I handle it?*
- » *What's one step I can take today to move closer to this goal?*

5. REFLECT AND CELEBRATE: ACKNOWLEDGE YOUR PROGRESS

Every step outside your comfort zone is a victory worth celebrating. Reflection helps you understand what you've learned and how you've grown, while celebrating progress reinforces the habit of challenging yourself.

- Examples in Action:
  - » After completing a challenging project, write down three lessons you learned and one way you've grown as a leader.
  - » Celebrate small victories with a reward, whether it's treating yourself to a favorite activity or sharing your success with friends or colleagues.

After completing my 180-mile cycling challenge, I took time to reflect, not just on the physical accomplishment, but on the mental resilience it built.

One thing became evident: I could do hard things without needing everything to be perfect. The hills, the pain, the moments I wanted to quit, they didn't stop me. They clarified what I was capable of when I stayed focused and kept moving.

I also realised how often we overestimate the risk of starting and underestimate the cost of staying still. That ride forced me to move forward, one pedal stroke at a time, and that's how real change happens.

That reflection reinforced my belief that resilience isn't built in comfort. It's built in motion, under pressure, when you choose to keep going, anyway.

Practical Tip: Keep a "growth journal" to track moments when you step outside your comfort zone. Review it regularly to remind yourself of how far you've come.

THE COMPOUND EFFECT OF EXPANDING YOUR COMFORT ZONE

Each small step you take compounds over time, expanding what feels possible and redefining your limits. By consistently challenging yourself, you'll not only grow, but inspire those around you to do the same.

Section 6: Resilience in the Face of Setbacks

"Setbacks aren't roadblocks; they're stepping stones for growth."

Stepping out of your comfort zone comes with inevitable challenges. Failure isn't just a possibility, it's often a necessary part of growth. How you respond to setbacks defines not only your journey, but also your resilience. Building resilience allows you to face difficulties with strength, learn from mistakes, and adapt for future success.

WHY RESILIENCE MATTERS

Resilience isn't about avoiding failure; it's about accepting it as a learning opportunity. Leaders who build resilience:

1. Adapt to Change: They see challenges as opportunities to innovate rather than obstacles to overcome.
2. Inspire Their Teams: A leader's ability to bounce back motivates others to approach setbacks with courage and confidence.
3. Strengthen Their Perspective: Reflection on failure deepens understanding and sharpens decision-making for the future.

When I was working for Selfridges & Co, I faced a project failure that shook my confidence. Despite careful planning, the initiative didn't deliver the expected results. My first instinct was to retreat, to avoid further risk. But I knew that wasn't the path to growth. Instead, I reflected on the experience, asking myself:

- *What went well, even in failure?*
- *What could I have done differently?*
- *What lessons can I carry forward into my next challenge?*

By shifting my perspective from defeat to learning, I grew stronger. That experience taught me that failure is only final if you choose not to learn from it.

One of my clients launched an Online Human Resources business that failed within a year. Financial losses, operational hurdles, and unforeseen challenges piled up, leaving her devastated. But instead of retreating, she made a bold decision to analyse what went wrong. She sought mentorship invested in coaching, refined her strategy, and launched a second venture with renewed focus. This time, her business exceeded expectations, achieving long-term success.

The turning point wasn't avoiding failure, it was facing it with a mindset of growth and adaptation.

THE COMPONENTS OF RESILIENCE

- Reflection: After a setback, take time to reflect on what happened. Identify the factors that contributed to the outcome, both internal and external.
- Adaptation: Use the lessons from reflection to adjust your approach. This could mean refining a strategy, seeking additional resources, or improving communication.

- Perseverance: Resilience requires the courage to keep moving forward, even when the path ahead feels uncertain.

PRACTICAL STEPS TO BUILD RESILIENCE

1. Create a Post-Setback Routine: After experiencing failure, take these steps:
   - » Write down three lessons you learned from the experience.
   - » Identify one immediate action you can take to improve your next attempt.
   - » Share your reflections with a mentor or trusted colleague for additional perspective.
2. Normalise Failure in Your Culture: If you're leading a team, model resilience by sharing your own setbacks and how you've grown from them. Create an environment where failure is seen as part of the learning process, not a reason for blame.
3. Celebrate Progress, Not Perfection: Focus on incremental improvements rather than expecting flawless results. Recognising small wins helps maintain motivation and builds confidence over time.

Section 7: Exercises to Build Comfort Zone Awareness

"To grow, you need to stretch your limits intentionally."

Awareness is the first step to expanding your comfort zone. By identifying the boundaries of what feels safe and exploring ways to gently push past them, you unlock opportunities for growth. These exercises are designed to help you recognise your limits, reflect on your experiences, and take intentional steps toward expanding them.

1. JOURNALING EXERCISE: REFLECTING ON MISSED OPPORTUNITIES

"Reflection turns missed opportunities into lessons for growth."

Writing about your experiences helps you uncover patterns in your behaviour and gain clarity about what holds you back. Journaling isn't about judgment. It's about self-awareness.

- Challenge: Reflect on a recent moment when you avoided stepping out of your comfort zone. Write about:
  - » What stopped you? (e.g., fear of failure, self-doubt, uncertainty)
  - » What opportunities did you miss by not taking the leap?
  - » How might you approach a similar situation differently in the future?
- Example in Action:
  - » *"Last month, I avoided volunteering to lead a high-visibility project because I doubted my ability to handle the responsibility. Looking back, I see it as a missed opportunity to showcase my skills. Next time, I'll remind myself that growth comes from trying, not just succeeding."*

Practical Tip: Dedicate 10 minutes each week to journaling about moments of hesitation or growth. Over time, you'll notice patterns and gain insights that help you make more confident decisions.

2. WEEKLY CHALLENGE: INCREMENTAL GROWTH THROUGH SMALL GOALS

"Small, consistent steps create lasting change."

Breaking out of your comfort zone doesn't require grand gestures. Setting and achieving small weekly goals helps build momentum and confidence over time.

- Challenge: Each week, set one small goal that pushes you slightly beyond your comfort zone. Examples include:
  - » Speaking up in a meeting.
  - » Trying a new skill, like learning a piece of software or giving a short presentation.
  - » Initiating a conversation with someone you don't know well.
- Example in Action:
  - » *"This week, I'll ask one question during our team meeting. It's a small step, but it's an opportunity to contribute and build my confidence in speaking up."*

Practical Tip: Track your emotions before, during, and after completing the goal. Notice how initial discomfort gives way to a sense of accomplishment.

3. ROLE MODEL REFLECTION: LEARNING THROUGH INSPIRATION

"Great leaders leave clues—follow them to discover your path."

Observing how others step out of their comfort zones can provide inspiration and guidance for your own journey. Role models show what's possible and demonstrate strategies for navigating uncertainty.

- Challenge: Identify someone you admire who consistently pushes their limits, whether it's a public figure, a colleague, or a mentor. Reflect on:
  - » What actions or habits make them stand out?
  - » How do they handle fear, failure, or uncertainty?
  - » What lessons can you apply to your own life?
- Example in Action:
  - » *"I admire how my mentor, Anja, always volunteers for challenging projects. She views setbacks as learning experiences rather than failures. This inspires me to approach challenges with a similar growth mindset."*

Practical Tip: Share your reflections with the person if possible. A conversation about their experiences might uncover valuable insights you haven't considered.

4. MICRO-EXPERIMENT: BUILDING FLEXIBILITY THROUGH DAILY CHALLENGES

"Small experiments help you discover what's possible."

Micro-experiments are a fun and low-pressure way to explore new experiences. They also stretch your limits. They help you build adaptability and confidence by stepping into the unknown in manageable ways.

- Challenge: For one week, commit to trying one new thing each day. Examples include:
  - » Taking an alternative route to work.
  - » Trying a new cuisine or restaurant.
  - » Learning a new skill, like a software shortcut or a mindfulness practice.

- » Starting a conversation with someone outside your usual circle.
- Example in Action:
  - » *"Today, I'll take a different route home from work. Tomorrow, I'll try a type of food I've never had before. Each day, I'll document how these small changes make me feel and what I've learned."*

Practical Tip: At the end of the week, review your experiences and note any patterns. Which activities were most challenging? Which were the most rewarding?

THE COMPOUND EFFECT OF AWARENESS

These exercises aren't just about stretching your limits, they're about understanding them. By reflecting on your comfort zone and intentionally stepping beyond it, you'll build the self-awareness, confidence, and resilience needed for meaningful growth.

Section 8: Reflection

"Comfort doesn't protect you; it delays you. Growth only begins when you choose to move through the tension, not around it."

Stepping outside your comfort zone doesn't require a dramatic transformation overnight. It starts with recognising the quiet discomfort that tells you it's time for change. Sometimes it's the voice that questions the work you're doing, the routine you're stuck in, or the version of yourself you've settled into. Other times, it's the moment you're forced to pivot, by a setback, a challenge, or a decision that feels bigger than you're ready for.

The goal of this chapter wasn't to tell you what to do. It was to get you to *look closer* at what's keeping you stuck, and show you that the discomfort you're feeling isn't a sign to stop. It's a signal to move. Growth lives just beyond where things start to feel hard.

This section is about pausing long enough to ask the right questions, not to dwell, but to notice the patterns, the missed chances, the small wins, and the moments that changed you. Awareness is the first shift. Intention is the next. Use these reflections not as a checklist, but as a tool for clarity. You don't have to leap. You just need to take the first real step.

Reflection Questions

SECTION 1:

What's one step you can take today to move beyond your comfort zone? How might leaning into discomfort uncover new strengths or opportunities for growth?

SECTION 2:

When was the last time you did something that truly scared you? What's one step you can take today to break free from the familiar and move toward growth?

SECTION 3:

What's a recent challenge or failure that felt overwhelming at the time? How can you use the lessons from that experience to fuel your growth?

SECTION 4:

What's one opportunity outside your comfort zone that you've been hesitant to pursue? How might saying yes to it open doors to new possibilities?

SECTION 5:

What's one step you can take today to expand your comfort zone? How can you make it a habit to challenge yourself regularly?

SECTION 6:

What's a recent setback that challenged you? How can you use that experience as a stepping stone for growth rather than a roadblock?

SECTION 7:

Which of these exercises resonates most with you? How can you integrate it into your routine to build greater awareness of your comfort zone?

CHAPTER 2

The Compass of Leadership

ALIGNING LEADERSHIP WITH EMPATHY, AUTHENTICITY, AND SELF-REFLECTION

> *"Your true direction isn't always the loudest voice; sometimes, it's the quiet certainty in your heart. Align with it and let it guide you through the noise."*

You're at a crossroads, pulled between external expectations and the voice inside you that knows what truly matters. Leadership isn't just about making decisions; it's about knowing which direction aligns with your values, your integrity, and the impact you want to have.

The noise around you: deadlines, opinions, pressure, can make it easy to drift. But real leadership is about tuning into your own compass, the one that keeps you steady when distractions threaten to pull you off course.

This chapter is about finding that internal guide and using it to lead with empathy, authenticity, and clarity.

Section 1: Interactive Reader Challenge

"Apply the compass principles and see your leadership evolve."

Leadership growth isn't just about reading concepts, it's about actively applying them. This interactive challenge is designed to help you integrate the principles of the leadership compass empathy, authenticity, self-assessment, and gratitude into your daily leadership style. Over the next 30 days, you'll focus on one principle each week, building habits that create trust, connection, and self-awareness.

THE 30-DAY LEADERSHIP COMPASS CHALLENGE

Each week, you'll focus on a specific principle from the leadership compass. By devoting time to practice and reflecting on these principles, you'll gain deeper insights into your leadership style and its impact on your team.

WEEK 1: EMPATHY—BUILDING TRUST THROUGH UNDERSTANDING

"Empathy isn't just about hearing words; it's about understanding what's beneath them."

Your goal this week is to create opportunities to understand your team members on a deeper level. Empathy develops trust and connection, helping leaders align their actions with their team's needs.

- Challenge: Schedule daily one-on-ones with team members. During these conversations:
  » Ask open-ended questions like:
    · *"What's been going well for you lately?"*
    · *"Are there any challenges you'd like to discuss?"*
  » Focus on listening without judgment or interrupting.
  » Share one meaningful take away from each conversation to demonstrate your understanding.

Ask yourself—What insights did you gain about your team's needs, and how can you act on them?

WEEK 2: AUTHENTICITY–LEADING WITH INTEGRITY
"Authenticity inspires trust because it reveals the real you."

This week, focus on showing up as your true self. Authenticity isn't about perfection; it's about aligning your actions and words with your core values.

- Challenge: Share a personal story during a team meeting that highlights your values or a leadership lesson you've learned. For example:
  » Reflect on a time when you faced a challenge and how your values guide your decisions.
  » Invite team members to share their own stories, creating an environment of openness and mutual respect.

Ask yourself—How did sharing your story impact your connection with your team? What did you learn from hearing their stories?

WEEK 3: SELF-ASSESSMENT–REFLECTING FOR GROWTH

"Leaders who grow are leaders who reflect."

This week, focus on developing the habit of self-assessment. Reflection helps leaders align their actions with their goals and identify opportunities for improvement.

- Challenge: Dedicate a period of 15 minutes each day to reflect on your decisions and actions. Use the following prompts:
  - » *What went well today?*
  - » *What could I have done differently?*
  - » *Did my actions align with my values and goals?*
  - » *Solicit feedback from peers or team members to identify blind spots.*

Ask yourself—What patterns or insights emerged during your reflections? How will you apply these lessons to improve?

WEEK 4: GRATITUDE–CREATING POSITIVITY AND RECOGNITION

"Gratitude isn't a grand gesture, it's a consistent practice that strengthens bonds."

This week, focus on creating a culture of appreciation by recognising the contributions of your team members.

- Challenge: End each workday by acknowledging at least one team member for their efforts. Be specific in your praise:
  - » *"Thank you, Alex, for your attention to detail in the client presentation. Your preparation made a significant difference in how it was received."*

> » Consider writing a personal thank-you note or sharing their contributions during a team meeting.

Ask yourself—How did your team respond to your gratitude? What changes did you observe in morale or engagement?

TRACKING YOUR PROGRESS

Throughout the 30-day challenge, keep a journal to record your reflections, observations, and lessons learned. Use these questions to guide your entries:

1. *What impact did this week's principle have on my leadership and team dynamics?*
2. *How did practicing this principle change my perspective on leadership?*
3. *What habits do I want to carry forward?*

At the end of the challenge, review your reflections to identify patterns and growth areas. Consider sharing your journey with your team to reinforce the importance of these principles and encourage collective growth.

Section 2: Leading with Empathy

"Empathy isn't just about listening; it's about understanding the unspoken."

In the crazy hustle of the corporate world, empathy is often overshadowed by deadlines, targets, and the drive for immediate results. Yet, it is empathy that transforms a leader from merely competent to truly extraordinary. Empathy creates connections, builds trust, and inspires loyalty qualities that drive not only short-term outcomes but long-term success.

WHY EMPATHY MATTERS IN LEADERSHIP

Empathy is the ability to step into someone else's shoes and understand their feelings, experiences, and challenges. For leaders, this isn't just a soft skill, it's a strategic advantage. When leaders genuinely care about their people, they create a culture of psychological safety, where employees feel valued and motivated to give their best.

Without empathy, teams can feel disengaged, undervalued, and even resentful. But with it, they feel seen, heard, and inspired.

It was in 2007 when I was working at a Fintech company dealing with Equities and Retail Stock Broking when I led my first team. I was laser-focused on hitting numbers and meeting objectives. To me, success was about results, and I assumed everyone else felt the same. I was continuously striving to hit targets and be the best, almost forgetting about the people around me and not giving a thought about them, just being focused on the damn numbers. It wasn't until I noticed one team member's consistent underperformance—not turning up on time, losing focus, never getting a response in meetings, behavioural changes. Realising this is when I knew I had to rethink my approach.

My initial reaction was frustration. Why weren't they keeping up? But instead of reprimanding them, I asked a simple question: *"Is everything alright?"* That conversation revealed a series of personal challenges affecting their work. By offering support, flexibility, and resources, I saw their performance improve dramatically. This is all it took, and it wasn't a hard task. More importantly, our relationship strengthened. That moment taught me that leading with empathy isn't an expense, it's an investment in your people, your culture, and your results.

When Satya Nadella took over as CEO of Microsoft in 2014, the company was stuck in internal competition, losing ground to rivals, and failing to innovate. Morale was low. One of the first changes Nadella made wasn't to the product line, it was cultural.

Early in his tenure, Nadella was handed a memo recommending that an underperforming engineer be let go. Instead of following protocol, he reached out and met with the employee. What he found wasn't incompetence, but a highly capable person burned out after caring for a terminally ill parent while managing intense project deadlines. Nadella didn't talk about KPIs. He asked about their family. He gave the employee paid time off, redirected their workload, and brought in support.

That employee stayed. And thrived.

Nadella's empathy didn't just keep one team member from falling through the cracks. It signaled a shift from a culture of internal rivalry to one focused on collaboration and care. Microsoft's performance followed, share price tripled, innovation surged, and employee satisfaction hit new highs.

PRACTICAL WAYS TO LEAD WITH EMPATHY

1. Ask Open-Ended Questions: Create opportunities for team members to share their thoughts, feelings, and challenges. For example:
   » *"How are you really feeling about the project?"*
   » *"Is there anything I can do to support you better?"*

2. Listen Beyond Words: Pay attention to body language, tone, and unspoken cues. Often, what's not said can reveal more than what is.

3. Be Flexible in Solutions: Empathy doesn't mean lowering standards; it means finding ways to support individuals so they can meet expectations. Offer accommodations where possible without compromising accountability.

THE RIPPLE EFFECT OF EMPATHY

Empathy isn't just about one-on-one relationships; it shapes the entire organisational culture. A leader's empathetic actions ripple outward, inspiring teams to mirror those behaviours. This develops collaboration, innovation, and a shared sense of purpose.

Section 3: Staying True to Your North Star

"Distractions may glitter, but they rarely guide."

We live in a world of enticing opportunities and endless possibilities, staying true to your purpose your North Star is one of the hardest yet most critical aspects of leadership. It's easy to be pulled in multiple directions by ideas that seem promising, but not all opportunities align with your true values and goals. Leaders who remain steadfast in their alignment create clarity, focus, and sustainable success.

WHY STAYING ALIGNED IS ESSENTIAL

Your North Star represents your core purpose and values the guiding principles that shape your decisions and actions. When you stray too far from it, your leadership loses focus, and the energy you pour into distractions can dilute your impact. Staying true to your North Star provides:

1. Clarity in Decision-Making: Knowing what aligns with your purpose makes it easier to say no to distractions.
2. Consistency in Leadership: Teams trust leaders who act with conviction and avoid chasing shiny objects.
3. Sustainable Success: Efforts concentrated on aligned goals lead to greater long-term impact.

In 2021, I was approached with an exciting proposal to start a mastermind business. On paper, it seemed like the perfect opportunity—financially rewarding, high-impact, and intellectually stimulating. But as I began investing my time and energy, I noticed my core coaching practice suffering. The more I reflected, the clearer it became: this venture, while promising, didn't align with my deeper purpose of helping individuals grow through one-on-one coaching.

Making the decision to walk away wasn't easy. It required reflection, humility, and courage to admit I had veered off course as well as having my wife remind me too. But as soon as I realigned with my North Star, my focus and energy returned, a lowing my coaching practice to take to great heights. It was the flame I needed to be reignited. That experience taught me that staying true to your purpose sometimes means saying no, even to good opportunities, so you can say yes to the right ones.

Take the story of Sarah Robb O'Hagan.

In 2006, Sarah landed what many would call a dream job, global marketing director at Nike. Big brand, big title, big salary. From the outside, it looked like success. But within months, she realised she was off course.

Sarah had always led with boldness and instinct. But at Nike, she found herself holding back, trying to fit into a system that didn't align with her values. It drained her. One morning, after yet another meeting where she stayed quiet to avoid rocking the boat, she asked herself: "Is this what success looks like for me?" The answer was no.

So, in 2008, she left Nike, without a new job lined up. She took time to realign. Later that year, she joined Gatorade as President. The brand was struggling and losing relevance fast. But this time, Sarah led on her terms. She took risks, overhauled the product line, and repositioned Gatorade as a performance-focused brand. It worked. The G Series relaunch turned the brand around and became a case study in how to rebuild from the core.

She didn't stop there. After Gatorade, she went on to lead Equinox as President, then became CEO of Flywheel Sports in 2016. And in 2020, she took on the role of CEO at EXOS, continuing her mission to drive human performance through aligned leadership.

Her story is a powerful example: walking away from a big opportunity might feel like failure, but it can be the first step toward something more aligned, more powerful, and truer to you.

PRACTICAL STEPS TO STAY TRUE TO YOUR NORTH STAR

1. Define Your North Star: Reflect on your core purpose and values. What drives you as a leader? Write it down and revisit it regularly.

2. Evaluate Opportunities Through the Lens of Alignment: Before committing to a new project or idea, ask yourself:
   » *Does this align with my purpose?*
   » *Will it distract me from my core focus?*
3. Say No with Confidence:
   » Practice saying no to opportunities that don't align with your North Star, even if they seem exciting at the moment.

Section 4: The Role of Self-Assessment

"Leadership without self-assessment is like sailing without a compass; you're moving, but you might just be lost at sea."

Self-assessment is a habit that separates leaders who merely manage from those who inspire. It's the practice of pausing to reflect on your actions, decisions, and values, ensuring that you remain aligned with your goals and the needs of your team. Without it, leaders risk drifting off course, making decisions based on habit rather than purpose. With it, they gain clarity, perspective, and the ability to grow.

WHY SELF-ASSESSMENT IS CRITICAL

1. Aligns Actions with Purpose: Reflection ensures that your actions are guided by your core values and long-term vision.
2. Reveals Blind Spots: Self-assessment helps identify areas where improvement is needed, preventing small issues from becoming larger problems.

3. Develops Growth: By regularly evaluating your performance, you create opportunities to refine your leadership approach and adapt to changing circumstances.

I was 27. Still early in my career, still trying to prove myself. I had just been handed a major project, multi-million-pound budget, multiple teams across time zones, and way more moving parts than I'd ever managed before. Looking back, it was probably too big for me to handle at that stage. But I wasn't going to say no. I wanted to show I could deliver.

And for a while, I did. We hit milestones. Things moved. But cracks started showing, delays, confusion, missed handovers. It didn't go the way I pictured it. I was frustrated, and my first instinct was to blame the obvious stuff: the unrealistic timeline, the resource gaps, the cross-team miscommunication. I thought, *It's not on me.*

That went on for weeks until it clicked. No one else was going to own this. And if I kept pointing fingers, I'd never grow. So, I shifted. I asked myself the tough questions:

- What actually went well?
- What could I have done better?
- Did I empower the team or did I try to control everything?

What came up hit hard. I wasn't delegating properly. I hadn't been clear about expectations. I was holding onto too much, trying to avoid being seen as weak or unprepared.

That moment of reflection changed everything. It wasn't about beating myself up, it was about being honest. From there, I refined my leadership style. I became clearer, more direct, and more trusting of the people around me.

And that shift has stayed with me ever since.

When Tim Cook took over as CEO of Apple in August 2011, he was stepping into the shoes of Steve Jobs, arguably one of the most iconic leaders in business. The expectation was simple: continue the momentum. The pressure? Immense.

But Cook didn't try to become Jobs. Instead, he paused and assessed what kind of leader he needed to be. Not just for the company, but for himself. That reflection changed the course of Apple.

In his first year, Cook faced criticism for not being bold enough. There were questions about innovation. Analysts wondered if Apple had peaked. Inside the company, the leadership style had to shift. Jobs was known for intensity. Cook operated differently, more collaborative, more measured.

Then came the moment in 2014 that defined his leadership mindset. Following a wave of internal feedback and external media scrutiny after the Apple Maps fiasco, Cook made a bold move. He publicly acknowledged the mistake, apologized to customers, and encouraged users to try competitors' apps until Apple could fix its own. That kind of humility was rare in Silicon Valley.

Behind the scenes, it was a turning point. Cook initiated a company-wide review of how decisions were being made. He pushed for more cross-functional alignment. He promoted leaders who challenged assumptions rather than just followed orders. And he made space for inclusion, privacy, and sustainability to become core pillars of Apple's long-term strategy, not marketing add-ons.

By 2022, Apple became the first company to hit a $3 trillion market cap. But more importantly, Cook's style of reflective, values-driven leadership became a case study in how self-assessment isn't about slowing down, it's how you move forward with intention.

PRACTICAL STEPS FOR EFFECTIVE SELF-ASSESSMENT

1. Set a Reflection Routine: Dedicate time at regular intervals, either weekly, monthly, or after key projects to evaluate your leadership.

2. Ask the Right Questions: Use these prompts to guide your reflection:

   » *What went well, and why?*
   » *What could I have done differently?*
   » *How did my actions impact my team's success or challenges?*
   » *Am I modeling the values I expect from others?*

3. Incorporate Feedback: Seek input from trusted colleagues or team members. Self-assessment is most effective when paired with external perspectives that provide a fuller picture.

SELF-ASSESSMENT IN ACTION: A PRACTICAL EXAMPLE

Imagine completing a high-stakes project that involved multiple departments. Instead of moving directly to the next task, take 30 minutes to reflect. Write down three things that went well and one area for improvement. Share your reflections with your team, emphasizing lessons learned and actions you'll take to address challenges in the future. This transparency not only enhances your growth but also strengthens trust within the team.

Section 5: Leading with Authenticity

"Authenticity isn't a tactic; it's a way of being."

Authenticity is the cornerstone of effective leadership. It's about staying true to your values and showing up as your genuine self, even in the face of challenges. Authentic leaders inspire trust, build deeper connections, and create environments where people feel empowered to bring their whole selves to work. It's not something you perform, it's a way of being.

WHY AUTHENTICITY MATTERS IN LEADERSHIP

- Builds Trust: Teams follow leaders they trust. Authenticity demonstrates integrity, which is the foundation of trust.
- Builds Connection: When leaders are genuine, it creates a sense of safety and openness, encouraging collaboration and communication.
- Drives Resilience: Authenticity helps leaders stay grounded during tough times, allowing them to lead with clarity and confidence.

In 2014, I experienced one of the toughest periods in my career, I was leading a large transformation programme for the luxury brand Selfridges. There was pressure from above to hit delivery milestones no matter what. Timelines were tight, budgets had already been cut, and leadership wanted results on paper fast. The message was clear: cut corners if you have to, just make it look like progress.

Do I, or don't I?

That was the question I wrestled with for weeks. On the surface, the "smart" move was to play along—adjust the metrics, smooth over the risks, and keep the execs happy. People around me said I was being too rigid. Some didn't need to say a word—the looks said it all: *He won't last if he doesn't play the game.*

It was a moment that tested everything. And I'll be honest, I almost gave in.

But I kept coming back to what my parents taught me: integrity, humility, hard work. These weren't just nice values; they were the foundation of who I am. I knew that if I compromised myself now, I'd be building my career on something that wasn't mine.

So, I didn't bend. I was direct about the risks. I reset expectations. And while it wasn't the popular route, it was the right one. We delivered, slightly later, but with quality and accountability intact.

That moment reinforced something I now carry into every part of my leadership: if the process is built on honesty and clarity, the outcome will take care of itself. That's the kind of leader I want to be, and the kind that people trust when it really counts.

In September 2022, Yvon Chouinard, the founder of Patagonia, gave away his entire company.

Not sold. Not IPO'd. Given away.

At 83, he transferred 100% of Patagonia's voting stock to the Patagonia Purpose Trust, and all non-voting stock to a nonprofit called the Holdfast Collective, set up to fight climate change and protect undeveloped land. From that moment, every dollar not reinvested back into the company went to environmental causes.

This wasn't some polished exit strategy. Chouinard never wanted to be a businessman in the first place. He was a climber, a surfer, and a blacksmith. The business only existed because he needed better gear for his outdoor life. As Patagonia grew, he kept pushing back against convention, closing stores on election day, suing a U.S. president over public land, and running ads that said, "Don't Buy This Jacket."

His leadership style wasn't driven by quarterly earnings or shareholder returns. It was built on values. He ran a company that cared more about its footprint than its valuation. He built a brand people trusted because he didn't fake it.

So, when it came time to think about succession, the question wasn't, "How do I maximise profit?" It was, "How do I protect the purpose?" And he did exactly that—no big headlines, no ego, just action.

That's what leading with authenticity looks like: not theory, but practice; not safe, but real. Chouinard didn't just talk about values—he lived them consistently for over 50 years, even when it cost him.

And that's why people still talk about Patagonia, not just for their products, but for what they stand for.

PRACTICAL WAYS TO LEAD WITH AUTHENTICITY

1. Identify Your Core Values: Reflect on the values that define you. Write them down and ask: *Am I leading in alignment with these values?*

2. Show Vulnerability: Authenticity isn't about perfection. Be willing to admit mistakes, share lessons learned, and show your humanity. This builds trust and connection with your team.

3. Live Your Values Daily: Ensure your decisions, actions, and communication consistently reflect your values. For example:
   » If humility is a value, give credit to your team regularly.

» If integrity is a value, prioritise transparency, even in tough conversations.

THE RIPPLE EFFECT OF AUTHENTIC LEADERSHIP

Authenticity doesn't just impact you; it influences your entire team. When leaders model authenticity, they give their teams permission to do the same, creating a culture of trust, openness, and innovation. This creates a ripple effect, where authenticity becomes the norm rather than the exception.

Section 6: Gratitude as a Leadership Tool

"Gratitude isn't just an act; it's a mindset that transforms challenges into triumphs."

It's easy to focus on what's next and forget to appreciate what's now. Yet gratitude is one of the most powerful tools a leader can wield. It grounds you, shifts your perspective, and reminds you to celebrate the journey rather than simply chasing the destination. Beyond personal reflection, gratitude has the power to transform teams, build trust, and create a culture of acknowledgment.

WHY GRATITUDE MATTERS IN LEADERSHIP

- Boosts Morale: Employees who feel appreciated are more engaged and motivated to contribute.
- Strengthens Trust: Genuine gratitude reinforces a sense of value, deepening trust within the team.

- Encourages Collaboration: Acknowledging contributions develop a positive environment where people feel encouraged to share ideas and work together.

While I was working for Ted Baker, the demands of growth and targets consumed my focus. I was constantly looking ahead, trying to achieve the next milestone. During one particularly intense stretch, I realised I wasn't acknowledging the team's incredible efforts that made those milestones possible.

So, I decided to make gratitude a daily practice. Each evening, I wrote down one thing I was grateful for and shared it with my team when appropriate. Whether it was a small win, someone's extra effort, or simply their positive attitude, expressing that gratitude strengthened our relationships and built a culture where everyone felt seen and valued.

In 1987, Howard Schultz bought Starbucks when it had just six stores. Over the next two decades, he scaled it into a global brand, but not by chasing numbers alone. Schultz always said, "We're not in the coffee business serving people; we're in the people business serving coffee." That wasn't a tagline; it was the foundation of how he led.

He introduced benefits most retail workers never expected: healthcare for part-time employees, stock options, and education programs. In a high-turnover industry, this sent a clear signal: "You matter here."

When Starbucks hit a wall in 2008—with slowing sales and declining quality—he returned as CEO. Instead of chasing short-term fixes, he shut down every U.S. store for a few hours to retrain baristas. The goal wasn't better coffee; it was a connection. He wanted employees to remember why they did what they did. That one move cost millions in lost revenue but earned back their trust. It sent a clear message: quality and people come before profit.

That culture of gratitude built long-term loyalty: employees stayed longer, customers felt it, and the business bounced back stronger. By 2010, Starbucks had regained momentum—expanding globally while holding onto the values on which it was built.

PRACTICAL WAYS TO LEAD WITH GRATITUDE

- Make Gratitude a Habit: Start or end your day by identifying one thing you're grateful for—whether it's a team member's effort, a lesson learned, or progress made toward a goal.
- Recognise Efforts Publicly: A simple "thank you" during a meeting or an acknowledgment in front of peers can significantly boost morale.
- Celebrate Small Wins: Leadership often focuses on big outcomes, but recognising incremental progress creates momentum and reinforces positivity.

THE RIPPLE EFFECT OF GRATITUDE

Gratitude doesn't just benefit the individual practicing it; it transforms teams and organisations. Leaders who regularly express appreciation set a tone that encourages others to do the same. This creates a ripple effect, where gratitude becomes embedded in the culture, developing a sense of community, belonging, and shared purpose.

In 2013, HubSpot launched a simple initiative called *"Cheers for Peers."* It began as an internal shout-out tool where employees could thank each other for small wins—helping fix a bug, stepping in on a tough client call, or simply showing up with a great attitude.

What made it truly successful wasn't the tool itself, but the leadership using it consistently. Executives didn't sit above it. They joined in. Public appreciation wasn't saved for end-of-year reviews. It happened every day. The thank-you appeared in Slack channels, on dashboards, and even during all-hands meetings.

This wasn't just a feel-good feature—it shaped behaviour. People went out of their way to help each other, not for credit, but because they knew their efforts would be seen and valued. Gratitude became embedded in the culture rather than an add-on.

By 2018, HubSpot ranked consistently as one of the best places to work. Employee engagement scores were among the highest in tech. Turnover was low. Despite their growth, the culture remained personal: gratitude wasn't a campaign—it was how people operated.

When asked why it worked, their Head of People Ops replied, "People don't leave jobs; they leave environments where they feel invisible. We make sure that never happens here."

Section 7: Practical Tools for Leadership Alignment

"The right tools align your actions with your purpose."

Leadership alignment is about ensuring that your actions, decisions, and behaviours consistently reflect your core values and overarching vision. It's all too easy for leaders to get caught up in the demands of the moment and lose sight of their purpose. Practical tools and routines can help you keep grounded—ensuring that your leadership remains intentional and aligned.

VISION CHECK-INS

"Alignment begins with clarity of purpose."

Your vision is your compass—guiding every decision and action. Regular check-ins with your leadership team help ensure that your collective efforts stay on course. Without these touchpoints, even the most well-intentioned teams can drift from their mission.

After a challenging quarter, hold a meeting with your leadership team to revisit your company's goals.

Begin the meeting with an open-ended question such as:

- *"Are we still aligned with our mission, or have immediate priorities caused us to drift?"*
- *"What adjustments can we make to ensure our daily actions reflect our long-term vision?"*

These check-ins don't just realign your strategy; they also reinforce a shared sense of purpose across the team.

EMPATHY EXERCISES

"Listening develops understanding; and understanding strengthens connection."

Empathy is a cornerstone of effective leadership. By deliberately creating opportunities to listen and understand your team, you demonstrate care and develop deeper connections. Empathy exercises encourage open dialogue and provide leaders with valuable insights into their team's challenges, aspirations, and perspectives.

Each week, schedule "walk-and-talk" meetings with individual team members. During these informal sessions, focus solely on listening—without judgment or interruption.

Use open-ended questions such as:

- *"What's been on your mind this week?"*
- *"Is there anything I can do to support you better?"*

This approach not only strengthens trust but also helps uncover barriers or opportunities that might otherwise go unnoticed.

REFLECTIVE JOURNALING

"Reflection transforms experience into insight."

Leadership can feel like a constant forward motion, leaving little time to pause and reflect. Reflective journaling creates a structured opportunity to evaluate your week, recognise successes, and identify areas for growth.

Dedicate 10 minutes every Friday to journal about your leadership experiences. Use prompts such as:

- *What's one leadership success from this week, and why did it work?*
- *What's one area where I could improve? How will I address this next week?*

Over time, these reflections become a valuable archive of lessons learned, helping you track your growth and refine your leadership style.

GRATITUDE PRACTICE

"Recognition fuels motivation and strengthens relationships."

Gratitude isn't just about saying "thank you"—it's about creating a culture where contributions is acknowledged and valued. By integrating gratitude into your routine, you inspire loyalty, develop collaboration, and improve team morale.

Begin each team meeting by spotlighting one specific contribution from a team member and its positive impact on the project. For instance:

- *"I want to thank Sarah for her detailed analysis on our recent proposal. Your work helped us identify key opportunities and made a real difference in our strategy."*

This simple act creates a ripple effect, encouraging others to show appreciation and building a stronger, more engaged team.

AUTHENTICITY AUDITS

"Self-awareness ensures your leadership stays true to your values."

It's easy to be swayed by external pressures or short-term demands. Authenticity audits help leaders evaluate whether their decisions and actions align with their core values, ensuring integrity and consistency.

Once a month, evaluate a recent leadership decision. Reflect on questions such as:

- *"Was this decision aligned with my core values?"*
- *"Did I act out of integrity, or was I influenced by external pressures?"*
- *"How did this decision impact my team's trust and morale?"*

By consciously assessing your decisions, you reinforce your commitment to authentic leadership and build credibility with your team.

The tools above aren't just about aligning your own leadership—they set an example for your team. When leaders demonstrate alignment between their values and actions, they inspire others to do the same.

This creates a culture where integrity, empathy, and accountability thrive—amplifying the impact across the organisation.

Section 8: Visualising the Leadership Compass

"A true leader navigates challenges with empathy, authenticity, self-awareness, and gratitude as their guiding points."

Imagine a compass guiding your leadership journey, with four cardinal points that ensure you remain aligned and impactful:

- Empathy (N): The foundation of trust and connection.
- Authenticity (E): The core of credibility and respect.
- Self-Assessment (S): The guide for continuous growth.
- Gratitude (W): The force that fosters positivity and resilience.

Each point is essential, and together, they form a holistic framework for effective leadership. When you lead with all four points in balance, your leadership direction remains steady, regardless of external challenges.

NORTH: EMPATHY—THE FOUNDATION OF TRUST AND CONNECTION

Empathy helps leaders connect with their teams on a deeper level, developing trust, collaboration, and open communication. It's about understanding not just what people say, but what they feel.

Create anonymous surveys to give team members a safe space to voice concerns they might hesitate to share openly. Use the feedback to identify areas where the team feels unsupported or disconnected—and act on it.

Reflect on a moment when you truly listened to a team member's unspoken needs. How did that empathy change the outcome of the situation?

Practical Step: Schedule regular one-on-one check-ins with your team members to understand their challenges, motivations, and aspirations. Use open-ended questions to encourage honest dialogue.

EAST: AUTHENTICITY—THE CORE OF CREDIBILITY AND RESPECT

Authenticity ensures your leadership is grounded in honesty and integrity. It's about showing up as your true self, even when faced with setbacks or difficult decisions.

Share a leadership failure with your team and explain the lessons you learned from it. For instance, describe a time when a decision didn't go as planned, and how adapting your approach strengthened future outcomes. Transparency inspires trust and fosters a culture of accountability.

Practical Step: Evaluate whether your recent actions and decisions align with your core values. If they don't, identify what adjustments are needed to restore alignment.

SOUTH: SELF-ASSESSMENT—THE GUIDE FOR CONTINUOUS GROWTH

Self-assessment is the tool that keeps leaders aligned with their goals and evolving in their roles. It encourages reflection on past actions and identifies opportunities for growth.

Implement 360-degree feedback within your team. Invite input from peers, direct reports, and supervisors to identify blind spots in your leadership style. This holistic feedback provides invaluable insights for improvement.

Recall a moment when you received constructive feedback that reshaped how you approached leadership. How did applying that feedback enhance your impact?

Practical Step: Dedicate time each month to reflect on your leadership performance. Use prompts like:

- *What feedback have I received, and how am I applying it?*
- *What's one area I can focus on improving this month?*

WEST: GRATITUDE—THE FORCE THAT CREATES POSITIVITY AND RESILIENCE

Gratitude creates a culture of acknowledgment and positivity. It reinforces relationships and motivates teams by showing that their contributions are valued.

Celebrate team milestones by writing handwritten notes to each team member, acknowledging their unique contributions. This simple gesture shows that you see and appreciate each individual's efforts.

Practical Step: Begin every team meeting by highlighting one specific contribution from a team member and its positive impact on the project. This practice not only builds morale, but also inspires others to do their best.

HOW THE COMPASS WORKS IN HARMONY

Each of these cardinal points works together to create balanced, impactful leadership:

- Empathy ensures connection.
- Authenticity builds credibility.
- Self-assessment drives growth.
- Gratitude promotes positivity and resilience.

Just like a compass, these elements provide direction. When all four are in harmony, your leadership becomes a steady force, guiding your team through challenges and toward shared success.

In June 2010, Brené Brown stood on stage at TEDx Houston and delivered a talk titled *The Power of Vulnerability*. She didn't rehearse it the way other speakers might. She didn't script her lines. She chose to tell the truth.

She spoke about shame. About breaking down during her own research. About being a control freak. She told the audience that after a decade of studying vulnerability, she realised she didn't believe in it herself—and that scared her. But she kept going, because she knew people needed to hear it.

That 20-minute talk changed everything. Within days, it went viral. Millions watched it. Publishers called. Speaking offers came in. But Brené wasn't celebrating.

She panicked.

She had been raw. Unfiltered. Honest. The kind of authenticity that doesn't come with a safety net. She later said, "I felt like I'd just walked into a party naked." Her instinct was to pull back, to disappear. But instead, she leaned in.

What followed was a decision to double down on authenticity—not step away from it. She refused to polish her image or become someone else's version of a leadership coach. She kept showing up, telling the truth, and giving credit not just to herself, but to the researchers, teams, and critics who had pushed her work forward.

She publicly thanked the TEDx organisers. She consistently acknowledged her research team in talks and interviews. And she built a culture of gratitude within her own organisation, encouraging staff to speak openly, challenge her, and be seen.

BROWN'S LEADERSHIP COMPASS?

- North: Empathy—listening to hard truths in her own life first.
- East: Authenticity—sharing the messy parts as well as the polished ones.
- South: Self-assessment—recognising her blind spots and insecurities.
- West: Gratitude—expressing it, living it, and building it into her leadership style.

Brown didn't teach theory—she embodied it. She modeled what it means to lead from within, even when it's uncomfortable.

Section 9: Common Pitfalls and How to Avoid Them

"Awareness is the antidote to leadership blind spots."

Leadership is a journey filled with opportunities to grow but it's also fraught with pitfalls that can derail even the most well-intentioned leaders. These blind spots often emerge when leaders become overly focused on immediate demands, losing sight of the bigger picture or neglecting the well-being of their teams and themselves. By becoming aware of these pitfalls and adopting proactive strategies, you can navigate leadership with greater clarity and balance.

1. MICROMANAGING

"Empowering others isn't about relinquishing control—it's about promoting growth."

Micromanagement stems from a desire for control, but it often stifles creativity and trust within a team. When leaders hover over every decision, they unintentionally signal a lack of confidence in their team's abilities, which can lead to disengagement and frustration.

Assign a small project to a junior team member, providing clear objectives while allowing them autonomy over execution. Check in only at predefined milestones, offering guidance without taking over. This approach builds trust and encourages independent problem-solving.

Reflect on a time when you delegated a task but struggled to let go. How did your involvement impact the team member's confidence and performance? What could you have done differently?

Practical Tip: Create a delegation checklist for yourself. Include steps like:

- Clearly define goals and expectations.
- Set milestones for check-ins.
- Resist the urge to intervene unless absolutely necessary.

2. OVER-PRIORITISING RESULTS

"Great leaders don't just deliver results, they build relationships that sustain success."

While achieving results is essential, over-prioritising outcomes at the expense of relationships can damage team morale and long-term performance. A relentless focus on metrics can make employees feel like cogs in a machine, rather than valued contributors.

Schedule quarterly team-building activities to strengthen relationships and create a sense of camaraderie. For instance, host a team lunch, organise a volunteer event, or dedicate a meeting to celebrating accomplishments and personal milestones.

In 2001, Richard Branson found himself facing one of the most critical junctures of his career. The tragic events of 9/11 severely impacted the airline industry, with a dramatic drop in passenger numbers and widespread financial uncertainty. Virgin Atlantic, Branson's flagship airline, was hit hard. Faced with the potential collapse of his company, Branson could have followed the common corporate approach: cut costs, lay off employees, and tighten up operations in a bid to survive. However, he chose a different path, one focused on his people.

Branson, known for his unconventional and people-centric leadership style, made a bold decision. Rather than slashing jobs to keep the airline afloat, he chose to protect his team and preserve the Virgin culture. Despite the mounting financial pressures, Branson pledged not to lay off a single employee. His reasoning was simple, yet powerful: "Take care of your employees, and they'll take care of your business." He knew that a demoralized workforce would hurt his company far more than a few extra months of financial strain.

To bolster his employees' spirits and morale, Branson took an active role in reassuring them. He communicated transparently, holding meetings to let his staff know that, while the company was facing difficult times, their contributions were vital for the future. He also led by example, taking personal financial risks to support

Virgin Atlantic. Branson even mortgaged his private island to secure a loan for the airline, demonstrating his commitment not just to the business, but to the people who made it all possible.

Branson's approach was risky, but it paid off. By 2003, Virgin Atlantic had not only survived but had also thrived, returning to profitability. More importantly, the airline emerged from the crisis with a loyal, dedicated workforce. Branson's focus on the well-being of his employees, rather than just immediate financial outcomes, built a foundation of trust and commitment that would continue to fuel the company's growth.

This example of leadership demonstrates how over-prioritising short-term results can sometimes undermine long-term success. Branson's decision to prioritise relationships and trust over immediate profits proved to be the right one. It wasn't just about cutting costs—it was about building a resilient, motivated team that would carry the company forward. His people-first approach, even in the toughest of times, showcased the power of leadership that looks beyond the next quarter and invests in sustainable success through people.

Practical Tip: Balance metrics with meaningful interactions by ensuring every performance-focused meeting includes a moment to recognise contributions or address team well-being.

3. AVOIDING TOUGH CONVERSATIONS
"Leadership isn't about avoiding discomfort, it's about addressing challenges with courage and care."

Many leaders shy away from difficult conversations, fearing conflict or damaging relationships. However, avoiding these discussions often allows problems to fester, leading to larger issues down the line. Addressing concerns promptly and constructively strengthens trust and accountability.

Use the "feedback sandwich" approach when delivering constructive feedback:

1. Start with a positive observation

   (*"I appreciate your dedication to the project."*)

2. Address the issue constructively

   (*"I noticed some deadlines were missed, and I'd like to understand the challenges you faced."*)

3. End with encouragement

   (*"I am confident we can address this and keep things on track moving forward."*)

Practical Tip: Prepare for tough conversations by scripting your key points beforehand and focusing on the issue, not the person. This helps ensure the discussion remains respectful and productive.

4. NEGLECTING SELF-CARE

"You can't pour from an empty cup—leaders need care, too."

In the pursuit of supporting teams and achieving goals, leaders often neglect their own well-being. Over time, this leads to burnout, reduced effectiveness, and diminished decision-making capacity. Prioritising self-care isn't selfish, it's essential for sustainable leadership.

Block out "non-negotiable" personal time in your calendar; whether for an exercise, meditation, or for spending time with your family. Treat this time with the same importance as a critical business meeting.

Recall a time when you felt burnt out from over committing. How did neglecting self-care impact your leadership? What strategies could you have implemented to regain balance?

Practical Tip: Start small. Dedicate just 15 minutes a day to an activity that recharges you, reading, walking, or even simply disconnecting from screens. Gradually build this into a consistent habit.

5. OVERLOADING WITH UNNECESSARY MEETINGS

"Time is a leader's most valuable resource—spend it wisely."

One common pitfall is allowing unnecessary or overly long meetings to consume valuable time and energy. This not only wastes resources—but also leaves team members feeling drained or disengaged.

Audit your weekly meetings. For each one, ask:

> » *"Is this meeting necessary, or can the information be shared in an email?"*
> » *"Can this meeting be shorter or more focused?"*

Practical Tip: Implement a "10-minute rule." For internal meetings, start with a 10-minute session to determine if further discussion is necessary. This keeps meetings concise and purposeful.

Section 10: Resilience Through Reflection

"Setbacks aren't roadblocks; they're stepping stones for growth."

Resilience is one of the most essential traits for effective leadership, especially when stepping out of your comfort zone. Challenges and failures are inevitable, but it's not the setback itself that defines your journey—it's how you respond to it. Resilience isn't about avoiding failure; it's about embracing it as a learning opportunity and using reflection to move forward, stronger, and more prepared.

WHY REFLECTION FUELS RESILIENCE

- Extracts Lessons: Reflecting or setbacks allows you to identify what went wrong and how to improve.
- Creates Adaptability: By analysing failures, you build the flexibility to adjust your approach for future challenges.
- Reinforces Confidence: Overcoming setbacks through reflection reminds you of your ability to navigate adversity, boosting self-belief.

In 2019, I faced a leadership challenge that tested me more than I expected—at a company I can not disclose. I had been tasked with integrating a newly acquired business into an existing legacy system, across multiple countries, with different time zones, cultures—all with conflicting ways of working. It was high-profile, politically sensitive, and had tight executive oversight.

From day one, it was chaos. The systems didn't align. The teams weren't speaking the same language (literally and figuratively), and expectations were completely misaligned. I found myself stuck in the middle, responsible for driving progress without stepping on toes, all while being expected to report polished, seamless outcomes to senior leadership.

Despite months of effort, we didn't land the integration cleanly. The data was inconsistent, the customer experience was patchy, and the go-live was far messier than we'd planned for. My first reaction?

Frustration. Embarrassment. I had led the work—and it hadn't delivered as expected.

But, as I sat with that disappointment, I realised I had a choice: justify it or learn from it.

So, I blocked time, shut out the noise, and asked myself the hard questions:

- Where did I avoid conflict instead of addressing it?
- Where did I assume alignment instead of confirming it?
- What did I miss early that became unfixable later?

What I found was not failure, it was feedback. I saw where communication had been too passive, where I hadn't challenged senior assumptions early enough, and where I'd tried to protect the team from pressure rather than expose the risks clearly.

That project changed how I lead. I don't wait to speak the hard truths now. I confront misalignment early—and I build teams that don't fear conflict—they know how to use it productively.

I worked with a senior leader who had just been promoted to a global role. On paper, it was the opportunity she'd been working towards for years. But within the first few months, things started to unravel. She struggled to manage time zones, cultural dynamics, and the weight of expectation from both her regional and global teams. Her confidence took a hit. She started second-guessing her decisions, became overly cautious, and her team started to feel the impact.

Rather than push through blindly, she reached out. Together, we unpacked the real issue: she was trying to lead the new role using the same mindset and habits that had worked in her old one. It wasn't about capability—it was about adapting.

We focused on shifting her approach—building a strategy that prioritised influence over control, clarity over volume, and trust over micromanagement. Within months, she wasn't just holding the role—she was reshaping it.

Her growth didn't come from getting it right the first time. It came from her willingness to pause, recalibrate, and take ownership without ego.

Resilience isn't about avoiding pressure. It's about recognising when your current tools no longer serve you and having the courage to build new ones.

PRACTICAL WAYS TO BUILD RESILIENCE THROUGH REFLECTION

1. Set Aside Time to Reflect: After a setback, schedule time to review the experience. Ask yourself:
   - » *What went well, even in the failure?*
   - » *What could have been handled differently?*
   - » *What steps can I take to improve in the future?*
2. Seek External Perspectives: Feedback from mentors, peers, or team members can provide valuable insights you might have missed.
3. Reframe Failure as Growth: Remind yourself that setbacks are part of progress. Each failure brings you one step closer to success when you reflect and adapt.

THE POWER OF REFRAMING SETBACKS

The way you frame failure matters. Instead of viewing it as a reflection of your abilities, see it as a chance to strengthen them. Leaders who embrace this mindset develop the resilience to take bold actions—knowing that every challenge is an opportunity to learn and grow.

Dwayne "The Rock" Johnson is a perfect example of resilience through reflection. Before becoming one of the highest-paid actors in Hollywood, he faced significant setbacks. Early in his life, Johnson dreamed of playing professional football. After a promising start, he was cut from the Canadian Football League just two months into his contract. At this point, his dreams of a football career seemed over, and he was left with little direction and no immediate plan.

Instead of letting this setback define him, Johnson took a step back and reflected on his life. He realised that the key to overcoming this failure lay in reinvention. Instead of continuing to pursue football, he turned to his other passion: professional wrestling. Within a short period, he reinvented himself as "The Rock," rising to WWE superstardom. His charisma and relentless work ethic quickly propelled him to the top of the wrestling world.

Even as he built his wrestling career, Johnson didn't stop reflecting on how he could elevate himself further. He transitioned into acting, but initially faced rejection, with many casting agents and producers telling him he didn't have the "look" for Hollywood. However, he used those rejections as motivations. Reflecting on his previous setbacks, he learned not to take rejection personally and instead focused on how he could improve his craft. Over time, his resilience, reflection, and growth as an actor turned him into a global star.

Today, Dwayne Johnson is more than just a Hollywood actor; he's a successful entrepreneur, philanthropist, and one of the most influential figures in entertainment. His story highlights how setbacks can become stepping stones when approached with reflection and a willingness to adapt. Johnson's ability to stay resilient, learn from his failures, and continuously reinvent himself is a powerful example of leadership and success.

Section 11: Leadership in Crisis

"A crisis doesn't define a leader; their response to it does."

Crises are the ultimate test of leadership. They strip away the luxuries of time and predictability, demanding immediate action, clarity, and resilience. How a leader responds during these moments not only defines their effectiveness but also sets the tone for their team's morale and trust. A leader's compass—empathy, authenticity, self-assessment, and gratitude—becomes indispensable when navigating uncertainty.

WHY CRISIS LEADERSHIP MATTERS

1. Stabilises the Team: A composed leader provides reassurance during chaos.
2. Builds Trust: Transparency and empathy during crises strengthen team loyalty.
3. Guides Adaptability: Leaders who embrace challenges as opportunities create creativity and resilience within their teams.

In 2018, I faced a sudden organisational shift when the CEO of Ted Baker unexpectedly stepped down. That change triggered a shake-up at the top, and with it, serious questions about the future of my department. The new executive team didn't believe testing and quality should exist as a standalone function, which meant potential cutbacks, or closures altogether.

My team felt it immediately—the uncertainty, the silence, and the fear of being sidelined. As the pressure mounted, I realised that how I responded would set the tone for how we would get through it.

So, I focused on what I could control. I kept communication open, checking in regularly—even if all I had to say was "I don't know yet, but I'll tell you as soon as I do." I leaned into empathy to acknowledge what people were feeling. I was honest when I didn't have answers. And I made sure to call out the effort and resilience I saw in real time.

That experience taught me something simple but critical: crisis leadership isn't about having all the answers; it's about being someone people trust to face the unknown with them.

In the early 2010s, Adobe was facing a major crisis. The demand for its traditional software products like Photoshop was declining as the industry began shifting toward cloud computing and subscription-based models. The company's future was uncertain, and drastic change to stay competitive in a rapidly evolving market.

Shantanu Narayen, CEO of Adobe, made the bold decision to transition Adobe from a product-based business model to a subscription-based model through Adobe Creative Cloud. This shift involved significant risks, disrupting the status quo by moving away from one-time software purchases and convincing long-time customers to adapt to a new way of paying for and using software.

Narayen's leadership during this crisis was marked by clear vision and transparency. He communicated directly with employees, investors, and customers about the importance of this transformation, emphasizing that it was not just about surviving the crisis, but about embracing future growth and innovation. The transition was not easy, many employees were worried about the impact on their jobs, and customers were skeptical about the shift in the business' model. But, Narayen's transparency and strategic focus on long-term sustainability helped build trust and keep morale high.

The result? Adobe not only weathered the crisis but thrived. The Adobe Creative Cloud became a highly successful product, and Adobe's annual revenue increased significant y. Narayen's decision to guide Adobe through this major business model shift turned a potential crisis into a period of tremendous growth and transformation.

STRATEGIES FOR LEADING DURING A CRISIS

1. Communicate Transparently: Keep your team informed with regular updates, even if you don't have all the answers. Transparency builds trust and prevents speculation.

2. Acknowledge Emotions: Recognise and validate the stress, fear, or anxiety your team may be feeling. For example, start meetings with a moment to check in on how everyone is coping.

3. Focus on What You Can Control: Shift the team's attention to actionable steps, even if they're small. This creates a sense of progress and purpose amidst uncertainty.

4. Demonstrate Resilience and Hope: Balance honesty about challenges with optimism about the team's ability to overcome them. Your composure will influence your team's mindset.

A strong example of crisis leadership is Mary Barra, the CEO of General Motors (GM). When she took the helm in 2014, GM was in the midst of one of the largest recalls in automotive history, stemming from a faulty ignition switch that was linked to multiple deaths. The crisis posed a real threat to the company's reputation, customer trust, and financial stability.

Barra's leadership during this crisis was marked by her unwavering commitment to transparency and accountability. She didn't shy away from the hard truths. Rather than waiting for the situation to resolve itself, she took immediate action, publicly acknowledging the fault and making it clear that GM would take full responsibility. This transparency was key in rebuilding trust both within the company and with customers.

But Barra's leadership didn't stop at communication. She focused on actionable steps to correct the problem. GM implemented a comprehensive review of its safety practices, working to overhaul the company's culture of accountability and safety. Barra's decision to address the underlying systemic issues, rather than simply focusing on the immediate recall, showed her long-term vision and commitment to the company's integrity.

Through her resilience and direct approach, Barra not only led GM through one of the most challenging moments in its history but also set the company on a path to recovery. GM emerged from the crisis with a stronger commitment to safety and a renewed focus on ethical leadership. Barra's handling of the crisis demonstrated that owning up to mistakes, clear communication, and implementing sustainable changes can turn a crisis into a pivotal moment of growth.

PRACTICAL STEPS TO BUILD CRISIS LEADERSHIP SKILLS

1. Practice Crisis Simulations: Conduct regular "what-if" scenarios with your leadership team to prepare for potential challenges. This strengthens your ability to adapt and respond quickly.

2. Build Emotional Resilience: Incorporate mindfulness or stress-management practices into your routine to maintain composure during high-pressure situations.

3. Create a Crisis Response Plan: Document key steps to take during a crisis, including communication protocols, decision-making structures, and team responsibilities.

Section 12: Reflection

"Leadership doesn't drift—you do. Check the compass. Recalibrate. Then move with intent."

Leadership isn't about having all the answers. It's about asking better questions, especially of yourself. It's easy to focus on output, chase results, and keep moving. But alignment doesn't come from speed. It comes from stillness. From the pause. From checking if who you are, how you lead, and what you're building actually match.

This chapter was never about becoming someone else. It was about getting clear on who you already are, and leading from that place. Whether it's listening better, showing up more honestly, making time to reflect, or simply thanking the people around you. Your leadership compass is built from small, intentional acts; Not from big declarations.

The questions that follow aren't about ticking boxes. They're about noticing patterns. Calling yourself out. And making quiet decisions that shift how you show up for others and for yourself.

Reflection Questions

SECTION 1:
Which of these principles do you feel most confident in applying, and which one challenges you the most? How can you commit to the full 30-day journey?

SECTION 2:
What's one step you can take today to show empathy in your leadership? How can you make it a consistent practice rather than a one-time effort?

SECTION 3:
What is your North Star? How do you ensure your daily actions and decisions align with your core purpose and values?

SECTION 4:
How often do you take time to reflect on your leadership? What's one self-assessment question you can start asking regularly to align your actions with your purpose?

SECTION 5:
What values define you as a leader? How can you ensure your daily actions and decisions reflect these values authentically?

SECTION 6:

How can you make gratitude a consistent part of your leadership? What's one step you can take today to acknowledge your team's contributions?

SECTION 7:

Which of these tools could you start implementing today to align your leadership with your values and vision? How will you measure its impact over time?

SECTION 8:

Which cardinal point on the leadership compass—empathy, authenticity, self-assessment, or gratitude—needs the most attention in your leadership? How will you begin strengthening it today?

SECTION 9:

Which of these common pitfalls resonates most with your leadership experience? What specific strategy will you adopt today to overcome it?

SECTION 10:

What's a recent setback you've faced? How can you use reflection to turn it into a stepping stone for growth?

SECTION 11:

How have you responded to challenges in the past? What elements of your leadership compass—empathy, authenticity, self-assessment, or gratitude—can you strengthen to prepare for future crises?

CHAPTER 3

Changing Gears– Mastering the Ride of Life

> *"Changing gears in life isn't about speed; it's about timing and knowing when to push harder or ease off. Master that, and you control the ride."*

You're moving forward, but something feels off. Maybe you're pushing too hard, burning out before you reach your goal. Or perhaps you're coasting; stuck in a rhythm that no longer challenges you.

Life—like cycling—isn't about maintaining one speed, it's about knowing when to shift gears. Too much resistance and you stall. Too little and you lose momentum.

This chapter is about mastering that balance. Learning when to push, when to ease off, and when to recalibrate so that you stay in control of the ride; no matter how steep the climb.

Section 1: Lessons from the Road

"The steepest climbs teach you what you're truly capable of."

When I signed up for a 180-mile bike ride, I expected it to be a physical test of endurance. What I didn't anticipate was how profoundly it would challenge my mindset and teach me about resilience, adaptability, and the importance of pacing myself through life's uphill battles. This journey wasn't just about cycling; it became a metaphor for navigating the challenges we face in leadership and personal growth.

THE UPHILL BATTLES

Forty-five miles into the first day, I encountered my first major hill. My legs burned so fiercely that I didn't know if I could stand it for one more pedal, let alone get up this hill. With every push of the pedals, my breathing was labored, and my thoughts spiraled into doubt. I vividly remember questioning why I'd started this challenge in the first place. It felt insurmountable, and every fiber of my being screamed to stop.

But something kept me going: a small, steady voice reminding me that growth comes through discomfort. With every excruciatingly painful pedal stroke, I discovered that pushing through discomfort didn't just strengthen my body; it sharpened my resolve. Every turn of the pedal, through the pain, became a small victory. Every push to keep going dissolved the doubts, because in these moments, I learned that pushing through discomfort strengthened my resolve on that hill and became fuel for the next one, teaching me that progress is made one stroke at a time.

THE BREAKTHROUGH MOMENT

The second day brought its own set of challenges. Fear lingered from the exhaustion of the previous day. I didn't sleep the best, suffered cramps most of it, and the thought of another grueling climb was daunting. But instead of succumbing to doubt, I adjusted my mindset and approach. Initially, I thought I didn't have it in me, but something inside me took over, and it felt like a shift in gear to get to that finish line.

I realised I didn't need to conquer the entire hill in one burst of energy. Instead, I focused on working with the terrain rather than against it—shifting gears intentionally, pacing myself, and conserving energy when possible. Each small adjustment allowed me to tackle the climbs more effectively.

By the time I crossed the finish line, I wasn't just a cyclist completing a challenge; I was someone who had learned the art of perseverance. The ride taught me that resilience isn't about brute force; it's about adapting to challenges, finding your rhythm, and trusting that small, consistent efforts will get you to the top.

KEY LESSONS FROM THE ROAD

1. Resilience Comes From Pushing Through Discomfort: The moments that feel impossible are often where growth begins. By leaning into discomfort rather than avoiding it, you build the strength to overcome greater challenges in the future.

2. Adaptability is Key to Perseverance: Facing the steepest hills taught me the importance of adjusting my approach. Whether it's shifting gears on a bike or reevaluating a strategy in leadership, adaptability allows you to navigate obstacles more effectively.

3. Progress is Made One Step (or Pedal) at a Time: Looking at the entire climb can feel overwhelming. Breaking it down into manageable pieces helps you stay focused and maintain momentum.

4. Your Mindset Shapes Your Journey: The second day of the ride taught me that fear and doubt don't need to dictate your actions. By shifting my mindset from "I can't" to "I'll try," and then "I get to" I unlocked the determination to move forward.

TAKEAWAYS FOR LEADERSHIP AND LIFE

1. Embrace Discomfort: Identify a challenge in your personal or professional life that feels like an uphill battle. Instead of avoiding it, take one small step toward addressing it.

2. Adjust Your Approach: Reflect on how you're currently tackling a problem. Is there a different strategy or perspective that could make the climb easier?

3. Focus on the Next Step: When faced with a daunting task, shift your focus from the big picture to the next small action you can take. Progress is made incrementally.

4. Celebrate the Finish Line: Take time to acknowledge your accomplishments, big or small. Crossing the finish line, whether literal or metaphorical, deserves recognition.

Section 2: The Science Behind Momentum

"Your brain is like a gear system when it functions well, you glide forward; when it falters, you stall."

Momentum isn't just about physical effort it's deeply connected to your mental state. During my rice, I learned that my physical endurance depended heavily on my ability to manage mental energy. The brain, particularly the prefrontal cortex, the hub of decision-making and focus is like the gears of a bike. When you engage the right gears, you glide forward efficiently. But when stress or overwork bogs you down, it's like riding uphill in the wrong gear, draining your energy without meaningful progress.

THE ROLE OF THE BRAIN IN MOMENTUM

The prefrontal cortex controls focus, planning, and emotional regulation. However, it is a finite resource. Prolonged stress, decision fatigue, or lack of rest can drain its capacity, leaving you stalled or overwhelmed. Just like a cyclist needs to shift gears to adjust to the terrain, your brain needs cycles of focus and recovery to maintain momentum.

FINDING THE RIGHT GEAR

On the first day of the ride, I tried to power through the climbs, relying solely on determination. I pushed myself relentlessly, visualising I was always getting nearer to the end, ignoring the warning signs of fatigue. By the end of the day, I was completely drained, both physically and mentally.

On the second day, I shifted my approach. I conserved energy by pacing myself, adjusting my gears, and taking intentional breaks to recover. This simple change transformed how I approached the challenges ahead. It wasn't about pushing harder; it was about working smarter. The lesson was clear: momentum is as much about energy management as it is about effort.

THE SCIENCE OF ENERGY MANAGEMENT

1. Focus and Recovery Cycles: Research shows that the brain thrives on alternating periods of focus and rest. Studies on productivity highlight the importance of working in focused bursts (such as the Pomodoro Technique) followed by short recovery periods.

2. Decision Fatigue: Constant decision-making depletes the prefrontal cortex, thus reducing your ability to think clearly and make sound choices. Taking breaks and simplifying decisions can help preserve mental energy.

3. The Power of Flow: Momentum often comes from achieving a state of flow, a mental state where focus, engagement, and productivity peak. To enter flow, balance the challenge of a task with your skill level and eliminate distractions.

Elite endurance athletes, such as marathon runners or professional cyclists, prioritise energy management. They know that starting too fast or ignoring rest intervals leads to burnout before the finish line. By pacing themselves, they maximize their performance and maintain steady progress throughout the race.

STEPS TO BUILD MENTAL MOMENTUM

1. Pace Yourself:
    » Treat your mental energy like a resource. Break tasks into smaller chunks and tackle them in focused sessions.
    » Example in Action: Work for 25–30 minutes with full focus, then take a 5-minute break to recharge.

2. Simplify Decisions:
    » Minimise decision fatigue by creating routines for repetitive tasks. For instance, plan your meals or schedule in advance so you can save your mental energy for bigger decisions.

3. Prioritise Rest:
    » Just like cycling uphill requires intentional pauses, your brain needs time to recover. Incorporate restorative activities like meditation, walking, or power naps into your routine.

4. Adjust Your "Mental Gear":
    » Recognise when you're overexerting yourself mentally. When a task feels overwhelming, try breaking it down into smaller steps or approaching it with a different strategy.

THE LINK BETWEEN MOMENTJM AND LEADERSHIP

The principles of energy management apply not just to physical challenges but also to leadership. A leader who burns out can't inspire or guide their team effectively. By learning to balance focus with recovery, leaders can sustain momentum—for themselves and their teams.

Section 3: Applying the 5 States of Optimisation

"Mastering the ride of life means knowing which gear to use and when to shift."

Life, much like a challenging bike ride, requires constant adjustments. The 5 States of Optimisation—Productivity, Planning, People, Prospect, and Performance—act like the gears on a bike. Each serves a distinct purpose, helping you navigate different terrains. Learning when and how to use these states ensures that you move forward efficiently, no matter the challenges ahead. Let's explore each state through the lens of my journey—and how it applies to leadership and life.

1. PRODUCTIVITY STATE: KNOWING YOUR STRENGTHS AND LIMITS

"It's not about doing everything; it's about doing the right things well."

On the bike ride, I learned a critical lesson about knowing my limits. On steep inclines, pushing too hard left me too depleted for the stretches ahead. Easing off wasn't a sign of weakness—it was a strategy for sustainable progress. Productivity isn't just about effort; it's about intentional effort.

Many leaders I've coached have struggled with burnout because they tried to do it all. By focusing on their core strengths and delegating non-essential tasks, they achieved greater results without sacrificing their well-being.

- Practical Application:
  - » Assess your workload and identify tasks that align with your strengths.
  - » Delegate or delay tasks that don't require your unique expertise.
  - » Regularly check in with yourself to ensure you're pacing sustainably.

2. PLANNING STATE: PREPARING FOR THE TERRAIN AHEAD

"Preparation doesn't eliminate challenges; it equips you to face them."

Before tackling my 180-mile ride, I didn't just hop on my bike and hope for the best. I studied the route, trained my body, and ensured I had the right tools to handle the journey. This preparation made the unexpected manageable and gave me the confidence to keep moving forward.

Effective goal-setting requires the same foresight. Breaking down objectives into manageable steps, anticipating potential hurdles, and having contingency plans ensures progress even when the road gets tough.

- Practical Application:
  - » Break large goals into smaller, actionable steps.
  - » Identify potential obstacles and plan how you'll overcome them.
  - » Regularly review your progress and adjust as needed.

3. PEOPLE STATE: THE POWER OF SHARED ENERGY

"Collaboration fuels resilience and amplifies success."

Cycling alongside others transformed the experience. When the hills felt insurmountable, encouragement from fellow riders kept me going. Their energy became my energy—from a simple smile to a nod of the head, every small acknowledgment reminded me of the strength found in collaboration.

In a team setting, developing trust and creating a culture of support can make even the most challenging goals achievable. Leaders who prioritise collaboration inspire innovation and resilience.

- Practical Application:
  - » Invest time in building trust within your team through consistent communication and accountability.
  - » Empower others by delegating meaningful responsibilities and recognising their contributions.
  - » Maintain a culture of mutual support by celebrating team wins—both big and small.

4. PROSPECT STATE: BUILDING MEANINGFUL CONNECTIONS

"Strong networks keep everything moving smoothly, like a well-maintained bike chain."

The relationships I built during the ride were invaluable—especially since I wasn't part of a cycling club and trained alone. The lonely training was tough. I didn't have anyone pushing me along. I tracked every ride myself, gradually extending the distance by 2 or sometimes 5 miles for each new ride.

But training wasn't just about riding a bike. Regular gym sessions, strength training, and conditioning, even resting at the right times, were needed. This was something new that made me realise riding a bike is a lot harder than I thought, especially with all the training that went on behind the scenes.

As for the relationships I built during the ride, they weren't about stopping and having a chat. It was more subtle: a nod when someone passed me, a shared moment at a pit stop. This wasn't about camaraderie; they provided accountability, inspiration, and perspective. Similarly, in business and in life, meaningful connections lead to long-term success and personal fulfillment.

Networking isn't about exchanging business cards, it's about building authentic relationships. Clients who shifted their focus from transactional networking to meaningful connections discovered both professional opportunities and personal growth.

- Practical Application:
  - » Focus on building genuine relationships by listening, offering value, and showing interest in others' goals.
  - » Create a habit of reaching out to maintain connections, even when you don't need something.
  - » Seek out diverse perspectives to broaden your understanding and enrich your network.

5. PERFORMANCE STATE: USING FEAR AS A DRIVER

"Fear isn't something to eliminate, it's something to channel."

Fear played a significant role during the ride, particularly on the steepest climbs. I feared falling off the bike and, let me tell you, I did more than once. Going up a steep hill, could I keep pedaling? What if I stopped? There was also a moment, when I was going downhill, and the speed I gathered on this descent was very fast. I feared losing control and crashing into something. But instead of letting this paralyse me, I used it as fuel to push harder and prove to myself what I was capable of achieving. Each uphill battle became a chance to grow stronger, both physically and mentally.

Fear of failure can hold leaders back, but it can also be a powerful motivator. Leaders who embrace fear and take calculated risks often achieve breakthroughs that transform their careers.

- Practical Application:
  » Reframe fear as a signal of growth and opportunity.
  » Break big risks into smaller, manageable steps to reduce intimidation.
  » Reflect on past successes where you overcame fear and use those experiences to fuel your confidence.

HOW THE 5 STATES WORK TOGETHER

Much like the gears on a bike, the 5 States of Optimisation aren't meant to be used in isolation. They go together. For example:

- Planning helps you anticipate challenges and prepare for them.
- People provide the support and encouragement needed when the road gets tough.
- Performance channels fear into action; thus helping you push through the hardest moments.

When applied intentionally, these states ensure that you are always moving forward, no matter the terrain.

Section 4: Leadership Lessons in Changing Gears

"Leadership requires the courage to shift when the terrain demands it."

Leadership, much like cycling, is a dynamic process. It's not just about knowing your destination, but about how effectively you adapt to changes along the way. The terrain will inevitably shift: steep climbs, flat stretches, and unexpected detours. Knowing when to change gears is what defines a leader's ability to navigate both challenges and opportunities with skill and resil ence.

LEADERSHIP AS GEAR-SHIFTING

Just as a cyclist must adjust gears to tackle changing terrain, leaders must recognise when it's time to recalibrate their approach. Some situations call for accelerating momentum, while others require slowing down, reflecting, and strategising for the next move. Leadership demands both decisiveness and adaptability.

When Tufan Erginbilgiç took over as CEO of Rolls-Royce in early 2023, the business was bloated, underperforming, and still recovering from the pandemic's impact on aviation. At his first company-wide address, he called it "a burning platform"—a rare and brutally honest warning from a leader.

Rather than opt for incremental improvements or cosmetic changes, he changed gears completely.

- He restructured the leadership team and cut layers of middle management to speed up decision-making.

- He introduced hard financial targets, linking them directly to accountability across functions.
- He froze expansion plans and focused instead on fixing core business units—civil aerospace, power systems, and defence.

This wasn't about growth for the sake of it. It was about restoring clarity and momentum.

By early 2024, profits more than doubled. The share price climbed over 60%. And for the first time in years, internal alignment and external confidence matched up.

Erginbilgiç didn't make popular choices. He made necessary ones. And he made them fast. That's what shifting into the right gear looks like when the terrain is falling apart beneath you.

Effective leaders know that progress isn't always about moving faster. Sometimes, slowing down to recalibrate can lead to greater long-term success.

ADAPTING STRATEGIES WHEN THE ROAD CHANGES

No journey is linear, and no strategy is foolproof. Leaders who thrive are those who recognise when a plan is no longer serving its purpose and have the courage to pivot.

When Apple shifted from being a computer-focused company to a broader technology leader with the introduction of the iPhone, it wasn't just launching a new product—it was a bold redefinition of the company's identity. This gear shift, led by Steve Jobs, transformed Apple into one of the world's most valuable companies.

Leadership requires the ability to identify when your current approach isn't aligned with your goals. This might involve downsizing a project, reallocating resources, or abandoning an initiative that's not yielding results.

EMPOWERING YOUR TEAM TO CHANGE GEARS

Leadership isn't a solo effort. A great leader knows that adaptability must be cultivated within the team. Empowering your people to make decisions, take risks, and embrace uncertainty creates an organisation that thrives under changing conditions.

At 29, I was working in the finance sector in London. I've been at my desk for twenty minutes and already my inbox has two flagged emails from my manager. One of them is a reply to a message I drafted for the wider team—he's rewritten three words and added a full stop. The other is a reminder: *"All emails to be reviewed by me before being sent. No exceptions."*

The job was high-pressure, but manageable. The manager? Not so much. He had to sign off every email, every meeting invite, every update—even internal ones. Once, I sent a status update without him reviewing it. Within minutes, I was called into his office.

He looked up from his screen. "You sent this without me checking it."

I paused. "Had I made a mistake?"

"No. But what if you had?"

That line stuck with me. *What if you had?*

It said everything about how little trust he had in his team. From then on, I second-guessed everything I wrote. I'd forward drafts to him, wait for feedback, delay simple decisions, and lose momentum. Eventually, I started doubting whether I could even write a basic email properly.

Years later, as a coach, I work with leaders who don't want to fall into that trap. I show them what it looks like to take a hands-off approach—not abandoning responsibility, but trusting others to deliver. Let them send the email. Let them book and lead the meeting. Let them run with the project. That's what ownership looks like. And the more you do that as a leader, the more capable your team becomes.

Create an environment where team members feel empowered to lead within their areas of expertise. Encourage autonomy while offering guidance and support when needed.

NAVIGATING RESISTANCE TO CHANGE

One of the biggest challenges leaders' faces is resistance to change both within themselves and their teams. Change—even when necessary—often feels uncomfortable. In 2024, Boeing was reeling again. Another 737 Max manufacturing incident had sparked a federal investigation. Airline customers were furious. Trust from regulators and the flying public was running on fumes.

Dave Calhoun, Boeing's CEO since 2020, had already been under pressure. But this time, he didn't go into PR mode or wait for legal guidance. Instead, he shifted gears.

On his first day back at the 737 factory after the incident, he made a quiet, deliberate move, he sat with engineers, not executives.

He didn't blame suppliers. He didn't soften the message. He admitted Boeing's failures in public:

"We have to change the way we work. Culture, safety, accountability—everything is on the table."

Internally, he triggered an audit of every process in production and quality control. Teams were given the green light to stop the line if something didn't look right. Calhoun put pressure on himself, announcing he would step down by the end of 2024.

This marked a shift from damage control to systemic correction—not trying to calm shareholders, not spinning to the media—just doing the hard, necessary work of rebuilding trust.

When leadership hits resistance, deflection is easy. Owning the failure and steering into structural change—that's gear-shifting leadership.

Understand the fears and concerns that accompany change and address them with empathy. Growth happens when leaders embrace discomfort and guide their teams through it with compassion.

CRISIS LEADERSHIP: SHIFTING INTO LOW GEAR

Leadership during a crisis is akin to cycling uphill; you can't maintain the same pace you had on flat terrain. It requires slowing down, reassessing priorities, and focusing on what truly matters.

In early 2020, Zoom was a mid-tier video conferencing tool. It wasn't the most popular. It wasn't the slickest. And it definitely wasn't built for a global overnight shutdown.

When the COVID-19 pandemic hit in March 2020, Zoom's daily users skyrocketed from 10 million to over 200 million in under a month. Their infrastructure was never meant to carry that load. Security issues exploded. Meetings were hijacked. Privacy advocates were calling them out. Schools, businesses, hospitals—everyone was suddenly relying on a platform that wasn't ready.

At that point, Zoom's founder and CEO Eric Yuan didn't pretend to have the answers. In April 2020, he stood up on a live webinar, admitted the flaws, and said: *"We moved too fast... I really messed up on security."*

Then he shifted gears.

- He froze all product development and reassigned engineering teams to work only on trust, safety, and reliability.
- He hired top security advisors and brought in former CISOs from tech giants to audit everything.
- He opened weekly town halls to take live questions, even the hostile ones.

And he kept showing up, taking hits publicly so his team could focus on fixing the platform.

By the end of 2020, Zoom had rebuilt its infrastructure, strengthened security, and added new controls, without losing momentum. Revenue rose 326% year-over-year. But the real win wasn't profit. It was trust. Yuan turned crisis into clarity—not by pushing forward blindly, but by knowing when to hit the brakes and rebuild from within.

This wasn't a leader accelerating into uncertainty. It was a leader downshifting at the right moment to avoid a crash. That's what changing gears really looks like.

BALANCING VISION AND ADAPTABILITY

Great leaders balance long-term vision with short-term adaptability. They know where they want to go but remain flexible in how they get there. Holding both perspectives simultaneously is what sets exceptional leaders apart.

I was working with a COO (Chief Operations Officer) at a medium to large enterprise tech company, and they were facing declining team performance. I observed that their clear vision for success wasn't enough. Their rigid management style was creating a disconnect. By introducing incremental changes—weekly one-on-ones, team input sessions, and greater emphasis on recognition—they regained their team's trust and productivity without abandoning their core objectives.

Regularly reassess your strategies to ensure they're aligned with your vision. Flexibility in execution doesn't mean compromising your goals, it means finding smarter paths to achieve them.

LESSONS IN LEADERSHIP GEARS

1. Listen and Adapt: Leadership isn't about having all the answers; it's about listening to your team and adapting to their needs.
2. Promote Resilience: Build a team culture where setbacks are seen as opportunities to learn and grow.
3. Reassess Regularly: Evaluate whether your strategies align with your goals and be willing to shift gears when they don't.
4. Encourage Ownership: Empower your team to take initiative and make decisions within their areas of expertise.
5. Lead with Empathy: Understand the fears and concerns that accompany change and address them with compassion.

Section 5: Reflection

"You don't burn out because you're weak. You burn out because you stayed in the wrong gear too long. Shift early. Shift often."

Life doesn't reward you for staying in the same gear. It demands that you adapt—hat you know when to push, when to hold, and when to pause. You don't control the terrain, but you do control how you respond to it. That is what shapes the ride.

This chapter wasn't about endurance. It was about awareness—the awareness to notice when something's no longer working, the humility to shift your approach, and the discipline to keep moving, even if it's slower than you hoped.

Changing gears isn't about losing speed—it's about regaining control. When the climb gets steep, don't double down blindly. Reassess. Adjust. Move with intent. Because the riders who last—the ones who reach the finish line—aren't always the fastest. They're the ones who know when to change gears and how to keep going.

Use the reflections below to check in. Not with the version of you that's powering forward. But with the one that's been grinding too long in the wrong gear, unsure whether to shift. That's the version that needs your attention now.

Ride with intention, shift with purpose, and enjoy the journey.

Reflection Questions

SECTION 1:

What's your equivalent of an "uphill battle," and how can you apply resilience, adaptability, and small, intentional steps to overcome it?

SECTION 2:

How can you adjust your mental "gears" to manage energy more effectively and sustain momentum in your personal and professional life?

SECTION 3:

Which of the 5 States of Optimisation do you need to focus on most right now? How can you integrate it into your daily life or leadership approach?

SECTION 4:

What's one area in your leadership where a gear shift might be necessary? How can you prepare yourself and your team to embrace this change?

SECTION 5:

What's one area in your leadership where a gear shift might be necessary? How can you prepare yourself and your team to embrace this change?

CHAPTER 4

The Fear of What If

"Fear is not your enemy; it's your compass. Follow it, and you'll find what matters most."

Imagine you're standing at the edge of a decision, gripped by the weight of "What if?" It's the voice in your head listing all the reasons to hesitate, to stay where it's safe, to avoid the risk of failure.

But what if fear isn't a warning sign to stop, but a signal that you're on the brink of something important?

This chapter is about shifting that perspective, seeing fear not as an enemy, but as a guide. Because on the other side of "What if?" isn't just uncertainty; it's growth, confidence, and the version of you that's ready to step forward.

Section 1: Shift Your Mindset— Turning Fear into Fuel

"Fear is a reaction. Courage is a decision."

Fear often feels like an immovable obstacle, a wall separating you from what you want to achieve. But what if fear is actually a signal of something greater? A sign that you're standing on the edge of growth? Too often, we focus on the "What ifs" of failure:

- *What if I mess up?*
- *What if everything goes wrong?*

But how often do we consider the "What ifs" of success?

- *What if this is the best decision I've ever made?*
- *What if this fear leads to my greatest breakthrough?*

Reframing fear doesn't mean ignoring it, it means using it as fuel to propel you forward.

Fear is not the enemy. It is a sign that you care deeply about what's at stake.

THE NEUROSCIENCE OF FEAR

Fear originates in the amygdala, the brain's alarm system, which triggers the fight-or-flight response. While this reaction is essential for survival, it often misfires in modern situations like presenting to a boardroom, making a bold career move, or stepping into a leadership role.

The good news? The prefrontal cortex, the brain's rational thinking hub, can override the amygdala's instinctive response. Techniques like mindfulness, breathwork, and reframing strengthen the prefrontal cortex, thus allowing you to move from reactive fear to focused clarity.

TURNING FEAR INTO ENERGY

Before delivering my first TEDx talk, fear was almost paralysing. My heart raced, my thoughts spiraled, and the "what ifs" consumed me: *What if I forget my lines? What if I fail to connect with the audience?*

But then I stopped and reframed those fears. I realised that my nerves were evidence of how much I cared about the message I was about to share. Instead of resisting the fear, I leaned into it, using it as energy to fuel my performance. By stepping into the fear, I transformed it into a driving force that allowed me to connect with the audience meaningfully.

Simone Biles, widely regarded as one of the greatest gymnasts of all time, has faced fear head-on throughout her career. At the Tokyo 2020 Olympics, she made the bold decision to withdraw from several events due to mental health concerns—a groundbreaking move in a sport where physical strength and perfection are paramount.

Simone's decision wasn't just about stepping back from the competition—it was about acknowledging her fear and understanding that mental clarity and emotional wellbeing are just as important as physical strength. She famously spoke about how her fear had affected her ability to perform safely and effectively—something many athletes would avoid addressing publicly.

Rather than letting fear be a limitation, Simone Biles used it as a tool to gain insight into her own needs. By recognising when she wasn't in the right mental state, she shifted focus toward protecting both her body and mind. This move wasn't about quitting—it was about recalibrating. She understood that to continue performing at her highest level, she needed to confront and manage her fear, not push through it recklessly.

Later, Simone returned to competition in a different event—and despite the adversity, she continued to prove her greatness. Her story is a powerful reminder that fear doesn't need to be avoided or suppressed. When faced with it, you can use fear to guide your decisions, recalibrate, and ultimately, come back stronger.

STRATEGIES TO TURN FEAR INTO FUEL

1. Reframe the "What Ifs"
   » Replace fear-based "What ifs" with possibility-focused ones.
   » Example in Action: Instead of *"What if I fail at this project?"* think, *"What if this project opens the door to new opportunities?"*

2. Practice Mindfulness
   » When fear arises, pause and ground yourself in the present moment. Techniques like deep breathing, body scans, or meditation help regulate the amygdala's response.
   » Example in Action: Before a big presentation, take five slow, deep breaths, focusing on the sensation of air entering and leaving your body.

3. Break Down the Challenge
   » Fear often feels overwhelming because the challenge seems too big. Break it into smaller, manageable steps to build confidence incrementally.
   » Example in Action: If you're preparing for a major pitch, focus first on crafting the introduction, then on refining key points, and finally on practicing delivery.

4. Visualise Success
    »   Picture yourself successfully navigating the situation that's causing fear. Visualisation activates the same neural pathways as actually performing the task, building confidence and familiarity.
    »   Example in Action: Before your next big moment, close your eyes and imagine yourself handling it with confidence, poise, and ease.
5. Acknowledge and Name Your Fear
    »   Simply naming what you're afraid of can help reduce its intensity.
    »   Example in Action: Say to yourself, "I'm nervous about *this presentation because I care deeply about making an impact.*" This reaffirms the positive intention behind your fear.

REFRAMING FEAR AS A LEADERSHIP TOOL

Fear isn't just a personal hurdle; it's a powerful tool for leaders. Leaders who acknowledge their fears and share how they're navigating them inspire trust and relatability. By demonstrating courage, they encourage their teams to do the same.

Section 2: Overcome Fear and Find Success

"Fear is a mirage; the closer you get to it, the more it fades away."
Fear is one of the most common barriers to success. It manifests in countless forms fear of failure, rejection, or even success itself.

Its power lies not in the reality of the situation; but in the stories we tell ourselves about what could go wrong. Yet, fear, when faced and understood, often dissolves, revealing opportunities we couldn't see before. The key is learning to reframe fear as a guide, rather than an obstacle.

CHANGING THE NARRATIVE AROUND FEAR

Fear is, at its core, a projection of "what ifs."

- *What if I fail?*
- *What if others judge me?*
- *What if I'm not enough?*

But what if you shifted the narrative?

- *What if I succeed?*
- *What if this challenge is the best decision I've ever made?*
- *What if this moment leads to my biggest breakthrough?*

Reframing fear changes the focus from avoiding failure to pursuing growth, allowing you to act despite the discomfort.

BUILDING CONFIDENCE ONE STEP AT A TIME

When I started my coaching business, fear loomed large.

- *What if no one trusted me?*
- *What if I couldn't deliver results?*
- *What if I failed completely?*

The doubts were paralysing at times. But instead of letting them hold me back, I broke the fear down into smaller, actionable steps. I started with just one client. That first engagement built my confidence and proved to myself that I could create value. Each success chipped away at the fear, and over time, I realised that fear wasn't the immovable force I thought it was—it was a mirage. The closer I moved toward it, the more it faded away.

FRAMEWORK FOR FACING FEAR

1. Acknowledge the Fear: Name it to Reduce its Power
   » Naming your fear helps diminish its intensity by making it tangible.
   » Examples in Action:
      · "I'm afraid of presenting because I don't want to appear unprepared."
      · Naming this fear allows you to focus on preparation, shifting your energy from worry to action.

2. Break Down the Fear: Understand Its Root Cause
   » Often, fear stems from uncertainty or inexperience. Understanding its origin makes it more manageable.
   » Examples in Action:
      · "I fear this project because it's my first time leading a team."
      · Acknowledge that it's natural to feel this way in new situations. Then, seek out resources or mentorship to build confidence.

3. Act Despite the Fear: Take One Small Step Forward
   » Fear loses its grip when you take action. Start small to build momentum.
   » Example in Action: If public speaking feels overwhelming, begin by presenting a single point to a trusted colleague. Gradually expand your audience as your confidence grows.

In 1994, Jeff Bezos was a senior vice president at an investment bank in New York. While his career appeared to be on a solid, upward trajectory—but he couldn't shake a growing sense that the internet presented a once-in-a-lifetime opportunity. At the time, the internet was still a relatively new concept for most people, and the idea of an online marketplace seemed risky. Yet Bezos was convinced that e-commerce had massive potential, despite the overwhelming doubts from those around him.

Bezos' fear wasn't about leaving his high-paying job or the uncertainty of starting a business—it was about taking a risk that could cost him everything. Launching an online bookstore was an audacious idea, especially since online shopping hadn't really taken off, and Bezos had no guarantee that anyone would trust the internet enough to buy books. Still, Bezos committed to the idea and made the bold decision to leave his secure job and venture into the unknown.

Rather than jumping into the deep end, he took a calculated approach. He started with books because they were universal, easily cataloged, and had a vast global demand. By focusing on a niche, Bezos was able to test his business model in a way that minimised the risk of failure. This approach, starting small but thinking big, allowed him to build confidence as Amazon slowly began to gain traction.

In fact, Bezos took incremental steps to ease into the vast world of e-commerce. Amazon's first day of business in 1995 was remarkably low key: it sold books out of Bezos' garage. With no grand marketing campaign, Bezos relied on word of mouth and a simple, effective user interface. The platform was easy to navigate, and the service was excellent, something that set it apart from other businesses.

Even as Amazon began to grow, Bezos faced immense fear. During the first few years, Amazon was operating at a loss, and many investors questioned his strategy. The skepticism was so widespread that in 1997, Bezos famously told his investors that Amazon might never turn a profit. Yet, his ability to maintain his vision remained unwavering. He believed in Amazon's potential and, more importantly, he understood that fear and setbacks were part of the process. Rather than focusing on the fear of failure, Bezos reframed it as an essential part of the path to success—an unavoidable consequence of doing something bold and transformative.

This strategic, fear-driven approach laid the foundation for what would become Amazon. By continuing to focus on customer experience, expanding the product offering, and reinvesting profits into innovation, Bezos turned a modest online bookstore into one of the most valuable companies in the world.

TURNING FEAR INTO SUCCESS: ACTIONABLE STEPS

1. Reframe the Narrative:
   » Replace fear-driven questions *"What if I fail?"* with opportunity-focused ones *"What can I learn?"*.
2. Break It Down:
   » Divide big challenges into smaller, manageable steps. Success in one area builds confidence in the next.
3. Find a Mentor or Role Model:
   » Surround yourself with people who've faced similar fears and succeeded. Their stories and guidance can provide valuable inspiration.

4. Celebrate Small Wins:

  » Each step forward, no matter how small, deserves recognition. Acknowledge your progress to build momentum.

Section 3: The Illusion of Regret

"Regret is the shadow of action left undone. Take the step and leave no room for shadows."

Regret doesn't often come from failing, it comes from not trying. It stems from the moments when fear holds us back, leaving us wondering, *What if I had just taken that chance?* While we worry about making the wrong decision, we overlook the fact that inaction is the only decision guaranteed to leave us unfulfilled. The truth is, regret isn't a reflection of failure; it's a reminder of opportunities left unexplored.

MARTIAL ARTS LESSONS: ACTING DESPITE FEAR

Earning my black belts required me to confront fear at every stage: fear of failure, fear of not being good enough, and even fear of physical pain. One moment stands out vividly: during a black belt grading, I faced an opponent who was faster, more experienced, and known for being ruthless. As we sparred, I hesitated. I let doubt creep in. *What if I make the wrong move?* And in that split second, I was struck.

That moment taught me something clear: hesitation costs more than failure. Getting struck that day wasn't the real loss—waiting was. Since then, I've trained myself to move. To trust my first instinct, even if I get hit again. Because every strike teaches you something. Each time I acted, I got sharper—not just in what I was doing, but in recognising that the decision to act was the real win. Skill grows, but so does self-trust—and that's what shifts everything.

LEARNING FROM REGRET

In many cultures, regret isn't seen as failure, but as a missed opportunity to grow. Eastern philosophies—like the mindfulness teachings in Buddhism—encourage us to focus on the present moment rather than dwell on what could have been. This perspective teaches us that every action, whether it leads to success or not, contributes to growth and learning.

In coaching leaders, I've often seen how fear of regret can paralyze decision-making. Leaders delay choices, worried about potential backlash or failure. But those who embrace action—even amid uncertainty—ultimately learn and adapt faster, building both resilience and confidence.

TURNING REGRET INTO ACTION

The key to overcoming regret is to shift your mindset from: *What might go wrong?* To: *What can I learn?* Every step you take, even if it leads to failure, offers lessons that move you forward.

- Practical Steps:
  1. Identify one opportunity you've avoided because of fear of regret.
  2. Reframe the situation: instead of focusing on the potential downside, consider the potential growth and opportunities.

3. Take one small, actionable step toward pursuing that opportunity.

MOVING BEYOND REGRET

- Reflect on the cost of inaction: *How has avoiding this opportunity impacted your growth or happiness?*
- Commit to taking one step toward addressing it. For example:
  - » If you've been hesitant to apply for a leadership role, start by updating your CV/Resume or reaching out to a mentor for advice.
  - » If you've avoided a difficult conversation, plan a time to speak openly with the person involved.

Section 4: Confronting Fear– Your Path to Unstoppable Growth

"Fear is the gatekeeper to your potential. Confront it, and you'll unlock doors you never knew existed."

Growth doesn't come from staying in the safety of your comfort zone. Growth is born from confronting fear and stepping into the unknown. Fear isn't a stop sign; it's a signal. It points to opportunities for transformation, a green light urging you to move forward. By embracing fear and using it as fuel, you can open doors to achievements and possibilities you never imagined.

TRANSFORMING FEAR INTO ENERGY

When I prepared for my first TEDx talk, fear wasn't just present—it was overwhelming. My hands were clammy, my thoughts raced, and self-doubt whispered incessantly. I questioned everything: *What if I forget my lines? What if the audience doesn't connect with my story?*

But deep down, I knew that stepping onto that stage was about more than conquering fear; it was about sharing a message I believed in, a message that could inspire others. As I walked onto the stage, fear didn't magically disappear. Instead, it transformed me. The nervous energy became a driving force, sharpening my focus and heightening my delivery.

That experience taught me a powerful lesson: fear isn't an obstacle, it's a companion. When you confront it, it doesn't go away; it evolves into a source of energy that propels you forward.

FEAR AS A COMPANION

Great leaders understand that fear is part of the journey to success. They don't seek to eliminate it; they choose to act despite it.

Muhammad Ali, widely regarded as one of the greatest boxers in history, was not only known for his athleticism but also for his ability to confront fear in the ring and beyond. Ali's story is a prime example of how fear can be used as a driving force—one that challenges the status quo and make a lasting impact on society.

Ali's career was marked by fearlessness, not just in the boxing ring, but in his personal convictions. One of his most defining moments came in 1967 when, at the peak of his career, he refused to be drafted into the Vietnam War, citing his religious beliefs and moral opposition to the conflict. At a time when many saw his defiance as unpatriotic,

Ali faced backlash, public scorn, and even legal repercussions. He was stripped of his boxing titles, and his livelihood was threatened.

But instead of succumbing to the fear of losing everything, Ali doubled down on his beliefs. He stood firm, despite the consequences, and in doing so, he became a global symbol for resistance and conviction. Ali's courage to confront fear and stand for what he believed in reshaped his identity; turning him from a champion boxer into a cultural and political icon. His actions off the ring resonated far beyond sports, inspiring millions to confront societal and personal fears, challenging injustice, and fighting for equality.

When he returned to boxing in 1970 after being reinstated, Ali's legendary matches, like the "Fight of the Century" against Joe Frazier in 1971 and the iconic "Rumble in the Jungle" against George Foreman in 1974, showcased his ability to face fear with unyielding resilience. His legendary statement, "I am the greatest," was not just a boast, but an affirmation of his belief in his ability to confront any challenge—on any stage.

Fear doesn't disqualify you from being a leader. Fear qualifies you. Your ability to act in the face of fear defines your strength and inspires those you lead.

STEPS FOR CONFRONTING FEAR

Confronting fear isn't about eliminating it; it's about changing how you respond to it. Here's a practical framework to guide you:

1. Identify the Fear: Naming your fear diminishes its power by making it tangible.
   » Example in Action: "I'm afraid of failing this project because it's outside my comfort zone."

2. Reframe the Fear: Shift your focus from what could go wrong to what could go right.
   » Example in Action: "This project could be my chance to demonstrate my ability to lead in new areas."
3. Take Incremental Steps: Fear often feels overwhelming when viewed as one giant leap. Break it into smaller, manageable actions.
   » Example in Action: Start by gathering resources, creating a plan, or seeking advice from a mentor.
4. Lean Into Discomfort: Recognise that fear signals growth. Instead of retreating, lean into the discomfort and take action despite the uncertainty.

THE RIPPLE EFFECT OF CONFRONTING FEAR

When you confront fear, you don't just transform your own mindset, you inspire those around you. As a leader, your courage becomes a model for your team. When they see you embrace challenges and step into uncertainty, they feel empowered to do the same.

Fear is a natural part of growth. By confronting it head-on, you transform it from a barrier into a stepping stone. Each time you step into fear, you move closer to your potential, unlocking doors you never knew existed.

Section 5: Face the Unknown– Transform Your Fear into Growth

"True growth begins at the edge of your comfort zone. Dare to step beyond it, and watch yourself transform."

The unknown is one of the most intimidating territories we face. It's where fears flourish, conjuring up every possible scenario of failure, rejection, or disappointment. However, here's the paradox: the unknown is also where possibilities reside. It's where growth, innovation, and transformation happen. The question remains, will you step into it?

EMBRACING UNCERTAINTY

When I transitioned from my corporate career into coaching, stepping into the unknown felt like venturing into an endless ocean with no clear shoreline. Some questions haunted me:

- *Would I find clients?*
- *Would people trust me to guide them?*
- *Was I making a mistake by leaving stability behind?*

The doubts were loud, but the alternative of staying in my comfort zone meant stagnation. I chose to embrace the uncertainty, starting with small but deliberate actions: designing my first program, pitching my services to potential clients, and refining my skills through continuous learning.

Each step brought clarity. What initially felt overwhelming began to transform into a clear path forward. The unknown, I realised, wasn't an empty void, but a blank slate, ready to be shaped by my efforts and decisions.

STRATEGIES FOR NAVIGATING THE UNKNOWN

1. Focus on the Next Step: The vastness of the unknown can feel paralysing when viewed as one massive challenge. Instead, break it down into manageable steps. Progress starts with one action.
   - » Example in Action: If you're considering starting a new venture, don't focus on the entire business plan. Start by identifying one target client or drafting a rough outline of your idea.

2. Reframe Uncertainty as Opportunity: Instead of seeing the unknown as a space filled with obstacles, view it as a blank canvas. Every step you take is a brushstroke that creates the bigger picture.
   - » Example in Action: Think of launching a new project not as a risk but as a chance to innovate and bring something unique to life.

3. Build a Support System: Surround yourself with people who've navigated similar uncertainties. Mentors, peers, or even inspiring stories can remind you that growth is possible and encourage you to keep moving forward.

THRIVING IN UNCERTAINTY

The most innovative leaders aren't those who wait for certainty; they're the ones who thrive in ambiguity.

Uncertainty isn't a reason to pause. It means a call to adapt. Leaders who step into the unknown inspire confidence in their teams, creating a culture that sees change as an opportunity rather than a threat.

TRANSFORM FEAR INTO GROWTH: ACTIONABLE STEPS

1. Identify Your Unknown: What's one area of your life or work where uncertainty is holding you back? Write it down to make it tangible.
2. Take One Small Step: Identify a single action you can take today to move closer to clarity. Whether it's a phone call, an email, or a brainstorming session, progress begins with action.
3. Reflect on Progress: After each step, take a moment to reflect. What did you learn? How has your perception of the unknown shifted?

In the early months of 2020, when the pandemic hit, companies around the world were forced to pivot, adapt, or face decline. Peloton, known for its premium indoor cycling bikes, faced its own set of uncertainties as gyms closed, and people were confined to their homes. But instead of seeing this as a threat, Peloton saw an opportunity.

While other fitness companies struggled to transition to the digital world, Peloton capitalized on the surge of people looking for home-based solutions. They quickly expanded their digital offerings, pushing out a wide range of fitness classes accessible on their app, from cycling to yoga, and strength training. They even expanded their marketing to target a new, broader audience. The result? Their subscriber base soared. In fact, by the end of 2020, Peloton had surpassed 3 million subscribers—up from just 1.09 million in early 2020—demonstrating how embracing the unknown can lead to explosive growth.

This turnaround came with its own set of challenges, from maintaining a high-quality user experience as demand increased, to scaling production at a rapid pace. Peloton's ability to pivot, innovate, and reframe a crisis as an opportunity not only set them apart but also, cemented their position as an industry leader in the new era of fitness.

HOW PELOTON EMBRACED UNCERTAINTY:

- Pivoted quickly from solely offering fitness equipment to including a robust digital platform with live classes.
- Innovated to meet new customer needs by expanding the range of workouts and engaging instructors.
- Saw a massive increase in demand and achieved growth through a combination of exceptional customer experience and smart marketing.

Peloton's story is a great illustration of how, by re-framing the unknown and embracing change, companies can not only survive but thrive.

The unknown is where the magic of growth happens. By taking intentional steps and reframing uncertainty as a space of opportunity, you'll find that the fears holding you back begin to fade. Step into the unknown; it's where your greatest potential lies.

Section 6: Creating a Fear-Free Workplace

"Fear stifles innovation and creativity. A culture of courage unlocks limitless potential."

Fear doesn't just affect individuals—it can seep into workplaces, creating cultures where employees hesitate to take risks, speak up, or innovate. As a leader, your role is to shift this dynamic by developing trust, psychological safety, and empowerment.

SUBTLE SIGNS OF FEAR IN WORKPLACES

Fear doesn't always show up dramatically. Sometimes it's the silence in meetings when new ideas are requested or the reluctance to admit mistakes. These are signs that employees feel unsafe or judged, often leading to disengagement and stagnation.

TRANSFORMING A TEAM THROUGH TRUST

I worked at a major bank in the Middle East where fear dictated how people behaved. The pressure to conform, avoid mistakes, and protect your job was real. People kept their heads down. You could feel the tension. Ideas were shut down before they were even shared. No one wanted to be the one who failed publicly.

Then, James arrived.

He came in from a firm that actually encouraged open thinking. Within days, he picked up on the culture of silence. It wasn't hard to spot. People rarely spoke up in meetings and when they did, it was only to agree with whoever was the most senior in the room.

James knew things had to change, and fast. His first step: build trust.

He set up weekly open forums, ro slides, no hierarchy. Just a space to think out loud. In these sessions, any idea was welcome, no matter how rough. He followed through too, publicly supporting small experiments and acknowledging the effort, not just the result. When one team failed to deliver on a new process, he didn't punish them. He asked what they'd learned and how it could be reused.

Within six months, the mood had shifted. Teams began to collaborate without being asked. They took more initiative. People stayed late, not out of obligation, but because they were invested. Productivity didn't just improve, it multiplied.

LEADERSHIP PRACTICES FOR A FEAR-FREE CULTURE

1. Celebrate Effort Over Results: Normalise failure by highlighting lessons learned, not just successes.
   » Example in Action: Share a story about a risk you took as a leader that didn't work out but taught you something valuable.
2. Promote Open Communication: Create spaces where employees feel safe to share ideas or concerns without fear of judgment.
   » Example in Action: Introduce anonymous feedback channels or regular one-on-one check-ins.
3. Lead with Vulnerability: Model the behaviour you want to see. Admit when you're uncertain or have made a mistake; showing that fear is part of the process.

A VISION FOR COURAGEOUS WORKPLACES

Imagine walking into an office where every voice matters, where risks are celebrated, and where mistakes are seen as stepping stones to innovation. This isn't a utopia—it's a workplace led by someone who recognises that courage, not fear, drives progress.

Section 7: Conquering Decision Paralysis

"Fear is the fog that obscures your path; clarity comes when you step through it."

Indecision is one of fear's most subtle and paralysing effects. It keeps you stuck in a loop, oscillating between options, afraid to commit in case the wrong choice leads to failure. But the reality is, inaction is often more damaging than making a wrong decision.

Growth happens when you take action—even if it's imperfect action.

WHY INDECISION HAPPENS

Indecision is rooted in fear, fear of failure, fear of judgment, or fear of making the "wrong" choice. It often arises because:

1. We Overestimate Risks: The mind exaggerates potential downsides, making challenges seem larger than they truly are.
2. We Underestimate Resilience: People often doubt their ability to recover from setbacks, forgetting that failure is a natural part of learning.

3. We Seek Perfection: The desire for a flawless outcome can delay progress, as no decision feels "good enough."

By staying in limbo, we miss opportunities to grow, learn, and adapt. Action, even if imperfect, creates momentum.

OVERCOMING PARALYSIS IN LAUNCHING A PROGRAM

When I was deciding whether to launch my 5 States of Optimisation coaching program, I found myself stuck in a decision paralysis. My thoughts were dominated by "What ifs": *What if no one signs up? What if it doesn't resonate with clients?*

The fear of failure loomed large, leading me to delay the decision in search of certainty that would never come. However, upon reflection, I realised that the cost of inaction far outweighed the risk of failure. By focusing on progress rather than perfection, I chose to launch.

Instead of trying to perfect it before launching, I did what most don't, I shared the whole thing. I brought in ten people I knew and trusted. Let's call one of them Simone. I gave her full access: tools, exercises, even live coaching sessions, a l exactly how I planned to run it for paying clients. No filters. I wanted their real feedback. Simone had just stepped into a senior leadership role at a company known for its rigid hierarchy and a culture of fear. She'd come from a different environment, one where openness and trust weren't optional, they were normal. So, when she saw the framework, her first reaction wasn't about tools, it was: *"This could actually help me change the way people work here."* That stuck with me.

The 5 States of Optimisation clicked for her because it wasn't abstract, it was real, in-the-room, usable. Over the weeks, I adjusted the delivery, refined the flow, and cut what didn't serve. The result? A program that now helps execs increase productivity, strengthen leadership, and get measurable results across life and work. That experience taught me a simple, but powerful lesson: waiting for the "perfect" time or solution leads nowhere. Progress starts with the first step.

BREAK THROUGH PARALYSIS

1. Define Success Clearly:
   - » What does a positive outcome look like? Often, indecision stems from a lack of clarity about what you truly want. Write down your desired result and align your actions with that vision.
   - » Example in Action: If you're deciding whether to pursue a new job opportunity, clarify what success looks like career growth, better work-life balance, or financial improvement. Use this clarity to guide your decision.

2. List the Worst-Case Scenario:
   - » Write down the worst possible outcome and ask yourself:
     - · *How likely is this to happen?*
     - · *If it does happen, can I recover?*
   - » Example in Action: If you're hesitant about starting a business, your worst-case scenario might be financial loss or a slow start. By acknowledging these risks, you can plan strategies to mitigate them, such as starting small or maintaining a safety net.

3. Commit to Progress, Not Perfection:
   » No decision is flawless, and no outcome is guaranteed. The goal is to move forward, learn from the experience, and adjust as needed.
   » Example in Action: Launching a project or initiative? Start with a minimum viable version, gather feedback, and improve as you go.

ACTING DESPITE UNCERTAINTY

Innovative leaders understand that waiting for perfect conditions is a recipe for stagnation.

In 2009, Travis Kalanick made a bold decision that would change the transportation industry forever: he co-founded Uber. At the time, the taxi industry was a traditional, highly regulated sector with limited innovation. The idea of using a smartphone app to request a ride from a private driver was unheard of, and many thought it was a risky, if not impossible, venture.

However, Kalanick and his co-founder, Garrett Camp, saw an opportunity. They took action. Despite knowing the idea would face major resistance from both taxi unions and regulators, Kalanick pushed ahead. They bet on the fact that people would embrace the convenience and affordability of ride-sharing, and that technology could radically improve an outdated service.

The early days were anything but easy. Uber faced legal battles, protests from taxi drivers, and a massive uphill struggle to prove the concept. But Kalanick's ability to act decisively, even when faced with an uncertain future, is what set Uber apart. He didn't wait for perfect conditions. Instead of letting the fear of failure paralyze him, he kept moving, learning from mistakes, and refining the business model.

In just a few short years, Uber transformed from a small startup in San Francisco to a global platform operating in hundreds of cities. Kalanick's boldness and refusal to wait for the perfect moment ultimately disrupted the entire transportation industry and established Uber as one of the most valuable tech companies in the world.

Kalanick's story is a powerful reminder that decision paralysis is a luxury you can't afford when you're pushing the boundaries of innovation. By taking action—even if it's not perfect—you create the momentum needed to succeed.

PRACTICAL EXERCISE: TAKE ACTION ON A PENDING DECISION

1. Identify a decision you've been avoiding.
2. Take 15 minutes to write down:
   » The best-case scenario if you act.
   » The worst-case scenario if you act.
   » The cost of inaction if you don't act.
3. Choose one small step to move forward today, whether it's seeking advice, researching options, or committing to a deadline.

Decisions, even imperfect ones, create momentum. By stepping through fear and taking action, you'll discover that clarity often lies on the other side of movement. The path may not always be clear, but the act of moving forward transforms fear into progress.

Section 8: The Power of Taking the First Step

"The only true failure is the failure to try. Each step forward, no matter how small, is a victory over fear."

Momentum is the antidote to fear. Often, the hardest part of any journey isn't the middle or the end; t's taking that very first step. Fear convinces you to stay where you are, whispering doubts about failure, inadequacy, or uncertainty. But here's the truth: the first step doesn't have to be perfect; it just has to happen. With every small action, fear begins to fade, and is replaced by a growing sense of capability and confidence.

WHY THE FIRST STEP MATTERS

The first step isn't about achieving mastery or solving every problem; it's about breaking the inertia that fear creates. Fear thrives in stillness, growing louder as we remain motionless, building a narrative of "what ifs" that keeps us stuck. Taking action, no matter how small, disrupts that cycle and proves to yourself that progress is possible.

When I started my martial arts training, I didn't begin as an expert. My first step was simply walking into the class. I didn't know what to expect, but I was willing to try. That single act of pushing through the fear of the unknown led to years of discipline, growth, and eventual mastery.

Each punch I threw, each form I practiced, and each belt I earned built momentum. What felt intimidating on day one became second nature through repetition. The journey didn't start with mastery, it started with a single, imperfect step.

MOMENTUM IN ACTION: STARTING MY COACHING BUSINESS

Starting my coaching business felt like stepping off a cliff. The fear of failure loomed large:

- *What if no one hires me?*
- *What if I'm not good enough?*

But instead of focusing on the overwhelming goal of building a successful business, I broke it down into small, manageable steps. I started by offering free sessions, gathering feedback, and refining my services. Each small win reinforced my belief that fear thrives on inaction but diminishes with momentum. The more I acted, the less power fear had over me.

STRATEGIES TO TAKE THE FIRST STEP

1. Start Small:
   - » Fear often stems from the perception that a challenge is too big. Break it into the smallest possible step and focus only on that.
   - » Example in Action: If your goal is to write a book, don't aim to draft the entire manuscript. Start with a single paragraph or brainstorming ideas.
2. Focus on Progress, Not Perfection:
   - » The first step doesn't have to be flawless; it just has to happen. Remember, perfection is the enemy of progress.

» Example in Action: Nervous about networking? Commit to sending a single LinkedIn message instead of trying to attend a major event right away.

3. Reframe Failure:

» Instead of asking, *"What if I fail?"* ask yourself, *"What can I learn from this?"* Every step forward, even if imperfect, provides valuable lessons.

» Example in Action: If you're hesitant to start a project at work, view it as an opportunity to test and refine your skills rather than aiming for immediate success.

MINI-CHALLENGE: TAKE ONE SMALL STEP TODAY

Identify one goal or challenge you've been avoiding because of fear. Within the next 24 hours, commit to taking the smallest possible step toward it.

- Examples of Small Steps:
  - » Send an email to someone who can guide or mentor you.
  - » Research a course or skill you've been wanting to pursue.
  - » Write down your thoughts in a journal to clarify your goals.

This single act creates the momentum needed to move forward, transforming fear into fuel for growth.

Every great journey starts with a single step. The hardest part is often deciding to move, but once you do, the path begins to reveal itself. Fear loses its power in the face of action, and with each step, you'll find yourself closer to the growth, success, and fulfillment you're capable of achieving.

Section 9: Reflection

"Fear will always exist, but its power over you is a choice. Choose to let it fuel your courage, not your hesitation."

Fear is not the enemy we've made it out to be. It's not a sign that you're weak, unprepared, or destined to fail. Instead, fear is your compass, pointing directly to what matters most. Fear shows up when the stakes are high because it recognises the potential for growth, learning, and transformation.

Think of every great achievement—yours or someone else's. Behind each one lies a moment of doubt, hesitation, or fear. That fear wasn't a signal to stop; it was a signal to start.

This chapter isn't just about recognising fear, but about learning to work with it. Fear isn't a roadblock; it's a green light signaling that you're stepping into a space where meaningful change can happen. Whether you're starting a new project, speaking in front of an audience, or building a team, fear is often the first sign that you're on the edge of something extraordinary.

We explored how fear operates in the brain, often overreacting to challenges that are manageable. You've seen how small, actionable steps can dismantle even the largest fears, turning hesitation into momentum. And you've seen how leaders who model courage not only inspire trust but also unlock creativity and resilience in those around them.

LOOKING AHEAD

Fear doesn't disappear, it evolves as you grow. The better you become at confronting it, the more equipped you'll be to handle life's challenges. In the next chapter, we'll explore how self-awareness deepens your ability to harness fear, leading to stronger connections and greater influence in your personal and professional life.

You don't need to eliminate fear to succeed; you simply need to act despite it. Courage isn't the absence of fear; it's the resolve to move forward, knowing the stakes are worth it. The life you want, the impact you're capable of making, and the connections you're destined to build all lie just beyond the "What if?"

The prompts below are here to help you look at where fear is showing up now—and how you can meet it with clarity, honesty, and action.

Reflection Questions

SECTION 1:
What fear are you currently facing, and how can you reframe it as an opportunity for growth?

SECTION 2:
What fear is currently holding you back? What's one small step you can take today to move closer to overcoming it?

SECTION 3:
How has regret shaped your decisions in the past, and how can you use that awareness to guide your actions moving forward?

SECTION 4:
What's one area in your leadership where a gear shift might be necessary? How can you prepare yourself and your team to embrace this change?

SECTION 5:
What unknown have you been avoiding because it feels overwhelming? Write down the first step you can take today to turn that uncertainty into an opportunity for growth.

SECTION 6:

What can you do in your role whether as a leader or a team member to create an environment where people feel empowered to take risks and innovate?

SECTION 7:

What decision have you been delaying because of fear or uncertainty? What's one action you can take today to step through the fog and gain clarity?

SECTION 8:

What small step can you take today that will begin to dissolve the fear holding you back? How will that one action pave the way for the next?

CHAPTER 5

Start Creating Your Masterpiece

> *"True masterpieces are born not from perfection, but from the courage to face doubts and the relentless pursuit of your authentic self."*

Imagine standing in front of a blank canvas. The possibilities are infinite, but so is the uncertainty. Where do you begin? What if you make a mistake? Too often, we let the fear of imperfection stop us before we even start. Yet, masterpieces aren't created in a single stroke; they emerge from layers, corrections, and bold decisions.

Throughout my life, I've stood before this metaphorical canvas many times. From leaving a stable corporate career to pursuing coaching, to moments of self-doubt about whether I was on the right path. Each decision became a stroke on my canvas, forming the masterpiece I'm still creating today.

This chapter is your invitation to pick up the brush and start painting your masterpiece—not merely as a reflection of who you are, but as a pathway to lead yourself and others from within.

Section 1: Your Life Is a Canvas

"Every brushstroke, bold or hesitant, contributes to the masterpiece of your life."

Your life is your greatest work of art. Every decision you make, every risk you take, and every lesson you learn adds a brushstroke to your canvas. Some strokes are vibrant and confident, while others may feel uncertain or chaotic. Yet together, they create the unique masterpiece that is your life—a reflection of your choices, values, and authenticity.

THE POWER OF OWNING YOUR CANVAS

For years, I felt like my canvas was being painted by someone else. I pursued goals that looked impressive on paper but left me feeling unfulfilled. My choices were driven by external expectations rather than my own values, and the colours of my life felt muted and constrained.

It wasn't until I took ownership of my canvas—choosing colours and strokes that aligned with who I was—that my life began to take on meaning. I made deliberate decisions that reflected my passions, even if they didn't align with what others expected. Each new stroke felt more personal and authentic, and over time, the picture of my life became one I was proud to call my own.

AUTHENTICITY OVER APPROVAL

Consider the life of Vincent van Gogh, one of the most iconic and influential artists in history. Born on March 30, 1853, in the Netherlands, van Gogh created over 2,000 works of art during his lifetime, yet he sold only one painting, *The Red Vineyard*, in 1890. Despite his lack of recognition, he stayed true to his artistic vision, which differed vastly from the more restrained art popular in his time. His works were filled with raw emotion and vibrant colour, setting him apart from the conventional styles that dominated the art world.

Van Gogh faced constant rejection and struggled with mental health issues, spending time in psychiatric hospitals, and even cutting off part of his own ear. His paintings were often misunderstood by society, and his personal struggles led to many periods of deep isolation. Despite these hardships, he continued to create, driven by an inner passion that couldn't be silenced by the opinions of others. His art was an authentic expression of his inner world, and it resonated deeply with his emotions—not the expectations of his time.

Nowadays, van Gogh's works are considered some of the most celebrated and valuable paintings in the world. His masterpieces, such as *Starry Night* (1889) and *Sunflowers* (1888), are admired for their emotional depth and the originality of their style. These paintings now hang in prestigious museums worldwide, and van Gogh's influence on modern art is undeniable. His journey, marked by perseverance despite overwhelming adversity, shows that greatness often comes from staying true to one's inner voice, even when the world doesn't understand.

Van Gogh's story serves as a powerful reminder that genuine success isn't about external validation, it's about creating your masterpiece—no matter the recognition you receive during your lifetime.

REFLECT ON YOUR CANVAS

Take a moment to examine the canvas of your life:

- Are the colours bold, vibrant, and exciting, or do they feel muted and constrained?
- Are the strokes deliberate and personal, or are they shaped by someone else's expectations?

The beauty of a canvas is that it's never too late to add a new stroke. One deliberate choice today, no matter how small, can change the entire picture.

ADDING INTENTIONAL BRUSHSTROKES

To create a life that feels authentic and fulfilling, you must paint with intention. Here's how to start:

1. Reflect on Your Canvas as It Stands Today:
   - » Identify parts of your life that reflect your authentic self. What choices, relationships, or activities bring you joy and align with your values?
   - » Acknowledge areas that feel like they were painted by someone else's choices driven by external expectations or fear of judgment.
2. Add One Small, Intentional Brushstroke:
   - » Make a deliberate choice this week to align your canvas with your authentic self.

» Examples in Action:
  · Say "no" to an obligation that feels misaligned with your priorities.
  · Say "yes" to an opportunity or activity that excites you, even if it feels outside your comfort zone.
  · Spend time nurturing a relationship or hobby that reflects who you are at your core.
3. Embrace the Messiness of Growth:
  » Remember that no masterpiece is perfect. Bold, messy strokes often add depth and character. Give yourself permission to make imperfect but authentic choices.

The beauty of a blank canvas is that it's never too late to create something meaningful. Every brushstroke, whether bold or hesitant, contributes to the masterpiece of your life. Start today by painting with your own colours and watch as your canvas transforms into a true reflection of who you are.

Section 2: The Foundation of a Masterpiece

"Without a strong foundation, even the most beautiful masterpiece will falter."

Every masterpiece begins with a solid foundation. Whether it's a painting, a building, or the life you're creating, the foundation provides the stability needed to support growth and complexity. In your life, this foundation is built on three essential pillars: self-awareness, resilience, and authenticity. Together, they form the framework that allows you to thrive, adapt, and lead with purpose.

THE THREE PILLARS OF A STRONG FOUNDATION

1. Self-Awareness: Self-awareness is the cornerstone of personal growth. It's knowing who you are, what you value, and what drives your decisions. It's about embracing your strengths and owning your weaknesses, using both as tools for growth.

2. Resilience: Resilience is your ability to recover from setbacks and turn challenges into stepping stones. It's not about avoiding failure but learning from it, using each stumble as an opportunity to grow stronger.

3. Authenticity: Authenticity is the alignment between your values and your actions. It's living and leading with integrity, making choices that reflect who you truly are rather than what others expect you to be.

It was 2011 that I would say I stepped into Leadership, because I was leading a group of people in multiple locations. I felt like I was navigating without a map. I was responsible for making decisions that impacted others, yet I questioned whether I was the right person for the role. Every difficult conversation, every mistake, every moment of doubt felt like a test of whether I truly belonged. It wasn't just about leading others; it was about leading myself through uncertainty.

But those moments also revealed my core strengths, empathy, adaptability, and a genuine desire to help others grow. By reflecting on what mattered most to me, I strengthened my self-awareness. By reframing failures as lessons, I developed resilience. And by aligning my coaching approach with my values, I found authenticity. Over time, the foundation that once felt fragile became the bedrock of my work and my life.

In 2010, Novak Djokovic was already a top player, but nowhere near the status of Federer or Nadal. He was inconsistent in Grand Slams, often battling health issues mid-match. At the time, he was known for retiring early and fading under pressure. Critics labelled him mentally weak.

Instead of ignoring the noise, Djokovic took a hard look at himself. He realised it wasn't just physical; it was emotional. Stress, breathing problems, even diet were holding him back. That level of self-awareness pushed him to overhaul everything. He changed his training, his team, and controversially, his diet. He went gluten-free and cut out dairy completely—a decision many dismissed at first.

The results were immediate. In 2011, he won 10 titles, including three Grand Slams, and finished the year as world number one. But that year wasn't just about trophies, it was the turning point in how he saw himself. He stopped trying to be liked and focused on being real. He embraced his role as the disruptor in a sport that didn't welcome change.

His resilience shone each time he clawed back from match points down, beat the crowd favourites, or returned from injury. Through it all he remained authentic—even when that invited criticism for speaking his mind or doing things differently.

Djokovic didn't just build a career; he built a foundation of self-trust. That's why, even now, people might doubt him, but he never doubts himself.

STRENGTHEN YOUR FOUNDATION

Building and maintaining a strong foundation requires regular attention. Start by identifying one pillar that feels underdeveloped and take a small, intentional action to strengthen it.

1. For Self-Awareness:
   - » Reflect on what drives your decisions. Ask yourself:
     - *What values guide my choices?*
     - *What strengths do I rely on, and what areas could I improve?*
   - » Action Step: Journal for 10 minutes about a recent decision and what it reveals about your priorities and motivations.

2. For Resilience:
   - » Reflect on a recent setback. Instead of focusing on the failure, ask:
     - *What lesson did this experience teach me?*
     - *How can I apply that lesson moving forward?*
   - » Action Step: Write down one way you'll use the lesson from a past failure to approach your next challenge differently.

3. For Authenticity:
   - » Identify areas where your actions may not fully align with your values. Ask yourself:
     - *Where am I compromising what matters most to me?*
     - *What changes can I make to live more authentically?*
   - » Action Step: Commit to one value-driven action this week, such as saying "no" to something misaligned or speaking up about what matters to you.

A strong foundation doesn't eliminate challenges, but it ensures you have the stability to weather them. By investing in self-awareness, resilience, and authenticity, you build a life that is both enduring and uniquely your own. Every action you take to strengthen these pillars brings you closer to creating a masterpiece that reflects your true self.

Section 3: The Art of Self-Expression

"Your masterpiece reflects not just what you create, but who you are."

Every masterpiece is a reflection of its creator. The bold strokes, intricate details, and vibrant colours are all infused with the artist's essence. Your life is no different. It's not about conforming to a mold or meeting external expectations—it's about allowing your true self to shine through everything you do. Self-expression is the bridge between who you are and what you create—and it's the defining feature of your personal masterpiece.

BREAKING FREE FROM THE MOLD

For a long time, I tried to fit into a mold of what I thought a successful leader should be. I prioritised looking professional over being authentic; presenting a polished version of myself while suppressing my true voice and personality. On the surface, it worked. I appeared capable and confident. But internally, I felt disconnected—as though I was wearing a mask.

The turning point came when I decided to lead from within. I stopped trying to fit the mold. I wore what I felt comfortable in a blue t-shirt or jumper, relaxed trousers and trainers instead of stiff suits. I stopped masking my energy in meetings. I'd bring up martial arts analogies, reference my latest bike ride, or say exactly what I thought without softening it to be liked. That's when things shifted. I wasn't trying to impress; I was just being myself. And the more I leaned into that, the more trust I built. Clients opened up more. Teams responded better. I wasn't drained pretending. I was energised. It didn't just improve my work—it changed how I showed up for people. And how they showed up for me.

Gary Vaynerchuk, better known as Gary Vee, is a prime example of someone who has mastered the art of self-expression and authenticity in the business world. His journey is one of bold self-belief, unapologetic authenticity, and the willingness to take risks—no matter how unconventional they may seem.

Gary's career began in the wine industry, where he took over his family's business and turned it into a multi-million-dollar operation by embracing the power of digital marketing. However, it wasn't just about the numbers for Gary. His true breakthrough came when he began showing up as his real self—flaws, quirks, and all. His candidness, particularly on social media, allowed him to connect with people in a way that was raw, relatable, and real.

He's openly shared his thoughts on the importance of patience, hard work, and the relentless pursuit of your passion. But what really sets him apart is his focus on vulnerability and self-awareness. Gary constantly emphasises that success isn't just about making money—it's about doing the work that fuels your passion and aligning with your true self.

In 2009, when Gary launched VaynerMedia, he made sure that it wasn't just another marketing agency. Instead, it was a platform built on the idea that business should be about connection, transparency, and creating value—not just selling products. His constant message to his audience is "be yourself" and "stop trying to fit into others' expectations."

Gary's authenticity, which some might call bold or even brash, is actually the cornerstone of his success. His presence on platforms like Instagram, Twitter, and YouTube has allowed him to build a massive following—not by pretending to be perfect, but by being his unapologetic self. This approach has helped him cultivate deeper relationships with his audience, and it's a crucial reason for his success.

Gary Vaynerchuk's journey is not just about business success; it's a testament to the power of embracing who you truly are and showing that to the world. In an era that often rewards conformity, Gary teaches us that real success comes from unapologetically being yourself—whether you're making a career shift, building a business, or pursuing personal growth. By focusing on authenticity, Gary has built a brand that resonates with people at a deep level, demonstrating that when you express your true self, the rewards follow.

WHY SELF-EXPRESSION MATTERS

Self-expression isn't just about creativity, it's about connection, authenticity, and fulfillment. When you express who you truly are:

1. You Build Deeper Connections: Authenticity resonates with others, creating trust and mutual understanding.
2. You Find Greater Fulfillment: Living and working in alignment with your true self creates a sense of purpose and joy.

3. You Inspire Others: By being authentic, you encourage those around you to embrace their uniqueness.

EMBRACING YOUR AUTHENTICITY

To express your true self, you first need to identify where you've been holding back. Ask yourself:

> » *Where in my life do I feel restricted or inauthentic?*
> » *What's stopping me from expressing my true self here?*

If you've been holding back your ideas in meetings, challenge yourself to share one perspective in the next discussion.

If you've avoided showing vulnerability in relationships, start with a small act of honesty, like sharing how you feel about a challenge you're facing.

Take one small step this week to remove a restriction and let your authentic self shine.

BUILDING THE COURAGE TO BE SEEN

Self-expression requires vulnerability. It's about letting go of the fear of judgment and trusting that your uniqueness is your greatest strength. Here's how to begin:

1. Identify What Makes You Unique: Reflect on the qualities, passions, and experiences that define you. How can you integrate them more fully into your work, relationships, or creative pursuits?
2. Start Small: Expressing your authentic self doesn't have to be a grand gesture. Begin with small, deliberate actions, like sharing your opinion in a group setting or pursuing a hobby you've neglected.

3. Celebrate Your Voice: Recognise the value of your perspective and contributions. Each act of self-expression strengthens your confidence and reinforces your authenticity.

Your masterpiece is uniquely yours, and its greatest beauty lies in its authenticity. When you express your true self boldly and unapologetically, you create something that's not only impactful, but deeply meaningful. Dare to embrace your uniqueness and let your masterpiece reflect the heart and soul of who you are.

Section 4: Break the Mold

"To create something extraordinary, you must step away from the ordinary."

Masterpieces aren't created by following a template; they're born from innovation, risk, and the courage to challenge conventions. Breaking the mold means stepping away from patterns, expectations, or limitations that no longer serve you. It's about giving yourself permission to create something that's uniquely yours, even when it feels uncertain or unconventional.

Starting my own business, it felt like stepping into the unknown. For years, I had followed the "rules" of stability and success: a secure job, a clear career path, and external validation. But over time, these rules felt more like restrictions, confining me into a mold that no longer reflected who I was or aspired to be.

Making the decision to leave wasn't easy. The fear of judgment, failure, and uncertainty was very real. But so was the excitement of creating something new, something that aligned with my values and passions. Breaking the mold allowed me to live and work authentically; and it became the foundation for a career that feels deeply fulfilling.

Steve Jobs wasn't the kind of leader who followed the rules. In fact, he made a career out of breaking all the rules.

In the mid-1970s, the world of technology was all about practicality and function. Most companies were focused on building machines that were efficient and utilitarian. But Jobs saw something different. He saw the potential for technology to be more than just a tool; he saw it as a medium for creativity and design.

In 1976, after dropping out of college, Jobs co-founded Apple with a bold vision: to make computers that were not only functional but also beautiful and easy to use. The idea of merging technology with design was a radical departure from the norm. Many in the industry believed that design was secondary to performance. But Jobs, driven by a relentless desire to challenge the status quo, believed the two were inseparable.

His willingness to break away from conventional thinking led to the creation of the Macintosh in 1984. It was a gamble. The product was radically different from anything else on the market. It wasn't just a computer; it was a statement. And while the Mac faced early struggles, its design laid the groundwork for what would later become one of the most valuable companies in the world.

Jobs didn't stop there. He broke the mold again and again with the creation of the iPod, iPhone, and iPad products that changed entire industries. Each of these innovations defied traditional business logic. Jobs had the vision to see what others couldn't.

Jobs' story reminds us that breaking the mold isn't about rebelling just for the sake of it. It's about seeing possibilities where others see limits, restrictions, and having the courage to pursue them. His legacy shows us that real innovation often comes from stepping away from the predictable path and creating something uniquely your own.

Just as Jobs did, you too can also break the mold not by rejecting tradition, but by recognising when it no longer serves you, and daring to create something extraordinary.

RECOGNISING THE MOLDS THAT HOLD YOU BACK

Think about the molds in your own life. Are there patterns, expectations, or routines that no longer serve you? These molds might feel safe or familiar, but they can also limit your growth. Breaking free doesn't always require a dramatic leap—it starts with one deliberate step:

- Exploring a new idea.
- Challenging a limiting belief.
- Saying "no" to something misaligned with your values.

Each small chip in the mold creates space for something extraordinary to emerge.

STEPS TO BREAK THE MOLD

1. Identify the Mold:
   » Reflect on an area where you feel stuck, whether it's a job, routine, relationship, or belief. Ask yourself:
     · *What's keeping me here?*
     · *Have I outgrown this pattern or expectation?*

2. Examine the Fear:
   » Fear often keeps us in molds that no longer fit. Ask yourself:
     · *What am I afraid of losing by breaking this mold?*
     · *What could I gain by stepping out of it?*
   » You may find that the fear of staying stagnant outweighs the fear of change.
3. Take One Small Action:
   » Change doesn't have to be dramatic. Start with one step that challenges the status quo.
   » Examples in Action:
     · If you're stuck in a routine, try something new, whether it's a class, a skill, or a different way of approaching a problem.
     · If you're in a job that feels restrictive, explore other opportunities by researching roles or networking with peers in your desired field.
     · If you're holding onto a limiting belief, challenge it by seeking evidence that supports a more empowering narrative.

THE RIPPLE EFFECT OF BREAKING THE MOLD

Each step you take to break the mold not only frees you, but also inspires others. When you challenge conventions, you pave the way for those around you to do the same. Your courage becomes a catalyst for change—both in your life and in the lives of those who witness your journey.

Breaking the mold isn't about rejecting tradition for its own sake— it's about recognising when the old ways no longer serve you and having the courage to create something new. Each step away from the ordinary brings you closer to the extraordinary, allowing you to craft a masterpiece that reflects your true self.

Section 5: The Courage to Be Imperfect

"Imperfection isn't a flaw—it's the soul of your masterpiece."

Perfectionism whispers that nothing is ever good enough. It convinces us that we can't start until every detail is flawless and every outcome is guaranteed. It tells us that mistakes are failures and imperfections are weaknesses. But here's the truth: imperfection isn't a flaw—it's what gives your masterpiece its soul, its character, and its authenticity.

BREAKING FREE FROM PERFECTIONISM

In my early coaching sessions, I fell into the perfectionism trap. I over-prepared for every session, trying to anticipate every question and outcome. I held myself to an impossible standard, fearing that any misstep would undermine my credibility.

But some of the most meaningful breakthroughs in my coaching journey didn't come from perfect plans. They came from moments of vulnerability when I admitted that I didn't have all the answers or allowed a conversation to take an unexpected turn. Those moments reminded me that authenticity and connection matter more than perfection.

THE BEAUTY OF IMPERFECTION

Wabi-Sabi is an ancient Japanese aesthetic and philosophical concept that celebrates the beauty of imperfection, transience, and the natural cycle of life. The term itself is derived from two words:

- Wabi: Originally, this term referred to the loneliness or solitude found in nature, but over time, it has come to describe the simple, rustic beauty of things that evoke a sense of humility and modesty. Wabi emphasises the idea of living in harmony with nature, embracing simplicity, and valuing the understated.

- Sabi: This refers to the beauty that comes with the passage of time. Sabi celebrates the weathered, aged, or patinaed elements of life, things that have been worn down or aged by time—yet still carry a sense of dignity and grace. It's the beauty of something that shows its age or its history, like a weathered stone or a vintage item that has been loved and used over the years.

THE CONCEPT OF WABI-SABI

At the heart of wabi-sabi is the appreciation of imperfection and impermanence. It is the recognition that nothing lasts forever and that there is an inherent beauty in the process of aging, breaking, and healing.

Wabi-sabi invites people to look at objects, experiences, and life itself from a different perspective; one that values authenticity over superficial beauty, and flaws over perfection.

KEY ELEMENTS OF WABI-SABI

1. Embracing Imperfection: In wabi-sabi, imperfections are not something to be hidden but rather something to be celebrated. A crack in a piece of pottery, the fading colour of an old painting, or the asymmetry of a handmade object all carry significance. These flaws reflect the passage of time and the stories behind the object, making them more valuable and meaningful than something that is flawless.

2. Transience and the Beauty of Aging: Wabi-sabi acknowledges that nothing in life is permanent. Everything is in a state of constant change, and this transience is what makes life beautiful. Just as leaves turn from green to gold and then decay, people, objects, and experiences are all part of a cyclical process of coming into being, changing, and eventually fading away. There is beauty in the fleeting, the temporary, and the aging.

3. Simplicity and Subtlety: Wabi-sabi encourages a life of simplicity. The aesthetic favors modesty, natural forms, and muted colours over extravagance or opulence. It's about appreciating the quiet elegance of a weathered fence, the plainness of a stone path, or the understated beauty of a raw wooden table. The idea is that the less something demands attention, the more it reveals its true beauty.

4. Natural Materials and Textures: In wabi-sabi, materials that show the signs of their natural origins are highly valued. This might include objects made from clay, wood, bamboo, and stone; materials that evolve and change over time. It's the

natural texture of these materials, their imperfections, and the way they change as they age that makes them so special.

WABI-SABI IN EVERYDAY LIFE

Wabi-sabi isn't just an aesthetic that applies to art, pottery, or nature. It's a way of living and thinking that can also shape how you approach personal growth, relationships, and self-acceptance. Here's how it can manifest in life:

- Personal Growth: Instead of striving for perfection, wabi-sabi teaches us to embrace our flaws and learn from them. We all have scars, both physical and emotional ones, that define who we are. These imperfections make us authentic, just as the cracks in an old vase add character. Wabi-sabi reminds us that we don't need to be flawless to be beautiful or valuable.

- Relationships: In relationships, wabi-sabi encourages acceptance of others' imperfections. Just like an old object that has been loved and used over the years, people are shaped by their experiences. The imperfections in relationships, the misunderstandings, the disagreements, the struggles, are all part of the journey. Rather than seeking out perfection, wabi-sabi teaches us to find beauty in the growth that occurs through time and hardship.

- Mindfulness: Wabi-sabi is also about living in the present moment, appreciating the here and now. By recognising that everything is temporary, we are encouraged to cherish each moment—not in a frantic, perfection-seeking way—but in a more relaxed, open-hearted manner. The fleeting beauty of a sunset, a cup of tea, or a conversation with a friend becomes something sacred in the wabi-sabi view of the world.

THE AESTHETIC OF WABI-SABI:

Wabi-sabi can also be found in art and design, where imperfection is deliberately incorporated into objects, architecture, and gardens. For example:

- Japanese Tea Bowls: Traditional Japanese tea bowls made for tea ceremonies often embrace wabi-sabi aesthetics. These bowls may have irregular shapes, rough textures, or even cracks that have been lovingly repaired with gold or silver (known as *kintsugi*). Rather than being discarded, the cracks are highlighted, symbolizing resilience and the passage of time.
- Gardens: In Japanese gardens, rocks, plants, and paths are arranged to create a harmonious balance with nature. The placement of each element is done intentionally, but with an acceptance that nature's growth and decay will alter the landscape over time. The garden's beauty evolves, just as the seasons change.

THE WISDOM OF WABI-SABI

Wabi-sabi can be seen as a way of finding peace in a world that often encourages perfectionism and constant striving. It teaches us that true contentment comes not from reaching a finished, perfected state, but from embracing life's unfinished nature. Whether it's in the way we look at an old building or our own wrinkles, wabi-sabi helps us see beauty where others might see flaws.

By adopting this mindset, we can learn to appreciate ourselves, others, and the world around us more deeply. We can focus less on seeking perfection and instead learn to appreciate the fleeting and imperfect moments that truly make life worth living.

What would change if you embraced imperfection as a natural part of the process? How would it free you to create with courage and authenticity?

WHY IMPERFECTION IS ESSENTIAL FOR GROWTH

1. Imperfection Reflects Humanity: Mistakes and flaws make us relatable. They show others that we're real, encouraging connection and trust.

2. Mistakes Lead to Learning: Every misstep is an opportunity to grow. By embracing mistakes, you gain insights that move you closer to mastery.

3. Progress Over Perfection: Waiting for perfection often leads to stagnation. Taking action, even imperfect action, builds momentum and confidence.

EMBRACE IMPERFECTION

1. Reframe Mistakes as Opportunities:
   » Instead of seeing mistakes as failures, view them as lessons. Ask yourself:
     · *What can I learn from this?*
     · *How can this experience shape my growth?*

2. Celebrate Progress, No Matter How Small:

» Focus on what you've accomplished rather than what remains undone. Progress s more important than perfection.

» Example in Action: If you've been hesitant to launch a project, celebrate the steps you've taken whether it's brainstorming ideas, drafting a plan, or seeking feedback.

3. Let Go of External Validation:

» Create for the joy of the process, not for approval from others.

» Example in Action: When working on a creative or professional project, focus on what feels meaningful to you rather than trying to meet others' expectations.

Imperfection isn't something to fear, it's something to celebrate. It's the cracks and flaws that add depth to your story and authenticity to your journey. By letting go of perfectionism, you free yourself to create with courage, connect with others on a deeper level, and find joy in the process. After all, it's the imperfections that make a masterpiece unforgettable.

Section 6: Create Boldly

"Bold action isn't reckless—it's intentional and transformative."

Creating boldly is about stepping into uncertainty with purpose and courage. It doesn't mean acting without thought; it means taking intentional risks, trusting the process, and believing in your ability to navigate challenges along the way. Bold action is the catalyst for growth, innovation, and transformation.

HOSTING MY FIRST WORKSHOP

When I decided to host my first workshop, doubt crept in at every turn.

- *Would anyone show up?*
- *Would my message resonate?*
- *What if I failed?*

Despite the uncertainty, I knew I had to try. The workshop wasn't perfect, I didn't get the turnout I expected, I stumbled over my words more than once, and the tech glitched halfway through. I was trying to do too much with too little prep. But it became a turning point. By putting myself out there, I saw what landed, what didn't, and what I needed to fix. More than anything, it gave me the confidence to keep going. Each subsequent workshop built on that foundation. The initial act of boldness—imperfect as it was—created a shift I couldn't have reached through planning alone. Now, I speak to large crowds, audiences that are fully engaged, and I connect with each one in a meaningful way. A far cry from where I started.

REDEFINING WHAT'S POSSIBLE

Daniel Ek's bold vision for the music industry forever altered how we listen to music. In 2006, Ek and his team launched Spotify, a platform that challenged the traditional model of music ownership. At the time, the music industry was dominated by digital downloads, CDs, and piracy, with little focus on streaming. Many believed that people would never pay for access to music when they could download or stream it for free elsewhere.

However, Ek boldly pushed forward with a different idea: a freemium model where users could listen to music for free with ads or pay for an ad-free, premium experience. Despite the skepticism and resistance from record labels, Spotify grew rapidly, revolutionizing the way we consume music. The success of Spotify was not just in its technological innovation; but in its ability to challenge the long-standing norms of the industry, reimagining how music could be accessed, shared, and monetized.

Ek's journey is a prime example of creating boldly. His ability to trust his vision and navigate the uncertainty of disrupting an entrenched industry demonstrates that bold action is more than just risk-taking, it's about envisioning a new future and making it a reality. His unwavering commitment to Spotify's growth, even in the face of early setbacks and industry pushback, is a powerful reminder that boldness isn't about instant success; it's about persistence, vision, and reshaping what's possible.

WHY BOLDNESS MATTERS

1. It Builds Momentum: Bold actions, even small ones, create forward motion. Each step reinforces your belief in what's possible and encourages you to take the next.

2. It Encourages Growth: Boldness pushes you out of your comfort zone, where the greatest opportunities for learning and growth reside.

3. It Inspires Others: When you act boldly, you demonstrate what's possible, inspiring those around you to do the same.

CREATE BOLDLY

1. Start with One Bold Action:
   » Identify one area where you've been hesitating and take a single, deliberate step forward.
   » Examples in Action:
      · Share a new idea in a meeting.
      · Reach out to a mentor or potential collaborator you admire.
      · Begin a project you've been putting off; even if it's just drafting an outline or making a plan.
2. Accept Mistakes as Part of the Journey:
   » Bold actions often come with missteps, but these are valuable learning opportunities.
   » Example in Action: After launching your first initiative, take time to evaluate what worked and what can be improved. Use these insights to refine your approach.
3. Reflect and Learn:
   » After each bold action, reflect on what you gained from the experience.
   » Example in Action: If you initiated a difficult conversation, consider how it shifted the dynamic and what you learned about yourself or the other person.

THE RIPPLE EFFECT OF BOLD ACTION

Boldness is contagious. When you take intentional risks and step out of your comfort zone, you inspire those around you to do the same. Your courage becomes a catalyst for innovation and progress, creating a ripple effect that extends far beyond your individual actions.

Boldness isn't about perfection; it's about action. Each deliberate step you take strengthens your confidence, expands your horizons, and transforms what once seemed impossible into reality. Trust the process, embrace the journey, and create boldly.

The masterpiece you are building is waiting for you to take the first step.

Section 7: Leave a Legacy

"Your masterpiece is a gift to the world—make it meaningful."

Your masterpiece isn't just about your personal growth or success, it's about the impact you leave on others. Legacy isn't measured by grand gestures or monumental achievements; it's built through the moments of connection, generosity, and purpose that ripple outward. Each action you take contributes to a larger tapestry, shaping how you'll be remembered and the mark you'll leave on the world.

One of the most rewarding aspects of coaching is seeing the ripple effect of real transformation. I've worked with clients who've had the courage to leave toxic work environments, like dealing with a boss who didn't get it, who expected 12-hour days, guilt-tripped them for missing family events, and piled on more pressure when they were already maxed out. When they finally made the decision to walk away and find work that aligned with their values, it didn't just change their lives—it gave the people around them permission to do the same, to stop tolerating burnout as the norm, and start taking back control. Every time someone chooses to lead with purpose or take meaningful action, it creates ripples that extend far beyond the immediate moment. Their actions inspire others. This creates a culture of courage, kindness, and positive change.

Usain Bolt is widely regarded as the greatest sprinter of all time, with his legacy etched in the history of athletics through his remarkable records and infectious personality. Bolt's name became synonymous with speed, as he set world records in both the 100 meters (9.58 seconds) and 200 meters (19.19 seconds), records that still stand today. He is also an 8-time Olympic gold medalist, having dominated the 100m and 200m events in three consecutive Olympic Games (2008, 2012, and 2016), solidifying his legacy as one of the most iconic figures in sports history.

OVERCOMING CHALLENGES AND BREAKING BARRIERS

Bolt's rise to prominence wasn't easy. Growing up in Jamaica, he faced numerous obstacles, including limited resources for training. He was always a gifted athlete, but early on, he struggled with consistency in his performances. It was his transition to focusing on sprinting at the senior level, along with the coaching from Glen Mills, that helped him realise his full potential. Bolt faced fierce competition from other sprinters like Tyson Gay and Asafa Powell. However, his unique combination of stride length, technique, and raw speed allowed him to stand out.

What set Bolt apart wasn't just his physical talent, but his attitude. His charismatic personality, playful nature, and famous victory pose, the "Lightning Bolt," made him an international sensation. He made sprinting more than just a race; he made it an event. His approach to racing was fearless and fun; adding an element of entertainment and charisma that had never been seen before in track and field.

MENTAL TOUGHNESS AND LEGACY

In addition to his physical talent, Bolt's mental toughness played a huge role in his success. He had the ability to remain calm under the intense pressure of major events, whether it was the World Championships or the Olympic Games. Despite the weight of expectations, he consistently delivered, becoming the first man in history to win the 100m, 200m, and 4x100m relay in three consecutive Olympics (2008, 2012, 2016). His dominance in the sport was not just about his speed but also about his mental resilience. He knew how to perform when it mattered most.

Now, his legacy is not solely defined by his records and victories on the track. Usain Bolt's impact extends far beyond athletics. He became a global ambassador for the sport and played a key role in raising the profile of track and field, particularly in countries where the sport hadn't seen as much attention. He inspired countless young athletes to pursue their dreams and show that with hard work, determination, and a little fun, anything is possible.

INSPIRING FUTURE GENERATIONS

Bolt's legacy also includes his philanthropic work and efforts to give back to the community. The Usain Bolt Foundation focuses on benefiting children and young people, particularly in Jamaica, through education and cultural opportunities. He has also worked to increase youth participation in track and field. He created programmes that encourage sportsmanship and discipline in the next generation.

In the years following his retirement, Bolt has remained an influential figure in sports. His name is now synonymous with excellence and joy, and he continues to inspire athletes to dream big. His legacy has shown that the fastest man in the world isn't just about breaking records. He is someone who uses his platform to make a positive impact and inspire others to push beyond their limits.

These legacies weren't built on fleeting achievements, but on consistent, and intentional actions rooted in their values and vision for a better world.

BUILDING YOUR LEGACY: KEY QUESTIONS

1. What Do You Want Your Legacy to Be?
    »   Reflect on the impact you want to leave behind. Is it a legacy of kindness, innovation, leadership, or transformation?
2. How Can Your Daily Actions Align With Your Legacy?
    »   Legacy isn't created overnight. It's the result of consistent choices that reflect your values and purpose.
    »   Examples in Action:
        ·   If you want to be remembered for empowering others, make time to mentor or uplift someone this week.
        ·   If sustainability is part of your legacy, evaluate how your daily habits align with that commitment.

START BUILDING YOUR LEGACY

1. Identify Your Core Values:
    »   Your legacy starts with understanding what matters most to you. Reflect on the values that guide your decisions and actions.
2. Take Consistent, Intentional Actions:

- » Small, deliberate choices add up over time. Focus on actions that align with your desired impact.
- » Example in Action: If you want to leave a legacy of compassion, prioritise acts of kindness, whether it's helping a colleague, volunteering, or simply being present for someone in need.
3. Inspire Others Through Your Actions:
   - » Lead by example. The way you show up in your work, relationships, and community can encourage others to follow suit.
4. Document Your Vision:
   - » Writing down your vision for your legacy helps clarify your goals and serves as a reminder to stay aligned with them.

Your legacy isn't about grand achievements, it's about the consistent and meaningful choices made every day. It's about how you show up for others, the values you uphold, and the ripples you create in the lives you touch. Your masterpiece, shaped by your actions and purpose, is a gift to the world. Make it meaningful.

Section 8: Celebrate the Imperfect

"Progress, not perfection, creates masterpieces."

Perfectionism is the great illusion that keeps us stuck. It tells us that we can't move forward until everything is flawless, and it magnifies our mistakes, turning them into insurmountable obstacles. But the truth is, perfection doesn't create progress, embracing imperfection does. Mistakes aren't failures. they're stepping stones for growth and opportunities to refine your craft.

EMBRACING THE MESSY PROCESS OF CREATION

In 2012, very early into my coaching, I fell into the trap of striving for perfection. I wanted every program, session, and idea to be flawless. I spent countless hours refining details that ultimately didn't matter as much as I thought they would.

But the moments that truly made an impact weren't perfect. They were raw, authentic, and often unexpected. Whether it was adapting a session on the fly or acknowledging a mistake during a workshop, these moments of imperfection taught me to trust the process and connect more deeply with the people I was serving.

Perfectionism had been holding me back, but embracing imperfection allowed me to grow, adapt, and create something real, something that resonated with others because it came from a place of authenticity.

THE VALUE OF IMPERFECTION IN MASTERPIECES

The Beatles, one of the most influential bands of all time, faced a multitude of failures and imperfections early in their careers. Before they became global superstars, they were rejected by record labels and told that their music wouldn't appeal to a wide audience. Their first audition with Decca Records in 1962 ended with a blunt dismissal: "We don't like their sound, and guitar music is on the way out."

But the band didn't let these imperfections hold them back. Instead, they embraced them, learning from their early setbacks and refining their sound. Despite the rocky start, they continued to experiment and grow, eventually revolutionizing the music industry with their innovative approach to songwriting, recording, and performance.

The Beatles' rise to fame wasn't a straight path. They faced setbacks, struggled with personal tensions, and encountered numerous moments of doubt. But each imperfect moment, whether it was a poor review or a failed audition, became a stepping stone toward their success. They kept evolving, and learning from their mistakes. Ultimately, they created timeless music that resonates with millions to this day.

Their story is a powerful reminder that imperfection is not something to avoid, but to embrace. The Beatles didn't start out perfect, and their journey to success was filled with flaws and failures. Yet, it was those very imperfections that allowed them to grow, innovate, and leave an indelible mark on music history.

WHY CELEBRATING IMPERFECTION MATTERS

1. It Creates Growth:
   » Mistakes reveal areas for improvement and provide valuable lessons.
2. It Builds Authentic Connections:
   » People connect with vulnerability and authenticity more than polished perfection.
3. It Encourages Progress:
   » Striving for perfection often leads to paralysis, while embracing imperfection allows you to take action and build momentum.

TURNING IMPERFECTION INTO PROGRESS

1. Set Realistic Goals:

   » Focus on progress, not perfection. Break big goals into smaller, manageable steps that emphasise learning and improvement.

   » Example in Action: Instead of waiting to launch a perfect project, start with a minimum viable version and refine it based on feedback.

2. Reflect on Lessons From Imperfections:

   » After every setback or mistake, take time to reflect:

      · *What did I learn from this experience?*

      · *How can I use this insight to move forward?*

   » Example in Action: If a presentation didn't go as planned, identify one or two changes you can make for next time.

3. Celebrate Small Wins:

   » Recognise and celebrate progress, no matter how small. Every step forward is a victory over perfectionism.

   » Example in Action: At the end of each week, write down one action or accomplishment you're proud of, even if it wasn't flawless.

Imperfection is not a weakness, it's what makes your journey uniquely yours. By embracing the messy, unpredictable process of creation, you free yourself from the constraints of perfectionism and allow progress to take center stage. Celebrate your imperfections. They're the strokes that make your masterpiece truly authentic and meaningful.

Section 9: Reflection

"A masterpiece isn't created when it's finished, it's created every time you choose to keep painting."

Masterpieces aren't made in moments of certainty. They're made in the mess, in the half-finished drafts, the wrong turns, the risks that didn't land, and the decisions you made, anyway. They're built with courage, not approval. And they always begin before you feel ready.

You don't need a blank slate. You already have a canvas. The question is: are you painting it with your own colours—or someone else's expectations?

This chapter wasn't about becoming perfect. It was about becoming real. Owning your voice. Letting go of the script. And starting now, even if the lines aren't clean yet. Because the work you avoid today becomes the regret you carry tomorrow.

These questions are here to help you notice what you've been avoiding, what needs to shift, and where you can pick up the brush again—with clarity, intention, and bo d honesty.

Reflection Questions

SECTION 1:

What part of your canvas feels unfinished? What small, intentional stroke can you add this week to make it more your own?

SECTION 2:

Which pillar of self-awareness, resilience, or authenticity feels the most underdeveloped in your life? What's one step you can take today to strengthen it and solidify the foundation of your masterpiece?

SECTION 3:

What's one area of your life where you've been holding back? What small step can you take this week to allow your authentic self to shine?

SECTION 4:

What's one mold you've been stuck in, and what's one small step you can take today to start breaking free?

SECTION 5:

What's one area of your life where perfectionism is holding you back? What would happen if you embraced imperfection and took the first step forward?

SECTION 6:

What's one bold step you've been hesitant to take? How can you start small and take that first step today?

SECTION 7:

Take a moment to reflect on the following questions:

- *What impact do I want to have on the people around me?*
- *What values do I want to be remembered for?*
- *What actions can I take today to start building that legacy?*

Write down one small, intentional step you'll take this week to move closer to creating the legacy you envision.

SECTION 8:

Take a moment to reflect on a recent mistake or imperfection in your work or personal life. Ask yourself:

- *What did this experience teach me?*
- *How did it help me grow or adapt?*
- *What's one way I can celebrate the progress I've made, even if it wasn't perfect?*

Write down your reflections and identify one step you'll take to embrace imperfection in the week ahead.

CHAPTER 6

The Power of Consistency in Leadership

"Consistency isn't about perfection. It's about showing up, day after day, with integrity and intention."

Imagine a lighthouse standing tall amidst a storm. Its light doesn't falter, nor does it dim. It shines steadily, guiding ships to safety regardless of the chaos around it. This is the power of consistency in leadership. To be a dependable force that others can trust, even when the path ahead is uncertain.

Leadership, much like a lighthouse, isn't about dramatic moments or grand gestures. It's about showing up every day with purpose, clarity, and integrity. Consistency may not always be visible, but it creates a foundation of trust and stability that can weather any storm.

This chapter explores how consistency serves as the backbone of effective leadership. From developing trust to creating a culture of reliability and innovation, we'll uncover why this often-overlooked trait is one of the most powerful tools in a leader's arsenal.

Section 1: Your Reliability is Your Brand

"Consistency creates trust, and trust creates teams."

Reliability isn't just a trait, it's a foundation of great leadership. When your team knows they can count on you to deliver, stay aligned with your values, and maintain your energy, trust grows organically. This trust forms the basis of productive relationships, effective teamwork, and sustainable success.

Consistency isn't about rigidity. It is about being dependable in your principles, while adapting to changing circumstances. Leaders who are reliable in their decisions and behaviours create environments where creativity and innovation thrive because their teams feel secure.

Reliability is the silent backbone of leadership. It's not just about showing up. It's about how you show up. When your team consistently sees you act with integrity and purpose, they gain confidence in your leadership. This confidence fuels collaboration and empowers individuals to take ownership of their roles, knowing that their leader has created a safe and stable foundation.

In 2023, I worked with the Founder and CEO of a global digital marketing business who was unpredictable. Some days, they were supportive and encouraging; other days, they were critical without explanation. This inconsistency made it difficult for the team to trust their guidance, and morale suffered as a result. That experience taught me that reliability isn't just about doing the right thing, it's about doing it consistently so that others can count on you.

Indra Nooyi served as the CEO of PepsiCo from 2006 to 2018 and is a prime example of how consistent leadership can lead a global company through transformation. Under her leadership, PepsiCo not only achieved financial growth but also placed a strong emphasis on corporate responsibility and sustainability. Nooyi consistently aligned PepsiCo's strategy with her vision of "Performance with Purpose," which aimed to grow the business while making a positive impact on society.

For instance, when she took the helm at PepsiCo, she saw an opportunity to shift the company's portfolio toward healthier products. This decision was in direct response to growing concerns over health and wellness. Nooyi recognised that the future of PepsiCo would depend on adapting to changing consumer demands. Despite facing resistance and criticism from those who feared the company would lose its identity, Nooyi remained steadfast in her commitment to this vision. By the time she stepped down as CEO, PepsiCo had made significant strides in offering healthier options, from reducing sugar and salt in products to expanding their lineup of nutritious snacks and beverages.

Nooyi's consistency in maintaining this dual focus, driving growth while also addressing health concerns, was instrumental in building trust within the company and with external stakeholders. Even during difficult times, including the global financial crisis of 2008, she stayed committed to her long-term vision of creating a sustainable and innovative company, which ultimately paid off. PepsiCo's revenue doubled during her tenure, and the company became a leader in corporate social responsibility initiatives.

Her leadership showed that reliability in decisions and values could lead to groundbreaking success; even in the face of resistance. Nooyi consistently aligned her actions with her core principles, ensuring that PepsiCo's leadership in the beverage and snack industries was not just about profits but also about positively impacting communities and the environment.

PRACTICAL STEPS

1. Evaluate Your Reliability: Reflect on your actions and ask yourself:
   » *Do my decisions consistently align with my values?*
   » *Am I following through on my commitments?*
2. Choose One Behaviour to Reinforce: Identify an area where consistency is needed, such as:
   » Responding promptly to emails or inquiries.
   » Holding regular feedback or check-in sessions with your team.
   » Maintaining a consistent tone and energy during challenging situations.
3. Track Your Progress: Make a plan to practice this behaviour consistently for a set period, such as one month, and reflect on its impact on your team dynamics.

Reliability is more than a leadership skill. It is your brand. It shapes how others perceive and trust you. By consistently showing up with integrity, purpose, and stability, you create an environment where your team feels supported, empowered, and ready to thrive. Make reliability the cornerstone of your leadership. Watch how it transforms your relationships, your team, and your results.

Section 2: The Unsung Hero of Leadership

"Consistency transforms aspirations into achievements, one steady step at a time."

When we celebrate quick wins and flashy successes, consistency is often overlooked. Yet it's the invisible engine behind every lasting achievement. It's not about bursts of inspiration, but about the steady effort that compounds over time to create exceptional results.

Consistency is the quiet force that turns potential into performance and aspirations into reality.

THE POWER OF INCREMENTAL PROGRESS

Consistency doesn't mean grand gestures every day; it means small, intentional actions repeated regularly. These actions, while seemingly insignificant in the moment, build momentum over time. Think of it like water carving through rock, not because of its strength, but because of its persistence.

When I started martial arts, I wasn't a natural. I was uncoordinated, lacked technique, and questioned whether I'd ever improve. Despite all these, I kept showing up. I drilled the same movements over and over, refining my form, increasing my speed, and building my endurance. As I progressed through the ranks, the training intensified. Preparing for black belt grading meant breaking bricks, striking through tiles, and sparring against opponents who pushed me to my limits.

Each session tested my patience, my resilience, and my ability to handle pain, both physical and mental. There were moments of frustration when I doubted if I could break that brick or execute a perfect technique under pressure. But the results didn't come from talent alone; they came from the relentless consistency of training, failing, adjusting, and trying again. By the time I earned my 3rd-degree black belt, I realised the most valuable lesson wasn't just about martial arts, it was about showing up every day, regardless of how I felt, and trusting that progress was happening, even when I couldn't see it.

Serena Williams didn't become one of the greatest athletes in history by accident. Her journey began when she was only three years old, in 1984, training under the guidance of her father, Richard Williams, who had no prior experience in tennis, but was determined to develop his daughters' potential. By the time she was a teenager, Serena was already playing at a highly competitive level, hitting thousands of balls during each practice session. This relentless practice would become a hallmark of her career. Even in the early days, she learned the value of showing up consistently, even when it was difficult, and building the discipline that would serve her throughout her career.

At the peak of her career, during the 2000s and into the 2010s, Serena's daily routine was grueling. She trained 4 to 5 hours a day, six days a week. Her training schedule was rigorous, including not only on-court drills, but also, strength training, cardio, and mental conditioning. Despite a number of setbacks, including injuries and personal challenges, Serena never abandoned her strict regimen. For example, after her serious foot injury in 2011, which sidelined her for nearly a year, Serena came back in 2012 with even greater focus, proving that consistency in training, recovery, and mindset would always be her secret weapon.

Her success wasn't just the result of raw talent or natural athleticism; it was built on consistent, unwavering work ethic. Serena had to put in the time, every single day, to refine her skills and maintain her fitness.

This wasn't about one-off bursts of brilliance; it was about showing up day after day, even when progress felt slow or the challenges seemed insurmountable. Each practice session, each recovery session, added up to create the powerhouse she became.

Serena's career is a perfect example of incremental progress. She often said that she wasn't always the most naturally gifted player on the court, but through years of hard work and repetition, she was able to hone her skills and sharpen her mental resilience.

Her dedication paid off when, in 2003, she won her first Grand Slam title at the French Open. This victory marked the beginning of a remarkable career that would include 23 Grand Slam singles titles, more than any other player in the Open Era.

Even during her personal struggles, including a life-threatening pulmonary embolism in 2011 and postpartum complications following the birth of her daughter in 2017, Serena stayed committed to her sport. She came back to win the Australian Open in 2017, just 10 months after giving birth. This reminded the world that the foundation of her success was built not just on her innate talent, but on an unwavering commitment to training, recovery, and mental toughness.

Serena's consistency allowed her to return to the top of her game multiple times after major setbacks. For instance, in 2018, at 36, she made a remarkable comeback to the US Open final. Despite taking a break for maternity leave, she won. This ability to come back stronger, again and again, proves that greatness doesn't happen in flashes of inspiration, it is built through persistent, focused effort over time.

THE SCIENCE BEHIND CONSISTENCY

Neuroscience shows that consistency rewires the brain through a process called neuroplasticity. Repeating small, positive habits strengthens neural pathways, making behaviours more automatic over time. This applies to everything, from learning new skills to developing positive leadership habits. Consistency isn't just psychological; it's biological.

PRACTICAL INSIGHT

1. Identify a Target Area: Choose one area of your leadership or life where consistency could make a difference, such as communication, decision-making, or personal growth.
2. Start Small: Commit to one daily action that aligns with your goal. For example:
   » Devote five minutes each morning to strategic planning.
   » Spend ten minutes each day to connect with a team member.
3. Track Your Progress: Use a simple journal or app to track your consistency over the next 30 days and reflect on the compounding effect.

Section 3: Mastering the Power of Consistency in Leadership

"Great leadership isn't about grand gestures, it's about disciplined, daily actions."

Consistency in leadership is about more than showing up. It's about how you show up. It's the discipline of aligning your actions with your values, even in challenging situations, and demonstrating the same energy, integrity, and focus every single day.

This predictability builds trust, develops a sense of stability within your team, and creates an environment where individuals feel empowered to excel.

WHY CONSISTENCY MATTERS IN LEADERSHIP

Consistency in leadership provides:

1. Trust: Your team knows what to expect from you, which reduces uncertainty and anxiety.
2. Stability: In moments of change or crisis, your steady presence becomes a source of reassurance.
3. Alignment: Consistent actions reinforce the organisation's mission, vision, and values, aligning everyone toward shared goals.

When leaders are unpredictable, changing direction frequently or reacting emotionally to situations it creates confusion and erodes confidence. Consistency ensures that your team feels secure, even when external conditions are uncertain.

I've seen firsthand how consistency can transform a team's dynamic. Early in my leadership journey, I observed that my team often hesitated sharing ideas or addressing challenges. At first, I did not understand why. However, upon reflection, I realised my energy and responses weren't always predictable. Some days, I was fully engaged; on others, I was distracted by competing priorities. Recognising this inconsistency was a turning point. I made a deliberate effort to show up with the same focus and support every day. Over time, my team began to open up, trust grew, and collaboration flourished. That experience reinforced for me that consistent leadership isn't just about strategy, it's about presence and intentionality.

In 2013, Toto Wolff took over as Team Principal and CEO of the Mercedes F1 team. At the time, Mercedes hadn't won a Constructors' Championship in the modern era. The team was technically capable, but it lacked cohesion and a consistent performance culture.

Wolff didn't try to be a charismatic saviour. He focused on discipline, clarity, and standards, applied every day.

He introduced a culture of radical transparency. Mistakes were acknowledged without ego, in front of the entire team. After every race—regardless of result—debriefs were consistent. Everyone from the lead driver to the most junior engineer was held to the same standard of accountability and preparation. No drama. No excuses.

From 2014 to 2020, Mercedes won seven straight Constructors' Championships and helped Lewis Hamilton win six Drivers' Championships. Their edge wasn't always the car—it was their internal consistency.

When the team underperformed in 2022 and 2023, Wolff didn't deflect or look for a quick fix. He publicly owned the results, recommitted to core values, and kept the team focused on process over panic. In a sport defined by chaos, his consistency became the stabilising force.

It's not the loud moves that built Mercedes into a dominant force—it was Wolff showing up the same way, every day, for over a decade.

WAYS TO CULTIVATE CONSISTENCY IN LEADERSHIP

1. Set Clear Expectations: Communicate your values and goals clearly to your team, ensuring everyone understands what success looks like.
2. Be Transparent: When challenges arise, share your thought process and decisions openly. Transparency creates trust, even when the outcomes are uncertain.
3. Maintain Emotional Steadiness: By consistently responding calmly and being supportive, this creates a safe environment where your team feels empowered to share ideas and take risks.

PRACTICAL INSIGHT

1. Choose one habit that aligns with your leadership vision, such as developing collaboration or improving communication.
2. Commit to practicing this habit consistently for the next 30 days:
   » Schedule daily check-ins with your team.
   » Dedicate time for reflection or planning each morning.
   » Reinforce team goals during weekly meetings.

3. Track its impact by noting changes in team engagement, productivity, or morale.

Section 4: Transform in 21 Days: A Framework for Leaders

"Small steps, consistently taken, lead to profound transformation."

Change isn't an overnight process. It's the result of intentional, incremental actions that build momentum over time. Just like a seed planted in the soil, transformation requires consistent nurturing before growth becomes visible. Leaders who integrate small, consistent habits into their routines can create powerful ripple effects, improving their leadership, influencing their teams, and creating long-term success.

During a particularly challenging phase in my business, I discovered the transformative power of small, consistent actions. I felt like everything was about to fall apart both in my business and in my life, as I was going through deeply uncertain marital challenges. I was struggling to generate a new business. I felt overwhelmed by competing demands and unsure of where to focus my energy.

After seeking support and guidance, I implemented a simple habit: spending five minutes each morning identifying three key priorities for the day. It seemed almost trivial at first, but by sticking to this habit daily for three weeks, I noticed a significant shift.

My focus improved, my decision-making became sharper; and I felt more in control of my time, and energy. That small habit, practiced consistently, became a foundation for greater clarity and productivity in my leadership.

THE 21-DAY FRAMEWORK

Change happens in three phases over 21 days. By breaking the process into manageable steps, leaders can build habits that last.

1. Week 1: Plant the Seed

   Identify one area where you'd like to improve and commit to a small, manageable habit. Keep the action simple to reduce resistance.

   » Example in Action: Devote five minutes a day to team communication or self-reflection.

   » Focus on consistency over results during this phase. The goal is to establish the habit, not to achieve perfection.

2. Week 2: Build Momentum

   Stick with your habit, even if the impact isn't immediately visible. This is often the most challenging phase because progress may feel slow.

   » Keep a journal or checklist to track your daily efforts.

   » Celebrate small wins to reinforce your commitment.

3. Week 3: Strengthen the Roots

   By the third week, your habit will start to feel more natural. Reflect on the progress you've made and identify how to maintain the habit moving forward.

   » *Ask: How has this habit improved my leadership?*

   » *How can I sustain it over the next month?*

When Reshma Saujani founded Girls Who Code in 2012, she had a clear but ambitious mission: to close the gender gap in technology.

Starting with just a small group of girls in a summer coding program, Saujani focused on making incremental improvements, building trust, refining the curriculum, and expanding outreach efforts.

At first, the progress was slow. However, through consistent efforts, her team steadily grew the program. They focused on creating a strong sense of community among young girls interested in coding, providing them with not only technical skills but also the confidence to pursue careers in technology.

By 2014, Girls Who Code had expanded to multiple cities across the U.S. By 2017, Saujani was able to leverage her consistent approach to secure substantial funding and partnerships with major tech companies, including Microsoft, Amazon, and Facebook.

Over the years, her focus on providing opportunities for mentorship, hands-on coding experience, and job-readiness programs for young women transformed Girls Who Code from a modest initiative into a national movement, thus inspiring thousands of girls to enter the tech world.

Saujani's story exemplifies how consistent, incremental improvements—focused on building community, refining educational content, and expanding outreach—can lead to transformative change. Her steady commitment to empowering young girls has not only changed their lives, but is also making a lasting impact on the tech industry itself.

STEPS FOR LEADERS

1. Choose a Small Habit: Identify one habit that aligns with your leadership goals, such as giving daily recognition to a

team member or dedicating five minutes each morning to strategic planning.

2. Track Your Progress: Use a visual tracker or app to log your consistency and reflect on how the habit is impacting your leadership.

3. Reflect and Adjust: At the end of the 21 days, reflect on what worked, what didn't, and how you can sustain the habit over time.

Section 5: Consistency Creates Culture

"Consistency in leadership shapes culture and turns excellence into habit."

A strong organisational culture isn't built overnight; it's the cumulative result of daily, consistent actions that reflect and reinforce the company's values. Leaders who embody these values through their decisions, behaviours, and communication set the tone for the entire organisation. Over time, these consistent actions create a culture where excellence becomes a habit—not a one-off event.

WHY CULTURE DEPENDS ON CONSISTENCY

An organisation's culture isn't defined by mission statements or lofty goals alone. Culture is defined by what happens every day. When leaders model the company's core values consistently, they create a ripple effect that influences every interaction, decision, and initiative.

However, inconsistency—such as promoting one value but acting against it—can quickly erode trust and alignment.

In 2018, I was part of a team for a global logistics organisation, where the stated value was collaboration—but the culture told a different story. Leadership rarely sought input from the team, decisions were made behind closed doors, and communication was inconsistent.

The result? Disengagement and frustration. When I had the opportunity to lead, I committed to consistently modeling collaboration—whether it was inviting input during meetings, being transparent about decisions, or publicly acknowledging contributions. Over time, those small actions reshaped the team's dynamic, proving that culture shifts when leadership walks the talk.

Toyota's approach to continuous improvement through the Kaizen philosophy has been a key driver behind its success in the automotive industry. Kaizen, a Japanese term meaning "change for better," emphasises the importance of making small, incremental improvements regularly, rather than aiming for large, disruptive changes. Toyota adopted this mindset after facing a severe production crisis in the 1950s.

A pivotal moment in Toyota's journey occurred in 1951 when Taiichi Ohno, a Toyota executive, introduced the "Just-In-Time" (JIT) production system. This relied on constant, incremental improvements. The goal wasn't only to reduce waste, but also to empower every employee to contribute ideas for improvement. Employees at all levels—from assembly line workers to managers—were encouraged to identify inefficiencies and suggest better ways of doing things.

For instance, Toyota implemented a system where workers could stop the production line if they noticed a problem, ensuring immediate attention to quality issues. This commitment to ongoing, small improvements—backed by a leadership that modeled Kaizen through daily actions—created a company culture where excellence wasn't just an aspiration, but a routine habit.

By focusing on consistent, small improvements rather than sporadic large-scale changes, Toyota built a reputation for reliability and quality. Over time, this ingrained culture of Kaizen allowed the company to innovate continuously while maintaining operational excellence, which became a competitive advantage in a market that values both quality and efficiency.

WAYS TO BUILD A CULTURE OF CONSISTENCY

1. Identify Core Values: Choose three values that align with your vision for the organisation. These might include collaboration, accountability, or innovation.
2. Model the Values Daily: Align your actions and decisions with these values. For example:
   » If transparency is a value, ensure that team updates are open and accessible.
   » If accountability is a value, own your mistakes and encourage others to do the same.
3. Recognise and Reward Consistency: Publicly acknowledge team members who consistently demonstrate the organisation's values. This not only reinforces the importance of the values but also inspires others to embody them.

PRACTICAL INSIGHT

- Schedule a weekly check-in with yourself or your leadership team to assess how well your actions align with your stated values.
- Encourage feedback from your team to identify areas where alignment could improve.

Section 6: The Key to Emotional Consistency

"Consistency in emotional responses builds trust and creates connection."

In leadership, emotional consistency is just as important as behavioural consistency. Teams look to their leaders for stability—especially in times of uncertainty or crisis. Leaders who maintain emotional consistency respond predictably, calmly, and constructively, creating an environment of psychological safety. This stability empowers team members to take risks, communicate openly, and perform at their best.

THE IMPACT ON TEAMS AND CULTURE

Emotional consistency has a profound effect on team dynamics and organisational culture. When leaders maintain steady emotional responses:

- Trust Deepens: Team members feel secure, knowing they can rely on their leader's composure and fairness.

- Stress Reduces: A stable leader mitigates anxiety, especially during high-pressure situations.
- Collaboration Increases: Calm and constructive responses encourage open dialogue, problem-solving, and creativity.

Inconsistent emotional responses, however, create confusion and fear. If team members can't predict how their leader will react, whether with encouragement, criticism, or silence, they may withhold ideas or avoid addressing problems altogether.

Over time, this uncertainty erodes collaboration, trust, and morale.

I vividly remember a time when a major global payments transformation project went off course. My initial reaction was frustration—and I unintentionally let it show during a team meeting. I lost the plot. I called out each member and almost ran a performance diagnostic on them. I surprised myself. The result? My team became visibly tense, hesitant to share ideas, and uncertain about my response to future setbacks. That moment was a turning point. I realised the importance of maintaining emotional steadiness, especially in times of crises. I started practicing intentional pauses and reflective questioning to respond more constructively.

Over time, the shift in my approach strengthened the team's confidence but also their willingness to collaborate openly—even during challenges.

TOOLS FOR EMOTIONAL CONSISTENCY

1. Active Listening: Listening attentively shows team members that you value their input, even during stressful situations. Repeat back what you've heard to confirm understanding and demonstrate engagement. For example:

> » *"What I'm hearing is that you're concerned about the timeline. Let's explore options to address this together."*

2. Reflective Questioning: Before reacting emotionally, ask yourself reflective questions like:
   > » *"What's the root cause of this issue?"*
   > » *"How can I address this constructively?"*
   >
   > These questions help shift your focus from reacting to problem-solving.

3. Intentional Pauses: In moments of stress or frustration, take a deliberate pause to collect your thoughts.
   > » A few deep breaths or even a brief moment of silence can prevent reactive responses and lead to a more thoughtful leadership.

When Angela Ahrendts joined Apple in 2014 as Senior Vice President of Retail, she stepped into an environment under pressure. The retail division was in transition after leadership changes. Staff morale was low, and customer satisfaction had started to dip. Many employees feared more disruption was on the horizon.

During one of her first store visits in early 2014, an employee broke down mid-shift, burned out and anxious about potential layoffs. Ahrendts didn't delegate the situation or gloss over it. She sat down with the employee, listened without judgment, and calmly acknowledged the uncertainty they were feeling. She didn't promise everything would be perfect, but her tone remained clear, steady, and respectful.

Then she followed through. Over the next five years, she continued visiting stores, meeting employees face to face, and maintaining that same grounded tone—no matter what challenges came her way. Her emotional consistency became a stabilising force.

By the time she left Apple in 2019, retail employee engagement was significantly higher, and Apple stores had evolved from transactional spaces to community hubs. Her steady, empathetic presence was a key driver of that transformation.

Ahrendts didn't fix culture with big speeches. She did it by staying calm, showing up, and treating people like people, every single time.

STEPS FOR LEADERS

1. Reflect on Your Patterns: Take time to evaluate how you typically respond to stress. Are your reactions consistent and constructive?
2. Practice Emotional Regulation: Incorporate mindfulness techniques like deep breathing, journaling, or meditation to enhance emotional stability.
3. Set a Calm Tone: Begin meetings or discussions with a steady, composed tone, especially when addressing challenges or delivering feedback.

Section 7: Cultural Wisdom on Consistency

"Every great tradition is built on the steady rhythm of consistency."

Consistency isn't just a modern leadership principle, it's a value deeply embedded in cultural philosophies across the globe. These traditions highlight how patience, deliberate effort, and incremental progress lead to lasting transformation.

Leaders can draw inspiration from these timeless practices to embed consistency into their own leadership styles.

CULTURAL PERSPECTIVES ON CONSISTENCY

1. The Japanese Principle of *Kaizen*: At the heart of Kaizen is the idea of continuous improvement through small, steady changes. This philosophy teaches that even the smallest improvements, practiced daily, can lead to significant long-term results. Toyota exemplifies this approach, embedding *Kaizen* into every aspect of its operations, from manufacturing to leadership, creating a culture of innovation and excellence.

2. Indigenous Wisdom and Deliberate Effort: Many Indigenous cultures emphasise the importance of patience and harmony with natural cycles. For example, indigenous farming practices often rely on observing and understanding nature's rhythms, applying consistent care to ensure sustainable growth over time. This approach mirrors how consistent, thoughtful leadership creates resilience and long-term success in organisations.

3. The Chinese Bamboo Tree Analogy: The Chinese bamboo tree offers a powerful lesson in patience and consistency. For the first five years, the tree shows little visible growth as it establishes its roots. But in the fifth year, it can grow up to 27 meters in just a few weeks. This reflects how consistent effort, even when progress isn't immediately visible, lays the foundation for exponential growth.

I first encountered *Kaizen* when working with a team that faced significant inefficiencies. Instead of overhauling everything at once, we focused on small, daily improvements streamlining a process here, adjusting a communication method there. At first, the changes seemed almost insignificant, but over time, they compounded into remarkable progress. That experience taught me that transformation doesn't always require sweeping changes; often, it's the small, consistent actions that create lasting impact.

WAYS TO INCORPORATE CULTURAL WISDOM

1. Adopt a Mindset of Continuous Improvement: Identify one small habit or process you can improve in your daily leadership, such as the way you provide feedback or conduct meetings. Focus on refining it incrementally over time.
2. Practice Patience in Results: Remind yourself that meaningful progress often takes time. Commit to consistent effort, even when immediate results aren't visible.
3. Celebrate Small Wins: Acknowledge the impact of minor improvements and recognise the efforts of your team, reinforcing the value of steady progress.

Section 8: Building Your Legacy with Consistency

"Your legacy isn't built in moments; it's built in habits."

Legacy isn't about a single achievement or grand gesture—it's about the consistent, reliable actions that define how others experience and remember you. It's the accumulation of your daily habits, the values you model, and the relationships you nurture over time.

True impact comes from the consistency of your character and commitment.

WHY CONSISTENCY SHAPES LEGACY

- Reputation is Built on Repetition: Your actions, repeated consistently, become your brand. If you're consistently supportive, reliable, and value-driven, that becomes your leadership identity.
- Steady Contributions Create Meaningful Impact: Small, reliable efforts often leave a greater mark than sporadic bursts of brilliance. A team member might not remember every project you led, but they'll remember how you consistently showed up for them.
- Legacy is Lived, Not Just Left Behind: Legacy isn't just about what you leave after you're gone; it's about the influence you create every day.

As a Lead Software Consultant for a boutique consultancy, I often focused on the immediate results—hitting targets, solving problems, and achieving goals. But as time went on, I realised that my legacy wouldn't be measured by numbers alone. It would be shaped by how consistently I lived my values and supported my team. Simple habits, like starting meetings by asking how people were doing or recognising small achievements, created an atmosphere of trust and collaboration. Over time, those consistent actions built a culture where my team felt empowered to lead with the same values, extending the legacy beyond me.

Nelson Mandela's legacy was not shaped by a single event or achievement but by his consistent commitment to justice, equality, and reconciliation over a lifetime.

After spending 27 years in prison, Mandela could have sought revenge or resented his oppressors. Instead, he consistently advocated for peace and unity, understanding that South Africa's future lay in reconciliation, not division.

Upon his release in 1990, Mandela didn't rush to lead with anger or retribution. Instead, he focused on building bridges between the divided factions of South African society. His actions over decades consistently reinforced his values of forgiveness and understanding. His refusal to retaliate and his dedication to peace, despite the personal and national cost, became the cornerstone of his presidency and the healing process for a fractured nation.

Mandela's impact, however, was not just in his presidency; it was in the way he lived out his principles each and every day, consistently demanding and working toward a better future for his people. His legacy isn't just the end of apartheid or his Nobel Peace Prize; it's the consistent application of his values over time, influencing not just a nation but the entire world.

WAYS TO BUILD A LEGACY OF CONSISTENCY

1. Define Your Vision for Impact: Reflect on how you want to be remembered as a leader. What values do you want to model consistently?
2. Adopt a Legacy-Building Habit: Choose one habit that aligns with your vision, such as:
   » Recognising team achievements regularly.

- » Being consistently present and engaged in one-on-one meetings.
- » Upholding transparency in your decision-making process.
3. Track the Ripple Effect: Pay attention to how your consistent actions influence your team or organisation over time.

THE MULTIPLIER EFFECT OF CONSISTENCY

Consistency creates ripples that extend beyond your direct influence. When you consistently embody values like integrity, empathy, or accountability, you inspire others to do the same. This multiplier effect ensures that your impact reaches far beyond what you accomplish personally.

Section 9: Consistency and Creativity: Partners, Not Opposites

"When the foundation is stable, creativity can thrive within the boundaries of trust and reliability."

A common misconception is that consistency stifles creativity, but the opposite is true. Consistency provides the structure that allows creativity to flourish. When your team knows the boundaries and expectations, they feel free to explore, innovate, and take risks.

WHY CONSISTENCY FUELS CREATIVITY

1. Stability Encourages Experimentation: Consistent leadership creates an environment where team members feel safe to

try new things without fear of unpredictable reactions or shifting priorities.

2. Reliable Processes Reduce Cognitive Load: Consistency in processes and expectations eliminates unnecessary guesswork, freeing up mental energy for creative problem-solving.

3. Momentum Amplifies Innovation: When small, consistent actions build momentum, they lead to breakthroughs over time. Creativity thrives when efforts are sustained rather than sporadic.

Pixar's remarkable ability to consistently produce some of the most groundbreaking animated films is rooted in its philosophy of balancing structure with creativity. One key element driving this is their internal process known as the "Braintrust." This regular, candid feedback forum brings together directors, writers, and other creative leads to come together to critique each other's work, all within a trusted and supportive environment. What makes this so powerful is that the feedback is direct yet non-hierarchical—there's no ego involved. The team trusts the process and trusts each other, creating a culture where creativity is nurtured within a structure that encourages improvement and growth.

This approach mirrors the way I work with executives through the 5 States of Optimisation. Just as Pixar has consistently refined its storytelling, animation, and production techniques, I help leaders refine their approach to leadership, performance, and decision-making. In my coaching, I focus on creating a reliable and repeatable process that frees up mental energy for innovation. This structured framework allows leaders to step outside the chaos of uncertainty and focus on delivering exceptional results while giving them the freedom to experiment, take risks, and embrace new ideas.

What's key is that consistency doesn't stifle creativity, it enhances it. Pixar's commitment to maintaining a stable process while simultaneously pushing creative boundaries has been central to their ability to innovate in the world of animation.

Similarly, when leaders have consistent systems and frameworks in place, they create space for innovative thinking and problem-solving, whether that's in business strategies, team management, or customer engagement.

Just like Pixar relies on consistent feedback and structured review to fuel creativity, my coaching ensures that leaders remain grounded in their core processes while constantly evolving to meet new challenges. It's about having the consistency of a proven system while cultivating the freedom to innovate and lead in new ways, ensuring that growth and creativity are not separate but intertwined.

Section 10: Practical Tools and Frameworks for Building Consistency

"Consistency is built on habits, and habits are built through deliberate systems."

Consistency doesn't happen by accident; it requires intentional tools and systems to reinforce your efforts. By integrating practical frameworks into your leadership, you can develop habits that make consistency sustainable.

1. HABIT STACKING

Pairing a new leadership habit with an existing one makes it easier to adopt. For example:

- If you already begin each morning by checking your calendar, add a brief reflection on your leadership priorities for the day.
- If you hold weekly team meetings, incorporate a quick review of team progress on long-term goals.

Habit stacking works because it ties a new behaviour to something already ingrained, thus creating a natural flow in your routine.

2. THE 2-MINUTE RULE

Start small to overcome inertia. The 2-Minute Rule suggests committing to a task for just two minutes:

- Instead of planning an entire strategy session, spend two minutes jotting down initial ideas.
- Instead of trying to solve a major challenge in one sitting, break it into two-minute brainstorming increments.

This approach reduces resistance and builds momentum, making it easier to maintain consistency over time.

3. THE WEEKLY REVIEW

Set aside 30 minutes each week to reflect on your consistency:

- Evaluate how well you followed through on your commitments.
- Identify areas where you slipped and adjust your approach.
- Celebrate small wins to reinforce positive habits.

The Weekly Review not only helps you course-correct, but also strengthens your self-awareness, a critical pillar of consistent leadership.

Section 11: Reflection

"Your legacy won't be built in the highlights. It'll be built in the habits you repeat when no one's watching."

Consistency doesn't shout. It doesn't look for credit. But it is what people count on when everything else is unpredictable. As a leader, your habits—how you show up, how you respond, how you follow through, become the standards your team works from. Not your mission statement. Not your slide deck. Your habits.

This chapter wasn't about building a brand. It was about recognising that you already are one. Your reliability, your energy, your discipline—all adds up. And it shapes how others show up around you.

This isn't about doing everything right. It's about showing up on the days you don't feel like it. Making decisions based on your values, not your mood. Sticking with the hard things long enough to let them work.

Look at your current routines. Which ones are building trust, and which ones are costing it? What's one small habit you can start—or stop—that will strengthen your leadership foundation?

The questions below aren't here to motivate you. They're here to help you notice. Because once you start noticing where consistency is missing, you can do something about it.

Reflection Question

SECTION 1:

What's one area where you could improve your reliability? How can you take a deliberate step today to strengthen trust and consistency in your leadership?

SECTION 2:

What's one area in your leadership or personal life where consistency could transform your results? What small, daily action will you start today to begin building momentum?

SECTION 3:

What's one area in your leadership where consistent actions could create greater stability or trust? How will you start implementing this today?

SECTION 4:

What's one habit you could commit to for 21 days that would align with your long-term leadership goals? How will you track and celebrate your progress along the way?

SECTION 5:

How does your current leadership behaviour reinforce or weaken your organisational culture? What's one action you can take today to align more closely with your core values?

SECTION 6:

What's one area of your leadership where emotional consistency could build greater trust or connection with your team? How can you start practicing it today?

SECTION 7:

How can you incorporate cultural wisdom about consistency into your leadership style? Consider adopting a mindset of continuous improvement or patience in your daily actions.

SECTION 8:

What consistent habit could you start today that aligns with the legacy you want to leave? How can you model this habit in your daily leadership?

SECTION 9:

How can you use consistency to create a stable foundation for your team's creativity? Consider how you can maintain predictable processes while encouraging innovation.

CHAPTER 7

Stop Waiting for Your Epiphany

Section 1: Take the First Step—Creating Your Own Moment

> *"Waiting for the perfect moment is a fool's game. The magic happens when you decide to create your own moment."*

Imagine you're waiting for that moment, the one where everything finally clicks, where clarity arrives like a lightning bolt, where you just *know* it's time.

But what if that moment never comes? What if waiting is the very thing holding you back? The truth is, clarity isn't something you wait for; it's something you create. Action, no matter how small, is what sparks progress.

This chapter is about breaking free from the illusion of the "perfect moment" and stepping into the reality that every step you take now shapes the future you want. Stop waiting. Start moving. Your breakthrough begins today.

For years, I fell into the trap of waiting for clarity to strike like lightning. I believed that one day, I'd wake up and everything would make sense what my purpose was, what steps I needed to take, and how to succeed. I told myself, *When the time is right, I'll know.*

But here's the thing: clarity doesn't arrive uninvited. It's not a divine moment of enlightenment. Clarity is something you cultivate, and it grows stronger with each deliberate action.

I was at a crossroads, deciding whether to transition fully into coaching a path that excited me but felt uncertain. I waited and over analyzed, convincing myself that I needed more time, more information, or more confidence. The waiting became unbearable—like standing at the edge of a cliff, staring at the horizon, but never jumping.

Then, I realised something powerful: the act of waiting was my biggest obstacle. The fear of taking the wrong step was keeping me from taking any step at all. I didn't need to know the entire path, I just needed to take the first step.

THE SMALL STEP THAT CHANGED EVERYTHING

That first step was small but transformative: attending a coaching workshop. It wasn't perfect. I didn't have a grand plan or ironclad confidence. But walking into that workshop, surrounded by like-minded people, sparked something inside me.

Suddenly, possibilities began to emerge. I connected with others who were on similar journeys, and their stories inspired me to keep going.

I learned new skills, gained valuable insights, and most importantly, realised that the only way to build momentum was to start.

Each step I took after that workshop—whether it was offering my first coaching session, refining my approach, or seeking feedback, added to a growing sense of clarity and confidence.

That one small action had sparked a chain reaction of learning, growth, and opportunities I never could have anticipated.

WHY WAITING HOLDS YOU BACK

Waiting often feels safer than acting. It gives the illusion of control, as though delaying a decision will make the path clearer or the stakes lower. But the truth is, waiting often amplifies fear and doubt, making the first step feel even harder. The act of waiting becomes its own obstacle, stealing time and potential.

You don't need to see the full picture before you begin. The magic of action is that clarity grows with every step forward.

THE POWER OF STARTING SMALL

Big transformations don't start with grand gestures. They start with small, deliberate actions. The first step doesn't have to be perfect; it just has to happen. Whether it's attending a workshop, signing up for a course, or simply having a conversation, each action builds momentum.

INSIGHTS TO TAKE YOUR FIRST STEP

1. Simplify the Decision: Break your goal into smaller, manageable steps. Instead of focusing on the end result, ask: *What's the smallest step I can take today?*

2. Start With Low Stakes: Your first step doesn't have to be life-altering. For example:
   » Attend a networking event.
   » Research a course or program.
   » Reach out to someone in your desired field for advice.
3. Embrace Imperfection: The first step is rarely perfect, and that's okay. It's about progress, not perfection.

Stop waiting for the "right moment." The magic lies in creating your moment through intentional action. Clarity and progress aren't gifts. They are rewards for starting, learning, and moving forward.

Section 2: The Myth of the Perfect Moment

"You don't have to see the whole staircase, just take the first step." –Martin Luther King Jr.

We've all been seduced by the myth of the perfect moment. Stories of sudden breakthroughs: Newton under the apple tree or Archimedes shouting "Eureka!" make us believe that success hinges on an extraordinary, transformative epiphany. These tales create the illusion that clarity or opportunity will arrive fully formed, waiting for us to seize it.

Those moments are rare. Even when they do occur, they're often the result of years of persistence and preparation leading up to that point. Success, more often than not, is built on the foundation of steady, incremental progress, not singular flashes of insight.

WHY THE MYTH OF THE PERFECT MOMENT HOLDS US BACK

The idea of the "perfect moment" is comforting. It feels like a safety net, protecting us from risk, failure, and uncertainty. It allows us to delay action, convincing ourselves that we're simply waiting for the right time.

But waiting comes with hidden costs:

1. Missed Opportunities: The longer you wait, the more likely you are to miss opportunities that could propel you forward. The window for action doesn't stay open forever.

2. Eroded Confidence: Inaction feeds self-doubt. The more you delay, the harder it becomes to believe in your ability to succeed.

3. Stagnation: Growth requires movement. By standing still, you limit your potential and risk being left behind.

WHY ACTION BEATS PERFECTION

Clarity and confidence don't come from waiting. They come from doing. Imperfect action teaches you more about what works (and what doesn't) than months or years of planning ever could.

J. K. Rowling's journey to creating the *Harry Potter* series is one of the most inspiring examples of resilience, persistence, and refusing to wait for the "perfect moment." In the early 1990s, Rowling was a single mother living on welfare in Edinburgh, Scotland. She struggled with depression, financial insecurity, and the demands of raising a young child.

Despite these personal challenges, Rowling found time to write the first book in the *Harry Potter* series, *Harry Potter and the Philosopher's*

Stone. However, even her passion and dedication couldn't shield her from the harsh reality of rejection. The manuscript was rejected by 12 publishers, with one of them even suggesting she get a second job, as her book was unlikely to succeed.

Yet, rather than waiting for an ideal moment, Rowling pushed forward.

In 1996, Bloomsbury Publishing took a chance on her; and in 1997, the first *Harry Potter* book was published. Rowling's life changed forever. The *Harry Potter* series went on to become a global phenomenon, with over 500 million copies sold and translated into over 80 languages. Beyond the books, the series expanded into movies, theme parks, and a massive fan following.

Rowling's story isn't one of perfect timing or waiting for things to align. It's about perseverance despite rejection, embracing imperfections, and continuing to pursue her dream. Her journey exemplifies how success often comes from continued effort and belief, even when everything around you seems to suggest failure.

Or think of a small business owner who launches a product before it's completely refined. By getting it into customers' hands, they learn what to improve, often faster and more effectively than if they'd waited for perfection.

The act of taking a step, no matter how small, creates momentum that leads to results.

VISUAL FRAMEWORK: THE MOMENTUM CYCLE

Breaking free from inaction follows a predictable cycle:

1. Take a Small Action: Break inertia with one deliberate step. It doesn't have to be grand, just enough to get started.

2. Achieve a Result: Even small progress creates a sense of accomplishment.
3. Build Confidence: Each win, no matter how small, reinforces your belief in your ability to succeed.
4. Repeat the Process: Use the confidence and momentum you've gained to take the next step.

The more you act, the more this cycle builds upon itself, compounding your progress over time.

THE GIFT OF IMPERFECTION

Imperfect action isn't just a tool for progress. It's a gift. When you embrace imperfection, you allow yourself to experiment, learn, and grow. You also set an example for others, showing them that success isn't about being flawless, it's about being bold enough to try.

Arianna Huffington's story is a compelling example of how the "perfect moment" often doesn't exist and that true success comes from learning to embrace failure, recalibrate, and push forward. Huffington, the founder of *The Huffington Post*, has built a career on challenging conventional definitions of success, both personally and professionally.

Her defining moment came in 2007, when she collapsed from exhaustion at her desk. This was a wake-up call for her, as she realised that her life had been defined by the relentless pursuit of professional success at the expense of her physica and mental health.

At that time, Huffington was already a highly successful entrepreneur, but this breakdown forced her to reconsider her values and the meaning of success.

Rather than waiting for the "perfect moment" to slow down or to focus on well-being, Huffington took action. She made self-care and well-being a central focus of her personal and professional life.

In 2016, she launched Thrive Global, a company focused on improving well-being and productivity by helping individuals and companies create healthier, more sustainable work environments.

Her ability to embrace failure, learn from it, and redefine success has made her a leader in the wellness space and a champion for a new approach to business and life.

Huffington's story reinforces that success doesn't come from waiting for perfection, but from taking the first imperfect step, learning from setbacks, and ultimately, finding a better balance in life.

WHY IMPERFECT ACTION WORKS

1. It Builds Momentum:
   » Action creates energy. Once you start, it's easier to keep going.
2. It Reduces Fear:
   » Taking a small step helps you confront uncertainty, making the challenge feel more manageable.
3. It Reveals the Path Forward:
   » Clarity often comes through doing, not waiting. Each action helps illuminate the next step.

J. K. Rowling and Arianna Huffington serve as strong examples of how success is rarely about waiting for ideal conditions. Rather, it's about taking action in the face of imperfections, learning from failures, and continuing to push forward with determination and resilience.

The myth of the perfect moment keeps you in a cycle of waiting. The reality? The perfect moment rarely exists. Instead, success is built through deliberate, imperfect actions that create momentum, build confidence, and open doors.

Section 3: Overcoming Fear of Failure

"Failure isn't the opposite of success, it's part of the process."

Fear of failure is one of the most powerful forces that keep people stuck. It whispers that mistakes are unacceptable, that setbacks define your worth, and that playing it safe is the better choice. Failure is not the end. It's a necessary step on the road to growth and success. Every mistake is an opportunity to learn, adapt, and refine your approach.

LEARNING TO EMBRACE FAILURE

Fear of failure felt like an ever-present weight. I remember my first workshop. I had poured endless hours into planning every detail; rehearsing my delivery, and anticipating potential questions. But when the day arrived, things didn't go as planned. Some attendees were disengaged, the pacing felt off, and my perfectionist tendencies left me overthinking every word.

Afterwards, I felt deflated. The voice in my head told me I wasn't cut out for this. Yet, as I reflected, I realised something powerful: the experience had taught me what I needed to improve. I learned to adjust my pacing, create more interactive elements, and focus less on perfection, and more on connection. Each subsequent workshop improved because I took those lessons to heart.

Looking back, that initial "failure" wasn't a setback. It was a stepping stone that made me a better coach. It showed me that failure, when viewed as feedback, is one of the most valuable teachers.

THE POWER OF REFRAMING FAILURE

Failure often feels like a dead end, but in reality, it's a redirection, a chance to reevaluate and pivot. Fear of failure is often rooted in the belief that mistakes define you, but the truth is, mistakes shape you.

1. View Failure as Feedback:
   » Every failure contains lessons about what works and what doesn't. Instead of dwelling on the outcome, focus on the insights you can gain.
2. Normalise Fear as Growth:
   » Fear often signals that you're venturing outside your comfort zone, the place where growth happens. If you're not feeling some discomfort, you're likely not challenging yourself enough.
3. Learn From Bold Examples:
   » Think of Simone Biles. Her path to becoming one of the greatest gymnasts of all time wasn't linear. Each stumble, fall, or missed routine wasn't a failure, it was a lesson. She used those moments to refine her skills, ultimately redefining what is possible in gymnastics.

THE HIDDEN COST OF AVOIDING FAILURE

While fear of failure can feel protective, it comes with a hidden cost:

- Missed Opportunities: By avoiding risks, you close the door to potential breakthroughs.
- Stunted Growth: Staying in your comfort zone limits your ability to learn and adapt.
- Eroded Confidence: The longer you avoid challenges, the harder it becomes to trust your ability to handle them.

EMBRACE FAILURE

1. Reframe the Narrative:
   - » Instead of asking, *"What if I fail?"* ask, *"What can I learn from this?"*
2. Start Small:
   - » Take manageable risks that allow you to build confidence while testing your limits.
3. Debrief After Setbacks:
   - » After a perceived failure, reflect on these questions:
     - · *What went well?*
     - · *What didn't go as planned?*
     - · *What can I do differently next time?*
4. Share Your Lessons:
   - » Talk about your failures with others. Vulnerability builds connection, and your experience might inspire someone else to take their own leap.

Michael Jordan, often regarded as the greatest basketball player of all time, faced countless failures that ultimately shaped him into the legend he is today. His story is a testament to how failure can become the greatest teacher if you are willing to learn from it.

In 1978, as a high school sophomore at Emsley A. Laney High School in Wilmington, North Carolina, Jordan was cut from his varsity basketball team. He didn't make the team, despite his strong desire to play. This rejection could have been devastating for many teenagers. but Jordan used it as fuel for his ambition. Instead of giving up, he channeled his frustration into relentless improvement. In his autobiography, he later reflected, *"I took that personally"* and this feeling pushed him to work even harder the following year.

Jordan's college years at the University of North Carolina were marked by challenges, but in 1982, at just 19 years old, he made a game-winning shot in the NCAA championship game against Georgetown. That moment was the first glimpse of his greatness. However, even at the peak of his college career, Jordan faced more setbacks. In his first year with the Chicago Bulls (1984-85), he was sidelined with a broken foot. Many questioned whether he would ever be the same player again; yet Jordan returned in 1986, scoring 63 points in a playoff game against the Boston Celtics—the most ever in a single playoff game at that time.

Despite these accomplishments, Jordan's career wasn't free from failure. Throughout his career, he missed over 9,000 shots in regular season games, and he lost nearly 300 games. But it was his mindset that made the difference. Each missed shot or lost game wasn't a sign of failure to Jordan, but a valuable lesson. He once famously said, *"I've failed over and over again in my life. And that is why I succeed."*

The ultimate symbol of Jordan's ability to embrace failure came during his time with the Chicago Bulls. After leading the team to a third consecutive championship in 1993, Jordan unexpectedly retired from basketball to pursue a career in baseball. While many saw this as a failure, he later returned to the NBA in March 1995. Jordan's comeback story is one for the ages, his return to the Bulls marked the beginning of a second three-peat, winning three more championships in 1996, 1997, and 1998.

Jordan's journey is a perfect example of how failure is not the opposite of success, but an essential part of the process. He embraced the challenges, learned from each defeat, and never allowed fear of failure to stop him. Today, his name is synonymous with greatness, not because he succeeded without effort, but because he faced setbacks head-on, learned from them, and became better because of them.

That first workshop I led wasn't perfect. But by treating it as a learning experience rather than a failure, I built the skills and confidence to deliver workshops that truly resonate.

Failure isn't something to fear, it's something to embrace. It's a teacher, a motivator, and a builder of resilience. Each stumble, when reframed as feedback, becomes a stepping stone to success. Don't let the fear of failure keep you from starting. Every great accomplishment begins with the courage to try.

Section 4: The Power of Action– Why Waiting Steals Your Potential

"Waiting is a trap that steals your time and potential."

Inaction is a thief. It whispers that waiting is the safe option, that the perfect conditions will come if you're patient enough. But every moment you spend waiting is a moment lost. It is time you could have spent growing, learning, and moving closer to your goals.

Action isn't about guaranteeing success. It's about creating momentum, discovering opportunities, and learning through doing. It's the antidote to fear, doubt, and indecision.

OVERCOMING THE PARALYSIS OF WAITING

When I started my coaching business, fear of failure loomed large. I found myself stuck in a cycle of overthinking:

- *What if I'm not good enough?*
- *What if no one trusts me?*
- *What if I fail completely?*

I convinced myself that waiting for more confidence or better conditions would make things easier. But the longer I waited, the more self-doubt grew. Waiting wasn't protecting me; it was paralysing me.

Finally, I realised that the only way forward was to take action, no matter how small. I began by offering free coaching sessions. They weren't perfect, but they gave me real-world experience, valuable feedback, and the confidence to refine my approach. Each session was a step forward, transforming my fear into progress and proving to myself that action—not waiting—was the key to building momentum.

THE HIDDEN COSTS OF INACTION

While waiting feels safe, it comes with hidden costs:

1. Lost Opportunities:
   » Opportunities often arise when you least expect them. By waiting, you risk missing chances that could propel you forward.

2. Eroded Confidence:
   » Inaction feeds self-doubt. The longer you wait, the harder it becomes to trust your ability to take the leap.
3. Stagnation:
   » Growth requires movement. By standing still, you limit your potential and allow fear to dictate your choices.

WHY ACTION IS MORE POWERFUL THAN PERFECTION

Taking action isn't about perfection, it's about progress. Each step forward teaches you something new, builds resilience, and opens doors to possibilities you wouldn't have encountered otherwise.

- Action Creates Momentum: Progress, however small, generates energy and enthusiasm, making it easier to take the next step.
- Action Sparks Learning: Every action, even imperfect, provides valuable feedback that helps you refine your approach.
- Action Uncovers Opportunities: The more you do, the more possibilities you uncover—possibilities that remain hidden when you're stuck in inaction.

In 1997, Reed Hastings returned a rented VHS of *Apollo 13* late and was hit with a $40 fee. It wasn't the money; it was the principle. The experience stuck with him. Most people would have just vented about it. Hastings acted.

He started thinking: what if video rentals worked like a gym membership? A flat fee, no late charges. Within weeks, he and his co-founder Marc Randolph tested the idea. They mailed a single DVD to themselves to see if it could survive the postal system. It did.

No one asked them to disrupt Blockbuster. The tech wasn't ready. DVD players were rare, and streaming was years away. Despite all this, they built the website, stocked a few titles, and launched anyway. Early customers didn't come in waves. They kept refining. They didn't know if it would work. But they kept moving.

By 2000, Netflix had just 300,000 subscribers and was losing money. Hastings offered to sell the company to Blockbuster for $50 million. Blockbuster laughed them out of the room.

Fast forward to 2007, they launched streaming, before internet speeds could fully support it. Another risk. Another bet on momentum.

Blockbuster filed for bankruptcy in 2010. Netflix kept growing.

Hastings didn't wait to be ready. He acted. He learned, adjusted, and repeated. If he had waited for better timing or a clearer validation, Netflix would not have existed today. Offering free coaching sessions wasn't glamorous, but it was essential. Each session taught me what worked and what didn't. They give me the clarity and confidence to build a thriving business. Think of any elite athlete. Their success isn't built on waiting for ideal conditions, but on showing up every day, even when conditions are less than perfect.

HARNESS THE POWER OF ACTION

1. Start Small:
    - » Identify one simple action you can take today to move closer to your goal.
    - » Example in Action: If you're considering a career change, update your CV or research one potential role.

2. Focus on Progress, Not Perfection:
   » Remind yourself that perfection isn't the goal; momentum is.
   » Example in Action: Launch your idea in its simplest form and improve it based on real-world feedback.
3. Set Clear Timeframes:
   » Avoid overthinking by giving yourself a deadline for your next action.
   » Example in Action: Commit to making a decision within 48 hours instead of waiting indefinitely.
4. Track Your Progress:
   » Keep a record of your actions and reflect on the progress you've made.
5. Celebrate Small Wins:
   » Acknowledge every step forward, no matter how small, to reinforce your confidence.

Waiting is a thief that steals your potential; while action transforms fear into progress. Each small step you take builds momentum, uncovers opportunities, and brings you closer to your goals. Don't wait for the perfect moment; it rarely comes. Instead, create your own momentum through deliberate, consistent action.

Section 5: What Will This Mean for You?

"Each step forward brings you closer to your goals."

Taking action isn't just about making progress; it's about transforming your mindset. Each deliberate step creates a ripple effect, shifting how you think, feel, and approach challenges. It's not just your external world that changes; action builds confidence, resilience, and a sense of purpose.

THE RIPPLE EFFECT OF ACTION

Action doesn't exist in isolation. Every step, no matter how small, creates momentum, opens doors, and reinforces belief in your abilities. Here's how:

1. Build Momentum: Progress; however small, generates energy that propels you forward. Each step leads naturally to the next, creating a cycle of growth.

   » Example in Action: Learning a new skill often begins with uncertainty. A writer, for example, might start with a few clumsy sentences. But over time, those sentences evolve into stories, articles, or even books. The initial momentum sparks mastery.

2. Discover Opportunities: Taking action exposes you to paths you couldn't see from a standstill. The more you do, the more opportunities arise.

   » Example in Action: When I signed up for my first coaching workshop, I didn't realise how transformative it would be. That single step connected me with mentors, peers, and ideas that helped me refine my vision. Opportunities I couldn't have anticipated emerged simply because I showed up.

3. Gain Confidence: Action replaces fear with belief. Each time you take a step and see results, your confidence grows, making the next step easier.

   » Example in Action: Nicole, a writer I coached, hesitated to submit her manuscript for fear of rejection. When she finally sent it, the feedback she received didn't just improve her writing, it validated her talent. That single act of bravery led to her first publication and transformed how she saw herself as a writer.

MY JOURNEY FROM FEAR TO ACTION

At the initial stages of starting my business, I felt overwhelmed by self-doubt.

Could I actually help people? Would anyone trust me?

Those questions kept me stuck for weeks—convincing me to wait until I felt more confident or better prepared.

One day, I decided to break the cycle. I reached out to someone I knew and offered a free workshop. I didn't have a polished program or years of experience, but I was committed to learning. That first session wasn't perfect, I stumbled over my words and second-guessed my advice; yet it was real.

That single action sparked a chain reaction. The people I trained provided positive feedback, and their encouragement gave me the confidence to offer more sessions. Each step taught me something new: how to ask better questions, how to adapt to different needs, and how to deliver meaningful outcomes. Looking back, those small, imperfect actions were what built the foundation of my career.

WHY THIS MATTERS

Taking action isn't just about achieving goals, it's about becoming the kind of person who takes ownership of their life. Here's what it will mean for you:

1. You'll Build Trust in Yourself:
   » Each step forward reinforces your ability to follow through on commitments, both to yourself and others.
2. You'll Expand Your Comfort Zone:
   » What once felt intimidating will become second nature and will empower you to tackle even greater challenges.
3. You'll Cultivate Resilience:
   » Action often comes with setbacks, but each one becomes a lesson that strengthens your ability to adapt and persevere.

Every elite athlete starts with small, consistent efforts. A runner's first mile isn't fast or graceful, but it's the foundation for future marathons.

Similarly, many successful businesses began with a single prototype or pitch. Action, even when imperfect, allowed them to gather feedback and refine their ideas.

Consider Kimberly, a senior executive I coached. She hesitated to share her social content because of self-doubt and fear of what other people would think. However, when she began preparing content that reflected her knowledge and story, and then pressed "post", the feedback she received not only boosted her confidence and dispelled her doubts, but also led her to create her own newsletter, and secure her new high-profile executive role. We're now in talks of her preparing for her first Tedx Talk.

STEPS TO HARNESS THE POWER OF ACTION

1. Start With What's Manageable:
   - » Identify one small step you can take today. For example, if you're exploring a career change, update your CV or research roles that interest you.
2. Focus on Learning, Not Perfection:
   - » Treat each step as an experiment. Reflect on what worked, what didn't, and what you can adjust.
3. Celebrate Progress:
   - » Acknowledge every step forward, no matter how small. Recognising progress reinforces your commitment and builds momentum.
4. Keep a "Win" Journal:
   - » Record your successes, either big or small. Over time, you'll see how far you've come and gain confidence in your ability to keep moving forward.

Each step forward brings you closer to your goals. But it also transforms who you are. With every action, you build momentum, uncover opportunities, and replace fear with confidence. Don't underestimate the power of small steps. They are the foundation of big transformations.

Section 6: Your Action Plan–Steps to Move Forward Now

"Clarity comes through action, not overthinking. Take the first step, and the path will reveal itself."

Success isn't built on grand plans or perfect strategies, it's built on consistent, intentional action. The best way to move forward is to simplify the process. Focus on what's manageable, and create momentum through small but deliberate steps. Here's your action plan to stop waiting and start making progress today.

1. THE "2-MINUTE RULE"–QUICK WINS BUILD MOMENTUM

If something takes two minutes or less, do it immediately. This rule eliminates procrastination and helps you build momentum by clearing small tasks that often clog your mental bandwidth.

- Examples in Action:
  » Instead of letting emails pile up, respond to straightforward ones right away.
  » If you've been avoiding scheduling a meeting, take two minutes to send the invite.
- Why It Works: These quick wins create a sense of accomplishment, motivating you to tackle larger challenges.

2. BATCH SIMILAR TASKS—MAINTAIN FOCUS AND EFFICIENCY

Switching between unrelated tasks wastes mental energy. Instead, group similar actions together to maximise focus and minimise distractions.

- Example in Action: Block out a specific time to respond to emails, schedule meetings, or brainstorm ideas, rather than scattering them throughout your day.

- Why It Works: Batching reduces decision fatigue, allowing you to stay in a focused state longer and accomplish more in less time.

3. GAMIFY PROGRESS—MAKE THE PROCESS ENGAGING

Turning progress into a game makes it more enjoyable and rewarding. Set milestones and create small rewards for achieving them.

- Examples in Action:
  - » If you're working on a big project, break it into milestones. Reward yourself with a coffee break, a walk, or a favourite activity after completing each one.
  - » For fitness goals, track your progress with apps that celebrate achievements or milestones.
- Why It Works: Gamifying tasks taps into your brain's reward system, making progress feel satisfying and fun, even for challenging goals.

4. SEEK FEEDBACK EARLY—LEARN AND IMPROVE FASTER

Don't wait for perfection to share your work or ideas. Early feedback helps you refine and improve while saving time and effort.

- Examples in Action:
  - » If you're writing a proposal, share a rough draft with a trusted colleague for input before perfecting every detail.
  - » When designing a product or presentation, test it with a small group to gather insights before rolling it out.

- Why It Works: Feedback highlights blind spots, refines your approach, and ensures your efforts align with your goals.

5. SET CLEAR DEADLINES—STOP OVERTHINKING AND START DOING

Ambiguity breeds procrastination. Give yourself specific timeframes for decisions and actions to avoid endless overthinking.

- Examples in Action:
  - » If you're launching a new initiative, set a deadline for each phase—such as drafting a plan, gathering resources, and executing.
  - » For personal projects, commit to starting within 48 hours and stick to it.
- Why It Works: Deadlines create urgency, helping you prioritise and act decisively.

When I opened my first martial arts class, I faced the same overwhelm I did when launching my workshops. There was a lot to manage: class structure, student engagement, refining techniques, and ensuring every session delivered real value. I found myself constantly tweaking lesson plans, over analysing feedback, and second-guessing my approach.

Instead of staying stuck in overthinking, I applied the same principles I now coach others on. I started batching tasks, setting aside specific times to plan lessons, communicate with students, and review techniques rather than jumping between them throughout the day. I gave myself deadlines to finalise drills instead of endlessly adjusting them. And most importantly, I sought early feedback.

Instead of waiting until I felt like I had the "perfect" teaching style, I paid attention to student reactions and made real-time adjustments.

One of the best changes I made was gamifying progress. I set small milestones—like mastering a specific drill or getting a student to execute a technique correctly—and rewarded myself with something as simple as a short break or a training session of my own. Those little wins kept me engaged, and before long, my confidence as an instructor grew. What once felt overwhelming became structured, intentional, and, most importantly, enjoyable.

WHY THESE STEPS WORK FOR EVERYONE

These strategies aren't about adding complexity, they're about simplifying and clarifying the path forward. They create structure, reduce procrastination, and ensure steady progress toward your goals.

HOW TO IMPLEMENT YOUR ACTION PLAN

1. Start With One Strategy:
   » Choose one of these steps that feels most relevant to your current challenge and implement it today.
2. Track Your Progress:
   » Keep a log of your completed tasks, feedback received, and milestones achieved.
3. Reflect and Adjust:
   » Regularly evaluate what's working and refine your plan as needed.

Your action plan doesn't need to be complicated; it needs to be actionable. By using simple strategies like the "2-Minute Rule," batching tasks, and setting clear deadlines, you can eliminate procrastination, build momentum, and move forward with clarity and purpose.

Success isn't about waiting for the perfect moment; it's about making progress, one intentional step at a time.

Section 7: Reflection Challenge– Take the First Step

"What's one decision or action you've been delaying?"
We all have decisions we've put off or actions we've delayed. Sometimes it's because we're waiting for the "perfect" moment; other times, it's because fear, doubt, or uncertainty holds us back. But here's the truth: the longer we delay, the harder it becomes to move forward. Taking the first step, no matter how small, is the key to breaking free from inaction.

THE COST OF DELAYING DECISIONS
When you delay action, you risk:

1. Missed Opportunities: The more time you spend waiting, the more potential opportunities slip away.
2. Eroded Confidence: Inaction often leads to self-doubt, reinforcing the fear that held you back in the first place.
3. Stagnation: Growth requires movement. Staying still means staying stuck, even as the world moves forward around you.

MY OWN FIRST STEP

I still remember the first coaching session I offered. It was a decision I had delayed for weeks, caught up in overthinking.

- *What if I wasn't good enough?*
- *What if I couldn't deliver value?*
- *What if I failed completely?*

The fear of those "what ifs" kept me in a holding pattern. But one day, I decided to write an email to someone I thought might benefit from coaching. It wasn't perfect, and I didn't have a polished program, but I offered to help. That email was my first step.

The session that followed wasn't flawless, but it taught me what worked and what didn't. It showed me that even imperfect action creates clarity and builds confidence. That single step turned into another, and then another, laying the foundation for a coaching career that has brought me fulfillment and growth.

WHY REFLECTION IS A POWERFUL TOOL

Reflection isn't about dwelling on the past, it's about gaining clarity to move forward. By reflecting on what's holding you back, you can identify the fears, doubts, or uncertainties keeping you stuck. Reflection gives you the perspective needed to take action with intention.

STEPS FOR YOUR REFLECTION CHALLENGE

Take 15 minutes to complete this simple but powerful exercise:

1. Write Down the Decision or Action You've Been Delaying:
   » Be specific. Whether it's starting a project, making a call, or pursuing a goal, name it clearly.

2. List the Best-Case Scenario:
   » Ask yourself, *What's the best possible outcome if I take this step?* Writing it down helps you focus on the potential opportunities rather than the risks.
3. List the Worst-Case Scenario:
   » Acknowledge your fears by asking, *What's the worst that could happen?* Then, evaluate how realistic those fears are and how you could handle them if they came true.
4. Identify One Action You Can Take Today:
   » Start small. Commit to one specific, manageable step, like sending an email, researching an opportunity, or setting up a conversation.

EXAMPLE IN ACTION:

- *Delayed Action:* Applying for a leadership role.
- *Best-Case Scenario:* I get the job and grow as a leader.
- *Worst-Case Scenario:* I don't get the job, but I gain interview experience and learn what I need to improve.
- *First Step Today:* Update my CV and submit the application.

THE IMPACT OF A SINGLE STEP

Taking the first step has a ripple effect. Once you act, momentum builds, confidence grows, and opportunities begin to appear. The hardest part is starting, but once you do, the path becomes clearer.

Reflection gives you clarity, and clarity fuels action. By taking just 15 minutes to examine what's holding you back, you can identify the fears and uncertainties that are keeping you stuck. More importantly, you can uncover the possibilities waiting on the other side of action.

The step you take today, no matter how small, could be the start of something extraordinary.

Section 8: The Big Impact of Small Steps

"Each small step is a seed. With care and persistence, it grows into something extraordinary."

Small steps can feel insignificant. But the truth is, they're foundational. Great achievements are rarely the result of one giant leap; they're the culmination of consistent, deliberate actions. Small steps, taken consistently, compound over time, creating the momentum and resilience needed to achieve extraordinary results.

BUILDING MY COACHING CAREER ONE STEP AT A TIME

I didn't launch a massive program overnight. I didn't have a grand strategy or a large client base. I started with one client. That first session wasn't perfect. I stumbled over my words, second-guessed my approach, and worried if I was providing enough value. But it was a step.

From that single session, I gained insights that shaped my next conversation, and then the next. Each small action added to my confidence and understanding, allowing me to refine my skills and grow my practice. Over time, those small seeds I planted one client, one session, one conversation grew into a thriving career and globally recognised business.

Looking back, I realise that the first small step was just as important as the bigger milestones that followed. Without those initial actions, I wouldn't have built the foundation that sustains my work today.

THE COMPOUNDING EFFECT OF SMALL STEPS

Small steps might feel modest in the moment, but their impact multiplies over time. Just as planting a seed doesn't yield a tree overnight, progress requires patience, persistence, and consistent effort.

Here's how small steps create big results:

1. Momentum Builds Confidence:
   » Each small step reinforces your belief in your ability to succeed. This confidence fuels your motivation to keep going.
2. Action Reveals Opportunities:
   » Starting small often uncovers paths you couldn't see before. Progress opens doors that waiting would have kept closed.
3. Consistency Creates Mastery:
   » Repetition and practice, even in small doses, build the skills and habits needed for long-term success.

Giannis Antetokounmpo, now an NBA champion and two-time MVP, didn't start his career with fame or fortune. Born in Greece to Nigerian immigrants, Giannis and his family struggled financially, often having to share shoes and clothes. But instead of focusing on the overwhelming dream of reaching the NBA, Giannis focused on taking small, consistent steps. He spent hours each day improving his skills—dribbling, shooting, strength training—regardless of the lack of resources or support.

When he entered the NBA as a raw prospect in 2013, Giannis wasn't an immediate superstar. He lacked many of the refined skills of other top players. However, he worked relentlessly, learning from his mistakes, improving his game, and adding muscle to his frame. Every season, he built on the small steps he had taken before.

In 2019, Giannis was named MVP. He had grown from a skinny teenager with raw talent into one of the most dominant players in the league. His story isn't just about a single, massive breakthrough but about a series of small, deliberate actions over many years that compounded to create extraordinary results.

Giannis's journey is a prime example of how small steps, when taken consistently, build momentum. He didn't start with a perfect shot or incredible athleticism, he started with persistence. By embracing the grind and focusing on the small steps, Giannis reached the pinnacle of his sport. Like in any great achievement, the little things make the biggest impact over time.

Starting with one client wasn't glamorous, but it was essential. That single step taught me more than any amount of overthinking or preparation ever could.

WHY SMALL STEPS MATTER

The beauty of small steps lies in their accessibility. You don't need perfect conditions or unlimited resources to begin. Small steps are manageable, actionable, and sustainable, making them the ideal starting point for any goal.

HOW TO START TAKING SMALL STEPS TODAY

1. Break Down Big Goals:
   » Identify a large goal and divide it into smaller, actionable steps.
   » Example in Action: If your goal is to write a book, start by drafting an outline or writing for 10 minutes a day.
2. Celebrate Micro-Wins:
   » Acknowledge every step forward, no matter how small. Recognising progress reinforces your commitment and builds momentum.
3. Track Your Progress:
   » Keep a journal or checklist of completed steps. Seeing your progress over time provides motivation and clarity.
4. Stay Consistent:
   » Commit to daily or weekly actions, even if they're small. Consistency over time creates exponential results.
5. Reflect on Your Growth:
   » Periodically review how far you've come since taking your first step. This reflection highlights the power of persistence.

THE DAY I ALMOST DIDN'T START

Before that first coaching session, I nearly convinced myself to wait. I thought, *What difference will one session make?* But taking that step taught me something invaluable: the hardest part of any journey is starting. Once you begin, the path reveals itself.

That single client grew into a network of referrals. Each session brought new insights that shaped my coaching approach. If I had waited for perfect conditions, I'd still be standing at the starting line.

Small steps are the foundation of big transformations. They may seem modest in the moment, but their impact compounds over time, creating momentum, confidence, and opportunities. Start where you are, with what you have, and take the first step. Each seed you plant today holds the potential for extraordinary growth.

Section 9: Reflection

"Stop waiting for a sign. The first step is the sign."

Most people don't lack ambition, they just spend too long waiting. Waiting for the right time. The perfect idea. A sign that they're ready. But the truth is, readiness is a result, not a requirement. You get it by doing.

This chapter wasn't about motivation; it was about momentum. Small steps taken consistently—not grand moments of clarity—are what change everything. Those who move forward aren't the ones with the perfect plan; they're the ones who got tired of standing still.

You don't need a breakthrough—You need to move. Clarity comes from action. Progress comes from starting. Your future self—the one you're working toward—will thank you for every step you take now, no matter how small it looks today.

Use the questions below to stop waiting and start shaping what comes next. The life you want doesn't need another delay—it needs a decision.

Reflection Questions

SECTION 1:

What's one action you've been putting off because you're waiting for the "right time"?

SECTION 2:

What opportunities might you be missing by waiting for "perfect" conditions instead of taking imperfect action?

SECTION 3:

What's one failure you've experienced that taught you a valuable lesson? How can you apply that lesson today to move closer to your goals?

SECTION 4:

What's one action you've been delaying because you're waiting for the perfect conditions? What's one step you can take today to move forward?

SECTION 5:

What's one action you can take today that will move you closer to your goals? How will this step create momentum for the next?

SECTION 6:

What's one strategy you can implement today to simplify your next step? How will it help you build momentum?

SECTION 7:

What's one decision or action you've been delaying? What's the smallest step you can take today to move closer to it?

SECTION 8:

What's one small step you can take today to move closer to your goal? How will that step create momentum for the next?

CHAPTER 8

Lead From Within

> *"True leadership begins where self-awareness meets action."*

Imagine walking into a room where one person stands out—not because they speak the loudest, but because their presence is undeniable. They don't force authority, yet they command respect. They don't push, yet people feel compelled to act. They don't demand trust, yet it's given freely. What makes them different? It's not their title or position; it's the energy they bring—rooted in self-awareness, clarity of purpose, and a deep alignment between their values and actions.

This chapter is about that energy—the force that fuels resilience, sharpens decision-making, and elevates leadership beyond strategy and execution. True leadership isn't about controlling others; it's about mastering yourself.

When your internal state is in sync with your external actions, you don't just lead, you inspire.

Section 1: Finding the Energy to Lead From Within

"Leadership starts from within; it's the energy you bring to every decision, every conversation, and every challenge."

Finding the energy to lead from within is about more than just physical stamina; it's about cultivating emotional and mental strength. This energy fuels your passion, drives your decisions, and inspires those around you, especially in challenging moments. Without it, even the most skilled leader can falter.

Leadership energy is finite. If not managed intentionally, it can become depleted, leaving you feeling overwhelmed and ineffective. Replenishing your internal energy isn't a luxury; it's a necessity. It requires self-awareness, deliberate effort, and the willingness to prioritise your own well-being alongside the demands of leadership.

RECLAIMING MY LEADERSHIP ENERGY

It was 2022, and I felt like I was running on empty. I was juggling multiple leadership responsibilities—from coaching clients, managing a growing team, to balancing personal commitments. I thought sheer determination would carry me through, but as my energy dwindled, so did my clarity. I became reactive rather than proactive, making decisions out of urgency instead of intention. My leadership suffered, and so did the people I was trying to lead.

The turning point came when I realised I couldn't lead effectively without managing my energy as carefully as my time. I began carving out moments for self-care, setting boundaries, prioritising activities that recharged me, and learning to say "no" to distractions. I realised that leadership wasn't about doing more; it was about doing what mattered most with intention and focus.

That internal recalibration transformed how I showed up for others. By protecting and nurturing my energy, I became more present, thoughtful, and aligned in my leadership.

THE LEADERSHIP ENERGY FRAMEWORK

To lead effectively, you must actively manage your energy. Here's a simple framework to guide you:

1. Recognise Energy Drains:
   - » Identify the activities, environments, or habits that deplete your energy.
   - » Example in Action: Endless back-to-back meetings without time to reflect can leave you drained and unfocused.
2. Prioritise Energy Boosters:
   - » Engage in activities that recharge you emotionally, mentally, and physically.
   - » Example in Action: Exercise, journaling, or a 10-minute mindfulness practice can help reset your focus and elevate your mood.
3. Establish Boundaries:
   - » Protect your energy by learning to say "no" to tasks or commitments that don't align with your priorities.
   - » Example in Action: Decline unnecessary meetings or delegate tasks that don't require your direct involvement.

THE POWER OF INTENTIONAL ENERGY

Angela Duckworth, in her seminal book *Grit: The Power of Passion and Perseverance*, explores the concept of grit—a combination of passion and perseverance that drives individuals to achieve long-term goals. Duckworth's research shows that talent alone is not enough for success; it is the ability to persist through challenges and stay focused on the end goal that truly sets high achievers apart.

Her work serves as a powerful reminder for leaders, especially those who face complex and unpredictable challenges in both their personal and professional lives. She argues that grit, more than intelligence or talent, is the defining factor in success. This is particularly relevant in leadership, where resilience, the ability to bounce back from setbacks, and staying committed to a long-term vision are key to thriving.

THE GRIT FORMULA: PASSION + PERSEVERANCE

In Duckworth's view, grit is made up of two key components:

- Passion: The deep interest in a long-term goal that sustains motivation over years. Passion fuels the drive to overcome obstacles and push forward when times get tough.
- Perseverance: The commitment to stay the course, even when success doesn't come immediately. This includes enduring failure and learning from mistakes, all while continuing to work towards the same vision.

Duckworth's research involved studying diverse groups—from students to corporate leaders, athletes to artists—and found that those who demonstrated grit were more likely to succeed than those with higher talent but less perseverance.

One striking example Duckworth uses in her book is that of West Point cadets. In a study she conducted, she found that the best predictor of success at the U.S. Military Academy was not physical fitness or academic achievement, but rather grit. Those who were able to persist, even when faced with overwhelming challenges, outperformed those who were physically or academically gifted but lacked resilience.

This concept applies directly to leadership. Leaders who exhibit grit inspire the same level of commitment in their teams. They are not deterred by obstacles, but are motivated by the larger vision, creating a culture of resilience and persistence within their organisations.

GRIT AND LEADERSHIP ENERGY

Leadership energy, as Duckworth's research suggests, is tied to grit. It's about sustaining the energy to face difficulties and persevering through them, despite short-term setbacks. The most effective leaders, according to Duckworth, are those who can channel their passion and perseverance to inspire others, even in tough times.

By applying Duckworth's principles of grit, leaders can cultivate their internal energy and create environments where teams stay motivated and focused, regardless of the challenges ahead. Leadership, at its core, is about knowing how to persist, and Duckworth's insights offer a roadmap for leaders to build lasting success through the power of grit.

CULTIVATE LEADERSHIP ENERGY

1. Start Your Day Intentionally:
   » Begin each morning with a grounding ritual that aligns your energy and focus.
   » Example in Action: Spend 5 minutes reviewing your priorities or practicing gratitude to set a positive tone.

2. Schedule Energy Breaks:
   » Incorporate short breaks into your day to recharge.
   » Example in Action: Step outside for fresh air, stretch, or take a mindful pause between meetings.

3. Reflect Regularly:
   » At the end of each week, evaluate what energised you and what drained you. Adjust your schedule accordingly.

4. Protect Your Non-Negotiables:
   » Identify the activities that are essential for your well-being and make them a priority.
   » Example in Action: Block time for exercise, family, or personal hobbies in your calendar as non-negotiable appointments.

Leadership energy isn't something you can leave to chance—it's something you cultivate. By managing your energy intentionally, you not only enhance your capacity to lead but also inspire those around you with your presence and purpose. Small adjustments can make a significant impact. Start by protecting what fuels you, and observe how it transforms the way you lead.

Section 2: Take Control of Your Inner Strength

"Leadership isn't about your title, it's about the example you set and the energy you project."

Great leadership starts with self-leadership. Before you can guide others, you must guide yourself with intention and clarity. This requires a deep understanding of your strengths, weaknesses, and values. Self-awareness becomes your compass, allowing you to navigate challenges with confidence, make decisions aligned with your principles, and project the energy that inspires trust and respect.

Leadership isn't a title or a position; it's a series of deliberate choices. It's about setting an example through your actions, even when no one is watching.

LEARNING TO NAVIGATE MY INNER TERRAIN

Becoming a business owner, I was so focused on achieving external success that I neglected my own self-awareness. I thought that as long as I worked hard and delivered results, everything else would fall into place. But I soon realised that my lack of alignment between my values and my actions was creating friction.

It became clear that to lead others effectively, I had to first take control of my inner world. Like a cyclist preparing for a challenging ride, I needed to understand my "terrain", my strengths, my limitations, and how to pace myself.

By reflecting on my values, acknowledging my blind spots, and embracing self-awareness, I started to lead with greater authenticity.

This internal recalibration didn't just make me a better leader, it made me a more confident and grounded person.

THE INNER STRENGTH FRAMEWORK

To take control of your inner strength as a leader, focus on three key areas:

1. Identify Your Core Values:
   - » Your values act as your leadership GPS, guiding your decisions and actions.
   - » Example in Action: If integrity is a core value, you'll naturally prioritise transparency and honesty in your leadership style.

2. Recognise Your Strengths and Weaknesses:
   - » Knowing what you excel at and where you need support helps you delegate effectively and seek growth opportunities.
   - » Example in Action: If you're a visionary thinker but struggle with details, surround yourself with detail-oriented team members to complement your skills.

3. Align Your Actions With Your Purpose:
   - » Leadership becomes effortless when your actions align with your beliefs and goals.
   - » Example in Action: If one of your purposes is to mentor others, carve out time for coaching and development sessions with your team.

LEADERSHIP AS A LONG-DISTANCE BIKE RIDE

Leadership, much like a long-distance bike ride, requires preparation, self-awareness, and adaptability. Knowing the terrain ahead allows you to pace yourself, conserve energy, and anticipate obstacles. Similarly, knowing your inner terrain—your strengths, limits, and triggers—equips you to handle external demands with resilience and poise.

On the Bike: You wouldn't approach a steep hill the same way as a flat road. You shift gears, adjust your pace, and conserve energy.

In Leadership: Adapting to challenges requires the same awareness and strategic adjustment. When you know your "gears" (inner strengths), you can navigate any terra n effectively.

THE POWER OF SELF-AWARENESS

One of the most powerful examples of leadership through self-awareness is Lewis Hamilton, a seven-time Formula 1 world champion. Since making his debut in Formula 1 in 2007, Hamilton has become a leader not only for his exceptional racing skills but also for his ability to lead both on and off the track.

In recent years, particularly in 2020, Hamilton has shown immense self-awareness by acknowledging the pressures of competition and the importance of mental health in a high-performance environment. He has been open about his struggles with mental health, using his platform to advocate for diversity and inclusion within motorsport. His decision to speak out on issues like racism and his support for the Black Lives Matter movement in 2020 highlighted his commitment to using his influence for positive change. His ability to continuously evolve and adapt is a testament to his leadership.

But Hamilton's leadership isn't just about his success on the track; it's about how he leads himself in the face of adversity. Over the years, he has consistently demonstrated the ability to reflect, seek feedback, and surround himself with experts. In 2018, after a challenging season, Hamilton acknowledged the need for personal growth, seeking new coaching and refining his approach to mental resilience. This focus on internal development has contributed not only to his success but also to his broader influence in the world of sports and beyond.

His example reinforces the idea that leadership is not defined by titles or positions but by the choices we make, our resilience, and the energy we project to others. Just as Hamilton shifts gears on the track to maintain control and stay ahead of the competition, effective leaders shift their internal gears to stay aligned with their purpose, adapt to challenges, and inspire those around them.

BUILD INNER STRENGTH

1. Conduct a Leadership Audit:
   » Reflect on your recent decisions and actions. Ask yourself:
     · *Were they aligned with my values?*
     · *What could I have done better?*
2. Identify Your Strengths and Gaps:
   » Write down your top three strengths as a leader and one area where you'd like to improve.
3. Set Intentional Goals:
   » Create one goal this week that aligns with your core values and strengths.

» Example in Action: If you value innovation, challenge yourself to brainstorm a new idea or approach with your team.
4. Seek Feedback:
  » Ask trusted colleagues or mentors for honest feedback on your leadership style.

Taking control of your inner strength is the foundation of effective leadership. By understanding your values, embracing self-awareness, and aligning your actions with your purpose, you project the kind of energy that inspires others. Leadership starts within. When you lead yourself with intention, you create a ripple effect that empowers your team and transforms your results.

Section 3: The People State– Embracing Social Awareness

"Social awareness bridges the gap between individuals and creates cohesive teams."

Social awareness is the glue that binds effective teams together. Within the 5 States of Optimisation, the People State highlights the importance of understanding team dynamics, recognising individual needs, and developing trust and collaboration. A socially aware leader doesn't just manage tasks; they connect with people, creating an environment where individuals feel valued and motivated to contribute their best.

At its core, social awareness is about listening, observing, and responding with empathy. It's what transforms a group of individuals into a cohesive, high-performing team.

THE POWER OF SOCIAL AWARENESS IN LEADERSHIP

A socially aware leader doesn't just focus on the "what" of leadership (results and tasks) they focus on the "who." They recognise that behind every project, deadline, or initiative there are people with unique strengths, challenges, and motivations.I remember leading a project where one team member consistently missed deadlines. Initially, I assumed they were disengaged, and I almost addressed it with a performance discussion. But after pausing to listen and observe, I realised that they were struggling with personal challenges that affected their focus. By creating space for an open conversation and adjusting their workload temporarily, they not only rebounded but became one of the most committed contributors to the project.

That experience reinforced a critical lesson: social awareness isn't just a leadership skill; it's a leadership superpower.

HOW THE PEOPLE STATE CONNECTS TO OTHER STATES OF OPTIMISATION

1. Productivity State: Social awareness ensures tasks are aligned with individual and team strengths, maximizing efficiency and engagement.
   - » Example in Action: Delegating a creative task to a team member with a flair for innovation instead of assigning it to someone whose strengths lie in analysis.

2. Planning State: Understanding team dynamics allows for more effective delegation and resource allocation, ensuring the right people are in the right roles.
   » Example in Action: Knowing who thrives under tight deadlines versus who performs best with detailed advance planning can shape project timelines.
3. Performance State: A socially aware leader prioritises morale and collaboration, which directly impacts team results.
   » Example in Action: Celebrating small wins and acknowledging individual contributions boosts team motivation and productivity.

EMPATHETIC LEADERSHIP

Naomi Osaka, a four-time Grand Slam champion, demonstrated the power of leadership by prioritizing mental health over the demands of competition. In May 2021, during the French Open, Osaka made the bold decision to withdraw from the tournament after facing scrutiny for refusing to participate in mandatory press conferences. She cited the toll that media obligations were taking on her mental health, sharing that she had been struggling with depression and anxiety for several years. Osaka's decision was a turning point in the world of professional sports, as she used her platform to spark an important global conversation about the mental and emotional pressures athletes face.

Instead of staying silent or pushing through, Osaka openly discussed her struggles, calling for better mental health support within the sports community. Her actions resonated with many;

encouraging athletes to take charge of their well-being and reshaping how the public and sports organisations approach the pressures of performance. Osaka's leadership showed that being vulnerable is not a weakness but a form of strength that can lead to positive change. Her decision to step away from competition for her mental health was a powerful reminder that leadership is not just about achieving success—it's about leading with empathy, listening to the needs of oneself and others, and fostering an environment where everyone feels supported and understood.

Her choice in 2021 to advocate for mental health led to increased discussions and reforms regarding how athletes are treated, emphasizing that empathy and care are crucial aspects of true leadership.

ENHANCE SOCIAL AWARENESS

1. Listen Intently:
   » Focus on truly understanding what's being said in conversations, both verbally and nonverbally.
   » Example in Action: During team meetings, ask open-ended questions and give space for diverse perspectives.
2. Observe Team Dynamics:
   » Pay attention to how individuals interact, contribute, and respond to challenges.
   » Example in Action: Notice who thrives in group discussions versus who prefers one-on-one interactions, and tailor your approach accordingly.

3. Create Safe Spaces:
    » Create an environment where team members feel comfortable sharing their thoughts and challenges.
    » Example in Action: Hold regular check-ins that focus on team well-being, not just performance metrics.
4. Adapt Your Leadership Style:
    » Adjust your approach based on the needs and personalities of your team members.
    » Example in Action: Provide clear guidance for those who value structure and more autonomy for those who prefer flexibility.

WEEKLY TEAM AWARENESS JOURNAL

At the end of each week, reflect on your team's dynamics by answering these questions:

- *Who on my team seemed energised and engaged?*
- *Who appeared disengaged or overwhelmed?*
- *What adjustments can I make to better support individual and team needs next week?*

THE RIPPLE EFFECT OF SOCIAL AWARENESS

When leaders prioritise social awareness, the impact goes far beyond team morale. It creates a ripple effect:

- Team Collaboration Increases: When individuals feel understood, they're more willing to contribute and collaborate.

- Retention Improves: Employees who feel valued and supported are more likely to stay and grow within the organisation.
- Innovation Thrives: A safe, connected team is more likely to take risks and generate creative solutions.

The People State isn't just a leadership skill—it's the foundation of cohesive, high-performing teams. By prioritizing social awareness, you connect with the individuals behind the tasks—creating an environment of trust, collaboration, and shared purpose. True leadership bridges the gap between people, empowering them to achieve more together than they could alone.

Section 4: The Social Battery–Protect, Recharge, and Redistribute

"Leadership requires energy knowing when to protect, recharge, and focus is key."

Leadership requires more than just vision and strategy; it requires energy. This energy, much like your physical energy, is finite. When depleted, it leaves you unable to lead effectively, make clear decisions, or inspire your team. Managing your social battery is essential for sustaining your leadership impact and avoiding burnout.

Your social battery is a measure of how much energy you have to engage with others, build relationships, and handle the interpersonal demands of leadership. By learning to protect, recharge, and redistribute this energy, you can lead with greater clarity, purpose, and presence.

LEARNING TO MANAGE MY ENERGY

I've had moments in my career where I stretched myself too thin taking every meeting, responding to every request, and trying to be available for everyone at all times. At first, I thought this was what leadership required: constant availability. But over time, my energy waned, my clarity faltered, and I found myself less effective in every area.

The breakthrough came when I realised that being a great leader wasn't about being available for everything, it was about being fully present for the right things. By setting boundaries, prioritising meaningful interactions, and carving out time to recharge, I not only protected my energy but also became a more focused and impactful leader.

THE SOCIAL BATTERY FRAMEWORK

Effectively managing your social battery requires attention to three key areas: Protect, Recharge, and Redistribute your energy.

1. PROTECT YOUR ENERGY

To lead effectively, you must first guard your energy against unnecessary drains. This means setting boundaries and being intentional about where you direct your focus.

- Say "No" to Tasks That Dilute Your Focus:
  - » Not every task requires your attention. Delegate or decline responsibilities that don't align with your priorities.
  - » Example in Action: If a meeting doesn't need your direct input, empower a team member to take ownership and provide you with a summary later.

- Set Boundaries to Prevent Overextension:
  - » Define your availability for meetings, emails, and social interactions. Boundaries protect your time and energy for what matters most.
  - » Example in Action: Reserve specific hours each day for deep work and let your team know you'll respond to non-urgent messages outside of that time.

2. RECHARGE YOUR ENERGY

Recharging is about filling your energy reserves so you can show up fully for your leadership responsibilities.

- Schedule Downtime to Reflect and Rejuvenate:
  - » Time off isn't a luxury, it's a necessity for sustainable leadership.
  - » Example in Action: Take a short walk between meetings or dedicate 15 minutes each morning to journaling or mindfulness.
- Engage in Activities That Bring You Joy and Clarity:
  - » Prioritise hobbies, relationships, and practices that energise you.
  - » Example in Action: Spend time with family, exercise, or pursue a creative outlet that allows you to disconnect from work.

3. REDISTRIBUTE YOUR ENERGY

Not every interaction or task deserves equal attention. Redistributing your energy means focusing on high-impact actions and meaningful conversations.

- Focus on Meaningful Interactions:
  - » Invest your energy in relationships and tasks that create the most value.
  - » Example in Action: Instead of attending every team meeting, prioritise one-on-one check-ins where you can offer tailored support and guidance.
- Prioritise Quality Over Quantity:
  - » Avoid spreading yourself too thin by concentrating on fewer, more impactful engagements.
  - » Example in Action: Rather than addressing surface-level concerns in a group setting, have in-depth discussions with key team members.

THE RIPPLE EFFECT OF MANAGING YOUR SOCIAL BATTERY

When you manage your energy effectively, the benefits extend beyond yourself:

1. Your Team Benefits: You show up as a more present, engaged, and supportive leader.
2. Your Decisions Improve: With greater clarity and focus, you make more thoughtful and strategic choices.
3. Your Well-Being Improves: By avoiding burnout, you sustain your energy and passion for leadership over the long term.

WEEKLY SOCIAL BATTERY CHECK-IN

At the end of each week, take 10 minutes to reflect on the following questions:

- *What activities drained my energy this week?*

- *What activities recharged my energy?*
- *What boundaries can I set or adjust to better protect my energy next week?*

MANAGING ENERGY WITH INTENTION

In 2019, Whitney Wolfe Herd was leading Bumble through global expansion while preparing for a potential IPO. As the youngest female CEO to take a company public, pressure came from all directions: media, investors, and internal teams.

She was flying city to city, reviewing product updates at midnight, and personally overseeing hiring for new markets. At first, she believed this hustle was the badge of a founder. But during a flight to London, after a week of 18-hour days, she broke down. In her own words, she was "running on fumes and completely disconnected from [her] own brain."

That's when she made the shift.

Wolfe Herd handed off daily operations to her COO, set strict limits on meetings (never more than four per day), and introduced "no-call Fridays" across the leadership team. She also blocked out one hour every afternoon—no meetings, no emails—to think, reflect, or decompress.

This boundary didn't stall growth; it accelerated it. Her decision-making became clearer. Her execs stepped up. Bumble's revenue grew by over 30% that year. By 2021, the company went public with a $13 billion valuation, and Wolfe Herd rang the NASDAQ bell holding her baby on her hip.

Her story is a reminder that protecting your energy isn't about working less; it's about working smarter, with presence and purpose.

Leadership requires more than just skill—it requires energy. By protecting your energy from unnecessary drains, recharging through intentional practices, and redistributing it to meaningful tasks and relationships, you can lead with clarity, purpose, and resilience. Managing your social battery isn't just about sustaining yourself, it's about showing up fully for the people and priorities that matter most.

Section 5: Why Do You Need to Take Action?

"Without action, leadership becomes stagnant. Self-awareness and social awareness are the tools that ignite progress."

Leadership is more than reflection, vision, or intention; it's about action. Without it, even the best ideas remain just that: ideas. Action is the bridge between what you aim to achieve and the tangible results you create. It transforms plans into progress and insights into impact.

Leading from within means taking the self-awareness you cultivate and the social awareness you build—channeling them into deliberate, meaningful action. It's how you align your internal energy and insights with external outcomes, creating momentum for yourself and those you lead.

THE COST OF INACTION IN LEADERSHIP

Inaction doesn't just stall progress; it creates ripple effects that undermine trust, confidence, and morale. A leader who hesitates to act can leave their team feeling uncertain, disconnected, and disengaged.

Imagine a leader who recognises a toxic dynamic within their team but avoids addressing it out of fear of conflict. The inaction allows tension to grow; eventually impacting productivity, collaboration, and morale. By avoiding action, the leader unintentionally amplifies the problem they sought to avoid.

WHY ACTION IS THE CATALYST FOR PROGRESS

Action isn't just about solving problems; it's about creating opportunities. Every deliberate step forward builds confidence, opens doors, and inspires others to follow.

1. Action Builds Momentum:
   - » Even small steps create a sense of accomplishment that propels you forward.
   - » Example in Action: Scheduling a single one-on-one meeting with a struggling team member can initiate a chain reaction of clarity, support, and renewed motivation.
2. Action Inspires Trust:
   - » When you take decisive action, your team sees you as someone who leads with purpose and resolve.
   - » Example in Action: A leader who implements changes based on team feedback demonstrates that they value input and are committed to progress.

3. Action Sparks Growth:
   » Every action whether it succeeds or fails offers valuable lessons that refine your approach and strengthen your leadership.
   » Example in Action: Launch ng a new initiative—even with uncertainty—provides insights into what works and what doesn't, equipping you for future decisions.

In November 2023, OpenAI was thrust into turmoil when its board made the unexpected decision to fire CEO Sam Altman. The move sent shockwaves through the company, leading to confusion and anger from employees and external stakeholders alike. However, instead of stepping back, Altman took immediate, strategic action to address the crisis. He reached out directly to employees, kept communication open, and listened to their concerns. He also engaged with key investors and partners to ensure they understood the situation and his vision for the company moving forward.

In the days following his firing, a dramatic shift occurred. Nearly the entire OpenAI research team, along with key executives, rallied behind Altman, threatening to resign unless he was reinstated. This show of solidarity reflected not just his leadership but the trust he had built with his team over the years. By November 21, 2023, just a week after the firing, the OpenAI board reversed its decision, and Altman was reappointed as CEO.

This swift and decisive action demonstrated that leadership is not about waiting for the perfect moment or clarity. Altman's ability to make bold decisions under pressure, rally his team, and stay committed to OpenAI's mission—even in the face of significant uncertainty—reaffirmed that act on, not inaction, is the key to navigating crises. His return marked a new phase of growth for OpenAI, where the company continued to make strides in advancing AI technologies.

MY OWN LEADERSHIP ACTIONS

I've learned firsthand how essential action is to progress. I once worked with a client in the financial sector who was stuck in a cycle of overthinking, waiting for the "perfect" strategy before launching a project. They feared making mistakes, so they avoided taking the first step.

Together, we broke the project into smaller, manageable actions, focusing on achievable milestones rather than perfection. The result? Each step built confidence, provided feedback, and revealed opportunities they hadn't considered. Their willingness to act, even imperfectly, became the foundation for their eventual success.

TAKE MEANINGFUL ACTION

1. Clarify Your Intentions:
   » Define what you want to achieve and why it matters. A clear purpose fuels focused action.
   » Example in Action: Before addressing a team conflict, identify the specific outcomes you're aiming for, such as improved communication or restored trust.
2. Start Small:
   » Break your goal into manageable steps to reduce overwhelm and build momentum.

» Example in Action: If you want to implement a new initiative, start with a pilot program or a brainstorming session with your team.

3. Focus on Progress, Not Perfection:
   » Action doesn't have to be flawless to be effective. Treat every step as an experiment that provides valuable insights.
   » Example in Action: Launch a project with a "minimum viable product" and refine it based on feedback.

4. Commit to Consistency:
   » Regular, deliberate actions create lasting impact.
   » Example in Action: Schedule weekly check-ins to track progress and address challenges proactively.

5. Reflect and Adjust:
   » After each action, evaluate its impact and refine your approach.
   » Example in Action: If a meeting didn't yield the desired outcomes, adjust the agenda or facilitation style for the next one.

Action transforms intentions into impact. Without it, even the best ideas remain unfulfilled. By aligning your self-awareness and social awareness with deliberate action, you create momentum, inspire trust, and drive meaningfu progress. Leadership is built step by step. Star today, and watch how each action brings you closer to your goals.

Section 6: What Will This Mean for You?

"Leading from within transforms you into a leader people trust, respect, and want to follow."

When you lead from within, you create a ripple effect that transforms not only your leadership but also the dynamics of your team and the results you achieve. Leadership rooted in self-awareness and social awareness promotes trust, loyalty, and meaningful progress. It equips you to navigate challenges, seize opportunities, and inspire others to rise to their potential.

Leading from within isn't just about achieving goals; it's about becoming a leader others choose to follow because they trust your character, respect your values, and believe in your vision.

THE IMPACT OF LEADING FROM WITHIN

1. Cohesive and Motivated Teams:
   - » When you lead from within, your authenticity develops trust. Your team feels valued and aligned, leading to greater collaboration, morale, and productivity.
   - » Example in Action: A manager who takes the time to understand individual team members' goals and strengths fosters a sense of belonging and purpose, making the team more motivated and resilient.

2. Personal Growth and Confidence:
   » Self-aware leaders are adaptable and confident. They learn from challenges, emb-ace growth opportunities, and lead with clarity.
   » Example in Action: A leader who reflects on feedback and adapts their approach demonstrates humility and strength, inspiring others to do the same.
3. Inspiring Ownership in Others:
   » Leading from within empowers your team to take ownership of their roles. When you model accountability and integrity, it encourages others to step up and contribute meaningfully.
   » Example in Action: By celebrating team members' contributions and offering autonomy, a leader creates a culture of trust and initiative.

THE MOMENT I REALISED THE POWER OF LEADING FROM WITHIN

In 2012 I was working on one of the largest e-commerce projects in the world for Tesco.com. I focused heavily on outcomes, meeting targets, delivering results, and staying on schedule. While this approach worked initially, I noticed my team's motivation and morale starting to wane. It wasn't until I shifted my focus inward reflecting on my leadership style, values, and approach that things began to change.

I started having open conversations with my team, asking for their input and understanding their needs. By aligning my actions with my values of collaboration and trust, I saw a transformation: my team became more engaged, creative, and motivated to take ownership of their work. This shift didn't just improve results, it strengthened relationships and created a culture of shared purpose.

WHY LEADING FROM WITHIN MATTERS

When you lead from within, your leadership is no longer about control or authority, it's about connection and impact. This approach creates:

1. Deeper Relationships:
   » Trust becomes the foundation of your leadership, developing stronger bonds within your team.
2. Sustainable Success:
   » A motivated and cohesive team sustains high performance, even in challenging times.
3. A Legacy of Leadership:
   » By inspiring and empowering others, you create a ripple effect that extends beyond your tenure.

STEPS TO LEAD FROM WITHIN

1. Prioritise Self-Reflection:
   » Regularly evaluate your leadership actions to ensure they align with your values and goals.
   » Example in Action: Spend 10 minutes each week journaling about your decisions and their impact on your team.
2. Promote Open Communication:
   » Create a culture where team members feel comfortable sharing feedback and ideas.

> » Example in Action:Hold monthly one-on-one check-ins focused on growth and collaboration.

3. Model Accountability:
   > » Take ownership of your mistakes and successes.
   > » Example in Action: If a dec sion didn't yield the desired result, acknowledge it and share what you learned with your team.

4. Celebrate Contributions:
   > » Recognise and reward the efforts of your team members.
   > » Example in Action: Publicly acknowledge a team member's innovative solut on during a meeting or in a written message.

THE RIPPLE EFFECT OF LEADING FROM WITHIN

When you lead from within, you become more than a manager; you become a source of inspiration, trust, and growth for your team. This ripple effect extends to every interaction, project, and decision you make. You set the tone for your team—empowering them to step up, collaborate, and thrive.

Leading from within transforms you into a leader who inspires trust, loyalty, and meaningful results. By aligning your actions with your values and building trust through self-awareness and social awareness, you create an environment where your team feels empowered and motivated to succeed. The impact of your leadership extends beyond tasks and outcomes; it becomes a catalyst for lasting growth and transformation.

Section 7: Energising Your Leadership

"Leading from within isn't about wielding power, it's about igniting passion and purpose in others."

Leadership is not about authority or control; it's about inspiring others to bring their best selves to the table. When you lead with energy and authenticity, you empower your team to embrace challenges, find purpose in their work, and thrive together.

Energising your leadership starts with understanding that your role is to ignite, not dictate. It's about cultivating an environment where passion and purpose are natural byproducts of how you lead and connect with your team.

HOW I LEARNED TO LEAD WITH ENERGY

I thought my role was to ensure everything was on track by micromanaging details and driving results. While this approach yielded some success, it came at a cost: my team felt disconnected, and I was burning out. I realised that true leadership wasn't about controlling outcomes but about empowering people.

I started shifting my focus to listening more, leading by example, and celebrating the team's successes. The transformation was immediate. My team became more engaged, innovative, and motivated. They didn't just work harder, they worked with purpose. That shift taught me that energising leadership is about inspiring people to see their value and potential.

THE IMPACT OF ENERGISED LEADERSHIP

When you energise your leadership, the ripple effects are profound:

1. Motivated Teams: People who feel seen, heard, and valued are naturally more engaged and committed to their work.

2. Greater Collaboration: An energised leader creates a sense of unity, encouraging individuas to support one another and work toward shared goals.

3. Sustainable Results: Teams driven by passion and purpose consistently deliver higher performance and find deeper satisfaction in their accomplishments.

ENERGIZE YOUR LEADERSHIP

1. LISTEN INTENTIONALLY

Great leaders prioritise listening—not just to respond but to understand. When you make space for your team to share their ideas, challenges, and feedback, you demonstrate respect and build trust.

- Example in Action: During a team meeting, ask open-ended questions like:
  » *"What's one challenge you're currently facing, and how can I support you?"*
  » *"What's one idea you've been considering but haven't had the chance to share?"*
- Why It Works: Intentional listenng fosters a culture of openness and collaboration, ensuring your team feels heard and valued.

2. LEAD BY EXAMPLE

The energy you bring to your leadership sets the tone for your team. If you model integrity, accountability, and resilience, your team will follow suit.

- Examples in Action:
  - » If you expect punctuality, consistently start meetings on time.
  - » If you value innovation, take risks yourself and encourage others to do the same.
- Why It Works: When you align your actions with your expectations, you build credibility and inspire your team to emulate your example.

3. CELEBRATE WINS

Acknowledging achievements—big or small—develops morale and unity. Celebrations remind your team that their efforts matter and encourage them to keep striving for excellence.

- Examples in Action:
  - » At the end of a project, host a team debrief to highlight individual contributions and celebrate collective success.
  - » Send a handwritten note or personalized email to a team member who went above and beyond.
- Why It Works: Recognising wins reinforces a positive team culture and motivates individuals to continue excelling.

ENERGISING THROUGH EMPATHY

Cheryl Bachelder, former CEO of Popeyes Louisiana Kitchen, revitalized the company using a leadership approach centered on serving and empowering others. When she took the helm in 2006, Popeyes was facing significant challenges, declining sales, a struggling brand, and a disengaged workforce. Instead of focusing on traditional top-down management tactics, Bachelder shifted the company's focus to its people, particularly the franchise owrers and employees.

Her leadership philosophy, which she called "servant leadership," was built on the idea that the role of a eader is to serve the needs of their team. She prioritised listening to employees, understanding their challenges, and helping them grow. Bachelder's focus on recognising and valuing the contributions of employees created a culture where people felt empowered to bring their best selves to work.

This cultural transformation had immediate results. In the first four years of her leadership, Popeyes' system-wide sales grew by over 50%, and its stock price increased by 144%. Under her guidance, Popeyes expanded significantly, with the brand's market share increasing and a renewed focus on both innovation and franchisee relationships. The company also became known for its strong ethical standards and commitment to quality.

Bachelder's leadership showed that when you focus on energising your team, through listening, supportirg, and empowering them, the results can extend far beyond immediate financial gains. Her tenure at Popeyes demonstrated that energising leadership is about creating a sense of ownership and passion in thcse you lead, ultimately driving sustainable success for the entire organisation.

THE RIPPLE EFFECT OF ENERGISED LEADERSHIP

When you energise your leadership, you don't just achieve better results, you create a thriving culture. Your team becomes more engaged, creative, and united, driving success that goes beyond metrics. Energised leadership isn't just about getting the job done—it's about transforming how people work, connect, and grow.

Energising your leadership isn't about working harder it's about inspiring your team to work smarter, more collaboratively, and with greater purpose. By listening intentionally, leading by example, and celebrating wins, you create an environment where your team thrives and your leadership impact grows exponentially.

Section 8: Leading From Within at Every Stage

"Leadership isn't defined by your experience, it's defined by your commitment to growth."

Leadership is a journey, not a destination. Whether you're stepping into your first leadership role or have decades of experience, the principles of leading from within apply at every stage. True leadership is not about the position you hold, but about your dedication to self-awareness, growth, and empowering others.

At each stage of leadership, the focus evolves, but the foundation remains the same: leading with authenticity, clarity, and purpose. By embracing these principles, you continuously elevate your impact, regardless of where you are on your leadership path.

NEW LEADERS: BUILDING A STRONG FOUNDATION THROUGH SELF-AWARENESS

For new leaders, the first step is understanding yourself. This means recognising your strengths, weaknesses, and values, as well as how they influence your leadership style. Self-awareness is the cornerstone of effective leadership; it helps you build credibility and earn the trust of your team.

- Focus Areas for New Leaders:
  - » Identify your leadership style and how it aligns with your values.
  - » Seek feedback early and often to refine your approach.
  - » Learn to balance confidence with humility.
- Example in Action: A newly promoted manager might start by reflecting on their communication style and seeking input from their team on how to improve clarity and engagement. This openness to feedback fosters trust and sets a strong foundation for future growth.

MID-LEVEL LEADERS: STRENGTHENING TEAM DYNAMICS THROUGH SOCIAL AWARENESS

As a mid-level leader, your focus shifts to understanding and optimising team dynamics. Social awareness becomes crucial. It's about recognising the unique strengths, challenges, and motivations of your team members and aligning them with organisational goals.

- Focus Areas for Mid-Level Leaders:
  - » Cultivate active listening skills to better understand team needs.

- » Adapt your leadership style to different personalities and situations.
- » Develop collaboration by building trust and encouraging open communication.
- Example in Action: A mid-level leader overseeing multiple teams may hold regular one-on-one check-ins to understand individual goals and challenges. By tailoring support to each team member, they create an environment where people feel valued and motivated.

SEASONED LEADERS: BUILDING A LEGACY THROUGH EMPOWERMENT

For seasoned leaders, the focus moves beyond individual or team success to creating a lasting legacy. This means empowering others to lead, fostering a culture of mentorship—ensuring the organisation thrives long after your tenure.

- Focus Areas for Seasoned Leaders:
  - » Prioritise mentorship to develop the next generation of leaders.
  - » Create opportunities for others to take ownership and grow.
  - » Emphasise purpose and values in decision-making to shape organisational culture.
- Example in Action: A veteran executive might create a leadership development program within their organisation, pairing emerging leaders with experienced mentors to ensure long-term growth and succession planning.

THE CONTINUUM OF LEADERSHIP GROWTH

While the stages of leadership emphas se different skills and priorities, they are interconnected:

1. Self-Awareness: The foundation at every stage.
2. Social Awareness: The bridge to understanding and empowering others.
3. Legacy-Building: The culmination of a leadership journey focused on purpose and impact.

LEADING ACROSS STAGES

I've experienced the distinct challenges and opportunities of each stage. As a new leader, I focused on proving myself, building credibility through self-awareness and action. As I advanced, I realised the importance of understanding and empowering my team, honing my social awareness to create stronger connections and collaboration.

Now, as a seasoned leader, my focus has shifted to legacy-building. I find immense fulfillment in mentoring others, sharing lessons from my journey, and watching the next generation of leaders flourish. Each stage has taught me that leadership isn't about arriving at a destination, it's about embracing the journey and continually striving to grow.

GROW AT EVERY STAGE

1. New Leaders:
    » Schedule regular self-reflection to identify your strengths and areas for growth.
    » Seek mentorship or guidance from more experienced leaders.

2. Mid-Level Leaders:
   » Conduct team assessments to understand dynamics and identify areas for improvement.
   » Practice situational leadership by adapting your approach to the needs of your team.
3. Seasoned Leaders:
   » Create opportunities for emerging leaders to take ownership and make decisions.
   » Focus on developing a culture that reflects your values and vision.

Leadership is not a one-size-fits-all journey. It evolves with your growth, experience, and commitment to learning. Whether you're a new leader building a foundation, a mid-level leader optimizing team dynamics, or a seasoned leader focused on legacy, the principles of leading from within remain constant. Embracing self-awareness, cultivating social awareness, and empowering others to thrive are the hallmarks of leadership at every stage.

Section 9: Reflection

"You can't lead others if you're disconnected from yourself. Clarity in, impact out."

Leading from within isn't a concept, it's a discipline. It's not something you switch on in moments of pressure. It's the daily work of aligning who you are with how you lead.

You've seen how self-awareness, energy management, and intentional action form the core of effective leadership. But none of these matters if it stays theoretical. This chapter is a reminder that leadership is built, not by title or expertise, but by presence, integrity, and action.

Your energy fuels the room before your strategy does. Your example shapes more behaviour than your directives ever will. And the version of leadership your team follows? It's the one you model daily.

So, take stock. Not of how busy you are—but of how aligned you are. Because the greatest shifts don't come from managing people, they come from mastering yourself.

Reflection Questions

SECTION 1:

What fuels your energy as a leader? Are you investing in activities that recharge you emotionally, mentally, and physically? What's one adjustment you can make this week to protect or replenish your energy?

SECTION 2:

What fuels your energy as a leader? Are you investing in activities that recharge you emotionally, mentally, and physically? What's one adjustment you can make this week to protect or replenish your energy?

SECTION 3:

How can you deepen your understanding of your team's unique needs and challenges? What steps can you take this week to strengthen your social awareness?

SECTION 4:

What's one boundary you can set this week to protect your energy? How can you prioritise an activity that recharges you?

SECTION 5:

Take five minutes to identify one area where you've been hesitating to act. Ask yourself:

1. *What's the best possible outcome if I take this step?*

2. *What's holding me back?*

3. *What's the smallest action I can take today to move forward?*

Write it down and commit to acting on it within the next 24 hours.

SECTION 6:

Take 5 minutes to reflect on the following questions:

1. *What aspects of your leadership already align with your values?*

2. *Where do you see opportunities to improve?*

3. *What's one action you can take this week to lead with greater authenticity and purpose?*

SECTION 7:

Take five minutes to reflect on the following:

1. *How often do I create space for my team to share their ideas and challenges?*

2. *What's one behaviour I could model to set a positive example for my team?*

3. *When was the last time I celebrated a team or individual achievement? What's one win I can acknowledge this week?*

Write down one action you'll take this week to energise your leadership and your team.

SECTION 8:

Take five minutes to reflect on the following:

1. *What stage of leadership are you currently in?*

2. *What's one area you can focus on to grow further?*

3. *What's one action you can take this week to apply the principles of leading from within?*

Write down your answers and commit to taking action on one specific area of growth.

CHAPTER 9

Risk Taking Mindset & Perceptual Positions

"Taking risks isn't about recklessness; it's about having the courage to turn fear into progress."

You stand at the edge of a decision, heart pounding, mind racing. Ahead lies the unknown; full of possibilities, challenges, and risks. Do you move forward, or retreat to what's familiar? Every breakthrough, every moment of success, every defining chapter of your life has come from stepping into uncertainty.

This isn't about blind leaps, it's about calculated courage. It's about shifting your mindset to see risk not as a danger, but as the catalyst for growth. Because the greatest risk isn't failing, it's staying still and never knowing what could have been.

True success isn't found in avoiding risks, but in embracing them with intention, learning from them, and using them as fuel for progress.

This chapter explores the power of a risk-taking mindset, the transformative impact of shifting perspectives, and how resilience and emotional intelligence allow you to navigate uncertainty with confidence.

Section 1: Embracing the Risk-Taking Mindset

"Risk is the heartbeat of growth. Embrace it, shift your perspective, and watch as possibilities unfold."

Risk-taking is often misunderstood. It's easy to view risks as dangerous or unnecessary, especially when comfort feels safer than the unknown. But the truth is, risk is the foundation of progress. Without it, innovation stalls, opportunities fade, and growth remains out of reach.

Embracing a risk-taking mindset doesn't mean throwing caution to the wind; it means reframing how you see risk. Instead of focusing on what could go wrong, shift your perspective to what could go right. It's about recognising that uncertainty holds the potential for breakthroughs.

TURNING FEAR INTO FUEL

In 2021, I had the opportunity to take on a leadership role that I didn't feel fully prepared for. I hesitated, what if I wasn't experienced enough? What if I made mistakes? The safer choice was to stay in my current position, where I was comfortable. But something inside me knew that staying put would mean limiting my growth.

Instead of letting self-doubt dictate my decision, I took on a calculated risk. I leaned into learning; sought mentorship, and accepted that I wouldn't have all the answers upfront. The transition wasn't perfect. There were missteps, lessons, and adjustments, but each challenge built my confidence and leadership skills. Looking back, stepping into that role was one of the best decisions I have ever made. It reinforced a key truth: risk isn't about having everything figured out, it's about trusting yourself to figure it out along the way.

THE MINDSET SHIFT: FROM FEAR TO POSSIBILITY

Embracing a risk-taking mindset requires a fundamental shift in how you approach uncertainty. Instead of seeing risks as threats, view them as opportunities to grow, learn, and innovate.

MINDSET SHIFTS:

1. Reframe Fear as Excitement:
   » Fear and excitement are two sides of the same coin. When you feel fear, ask yourself: *What about this excites me?*
2. Focus on Potential Rewards:
   » Shift your thoughts from *What if I fail?* to *What if this works?*
3. Treat Risks as Experiments:
   » Approach risks with curiosity. See them as opportunities to test ideas and gather valuable feedback.

BUILD A RISK-TAKING MINDSET

1. Start Small:
   » Take manageable risks to build your confidence.

» Example in Action: If you're considering a career change, start by networking with people in your desired field or taking a relevant course.

2. Seek Support:
   » Surround yourself with people who encourage and challenge you.
   » Example in Action: Share your goals with a mentor or trusted friend who can provide guidance and accountability.

3. Celebrate Every Step:
   » Acknowledge and celebrate progress, no matter how small.
   » Example in Action: After completing a step—like attending a workshop or sending a proposal—pause to reflect on what you've achieved.

In 1998, Sarah Blakely was a 27-year-old selling fax machines door-to-door with no experience in fashion or manufacturing. Her idea for Spanx, a line of footless pantyhose designed to smooth and shape the body, seemed like a far-fetched dream, especially since she had no background in the industry, no investors, and no professional connections.

Instead of waiting for the "perfect" opportunity, Blakely decided to take a significant risk. She used her entire $5,000 life savings to develop a prototype. She faced rejection after rejection, including hosiery manufacturers who told her the idea would never work. Undeterred, Blakely took matters into her own hands, teaching herself about the manufacturing process, pitching her idea to hosiery mills; and even designing the packaging herself.

In 2000, Blakely's persistence paid off when Oprah Winfrey featured Spanx in her "Favorite Things" segment on her show. That moment propelled Spanx into the public eye, and within a year, sales skyrocketed. By 2007, just seven years after she started with a small investment and no formal fashion training, Blakely had turned Spanx into a billion-dollar company.

Her story is a powerful testament to the potential rewards of taking risks, investing your time, money, and energy in an idea you believe in—even when the odds are against you. Sarah Blakely's leap into the unknown, fueled by resilience and belief, shows that risk-taking isn't about having everything figured out upfront—it's about having the courage to start, learn along the way, and pivot when necessary.

THE RIPPLE EFFECT OF EMBRACING RISK

When you embrace risk with intention and clarity, the impact extends far beyond the initial decision. You build confidence, expand your comfort zone, and create opportunities that wouldn't exist otherwise. Risk isn't just a challenge—it's a catalyst for growth.

Risk is the gateway to transformation. By shifting your mindset from fear to possibility, you open yourself up to growth and innovation. Start small, take the leap, and trust in your ability to navigate uncertainty. The rewards are waiting on the other side.

STEP INTO RISK

Take 10 minutes to reflect on the following:

1. What's one risk you've been avoiding?
2. What's holding you back—fear of failure, uncertainty, or something else?

3. What's one small step you can take today to begin
    addressing that risk?

Write down your thoughts. Commit to taking that step within the
next 24 hours.

Section 2: Expanding the Perceptual Positions Framework

"Perceptual positions broaden your perspective, allowing you to approach challenges with clarity and creativity."

One of the most powerful tools in decision-making and problem-solving is the ability to shift perspectives. The three perceptual positions first, second, and third allow you to see situations from multiple angles—fostering creativity, empathy, and clarity.

By learning to move fluidly between these positions, you expand your understanding of challenges and unlock solutions that would otherwise remain hidden.

THE THREE PERCEPTUAL POSITIONS: A DEEPER DIVE

1. First Position: Your Own Perspective
    »   This is your default position, where you focus on your own thoughts, feelings, and instincts. It's essential for understanding your emotions and motivations.
    »   When to Use It: Making decisions that align with your values and goals.

» Example in Action: If you're leading a project, the first position helps you assess your personal priorities and vision for success.

2. Second Position: Someone Else's Perspective
   » Stepping into someone else's shoes helps you build empathy and understand their motivations, concerns, and needs.
   » When to Use It: Resolving conflicts, negotiating, or fostering collaboration.
   » Example in Action: During a team disagreement, viewing the situation from a colleague's perspective can reveal underlying concerns and lead to a resolution.

3. Third Position: The Impartial Observer
   » This position allows you to detach emotionally and view the situation objectively, as though you're an outsider. It's ideal for gaining clarity and reducing bias.
   » When to Use It: Evaluating complex situations or making high-stakes decisions.
   » Example in Action: Before presenting a strategy, viewing it from the perspective of a neutral stakeholder helps ensure your approach is clear and compelling.

SHIFTING PERSPECTIVES IN LEADERSHIP

A Founder and CEO client running a 30-million-dollar Beauty AI business was struggling with leadership dynamics. From their perspective (first position), the issue seemed rooted in a lack of respect from the leadership team. However, by stepping into the perspective of the team (second position) it became clear that the team felt undervalued and unheard. Viewing the situation from the third position revealed a systemic issue: misaligned communication styles.

By shifting through these perceptual positions, my client was able to address the root cause rather than the symptoms, ultimately rebuilding trust and improving collaboration.

Sundar Pichai's leadership at Google offers a compelling example of shifting perspectives to navigate both technical and organisational challenges. When Pichai became the CEO of Google in 2015, the company was already an established tech giant, but the landscape was rapidly changing with new competitors and emerging technologies.

- First Position: Pichai had to consider his own leadership style and the future of Google. He knew that staying ahead of the curve would require a balance between maintaining the core values of the company and embracing innovation. He focused on Google's transformation from a search engine company to a multifaceted tech powerhouse, with AI and cloud computing at the forefront.

- Second Position: Pichai also needed to think from the perspective of employees, users, and partners. By emphasizing employee empowerment and inclusivity, he fostered a culture of innovation. His understanding of Google's user base guided strategic moves such as the development of Google Assistant and the expansion of Google Cloud.

- Third Position: From a broader perspective, Pichai had to navigate the challenges Google faced in the global market. He recognised that with the rapid growth of AI, data privacy concerns, and regulatory challenges, Google's next moves had to be mindful of societal impact while driving business growth.

Through his ability to fluidly shift between these perceptual positions, Pichai ensured that Google not only maintained its dominant position in search but also became a leader in AI, cloud computing, and other innovative technologies—all while keeping a keen eye on user trust and corporate responsibility.

STRATEGIES FOR APPLYING PERCEPTUAL POSITIONS

1. Pause and Shift Perspectives:
   - » Before reacting, consciously move through each position.
   - » Example in Action: During a conflict, start by acknowledging your emotions (first position), consider the other person's perspective (second position), and then view the situation as an outsider (third position).
2. Use Questions to Gain Insights:
   - » First Position: *What do I want or need in this situation?*
   - » Second Position: *What might the other person be thinking or feeling?*
   - » Third Position: *What would a neutral observer notice about this situation?*
3. Journal Your Insights:
   - » Documenting what each position reveals helps you identify patterns and solutions.

THE POWER OF PERSPECTIVE IN EVERYDAY LIFE

The ability to shift perspectives isn't just a leadership skill, it's a life skill. Whether you're navigating a disagreement with a loved one, making a career decision, or resolving a customer issue, perceptual positions help you see the bigger picture.

When planning a major career change, shifting to the second position helped me understand how the transition would affect my family. Moving to the third position provided clarity on the long-term benefits versus short-term disruptions, ultimately guiding me toward a confident decision.

Expanding your perspective through perceptual positions is a game-changer. It creates empathy, enhances clarity, and unlocks creative solutions to challenges. Whether you're resolving conflicts, making decisions, or navigating uncertainty, these positions help you see the full picture and act with confidence.

MAP A CHALLENGE THROUGH PERCEPTUAL POSITIONS

Take 10 minutes to reflect on a recent challenge or decision. Answer the following questions for each position:

1. First Position (Your Perspective): What are your priorities, concerns, and goals?
2. Second Position (Another Person's Perspective): How might someone else involved view the situation? What are their concerns or motivations?
3. Third Position (Observer's Perspective): What would a neutral third-party notice about this situation?

Write down one action you can take based on the insights from these perspectives.

Section 3: The Role of Emotional Intelligence in Risk-Taking

"Emotional intelligence is the foundation for taking risks with clarity and confidence."

Risk-taking is often perceived as a logical calculation, but logic alone isn't enough. The ability to navigate risk effectively requires emotional intelligence (EI) the capacity to understand and manage your emotions and the emotions of others. EI empowers you to handle fear constructively, make balanced decisions, and remain grounded in uncertain situations.

By developing emotional intelligence, you can approach risks not as threats, but as opportunities for growth. Self-awareness allows you to identify the emotions driving your decisions. Empathy helps you understand how risks impact others, and emotional regulation ensures you respond with clarity rather than reactivity.

HOW EMOTIONAL INTELLIGENCE TRANSFORMED MY RISK-TAKING

Fear was my constant companion in every career transition. It wasn't just the uncertainty of leaving a steady income—I worried about how the decision would impact my family and whether I had what it took to succeed.

At first, the fear felt overwhelming, but I realised that avoiding it would only keep me stuck. I leaned on emotional intelligence to guide me. I practiced self-awareness by naming my fears and understanding their roots. I used empathy to consider how my family might feel about the decision, and applied emotional regulation to stay calm during moments of doubt.

Instead of letting fear dictate my actions, I reframed it as a sign that I was stepping into growth. That mindset shift, powered by emotional intelligence, gave me the courage to take calculated risks and build a career aligned with my purpose.

THE KEY COMPONENTS OF EMOTIONAL INTELLIGENCE IN RISK-TAKING

1. Self-Awareness:
   - » Recognise your emotions and how they influence your decisions.
   - » Example in Action: Before taking a risk, pause to identify whether your hesitation stems from fear, doubt, or excitement.
2. Empathy:
   - » Understand how your decisions impact others.
   - » Example in Action: When considering a bold move, think about how it might affect your team, family, or colleagues.
3. Emotional Regulation:
   - » Manage your emotions to stay calm and focused under pressure.

» Example in Action: Use breathing techniques or mindfulness practices to ground yourself when anxiety arises.

4. Motivation:

» Use your intrinsic drive to push through uncertainty and stay committed to your goals.

» Example in Action: Visualize the long-term rewards of taking the risk to maintain focus and determination.

STRATEGIES FOR USING EMOTIONAL INTELLIGENCE IN RISK-TAKING

1. Reframe Fear as Growth:

» Fear is often a signal that you're stepping outside your comfort zone, the very place where growth happens.

» Actionable Tip: When fear arises, ask yourself: *What about this risk excites me? What's the best possible outcome?*

2. Visualise Success:

» Picturing a positive outcome helps shift your focus from what could go wrong to what could go right.

» Actionable Tip: Spend five minutes imagining the best-case scenario, focusing on how it will feel and the benefits it will bring.

3. Practice Emotional Regulation:

» Grounding techniques keep fear from escalating into paralysis.

» Actionable Tip: Try box breathing (inhaling for 4 seconds, holding for 4 seconds, exhaling for 4 seconds) to calm your nervous system before making a decision.

4. Engage in Reflective Journaling:

» Writing down your thoughts and emotions can help you process them and identify patterns in your risk-taking behaviour.

» Actionable Tip: After each decision, journal about what emotions influenced your choice and how EI played a role.

In 2018, LeBron James faced a career-defining risk. He chose to leave the Cleveland Cavaliers, where he was a hometown hero, for the Los Angeles Lakers, a team in disarray. They hadn't made the playoffs in five years. He was 33 years old, with nothing left to prove, and critics were ready to call him past his prime. But LeBron wasn't just thinking about basketball. He was thinking bigger; about legacy, leadership, and impact.

That decision wasn't based on pure logic. It was driven by emotional intelligence.

First, he used self-awareness. LeBron recognised he needed a new environment, not for validation, but for growth. He knew staying in Cleveland might have been easier, but it wouldn't stretch him. He also understood his brand, his influence, and the emotional weight of his choices.

Second, he showed empathy, toward his family, toward young Lakers teammates, and even toward the city he left. He didn't burn bridges with Cleveland. He wrote an open letter thanking the fans, showing maturity that earned respect even from critics. In LA, he took time to mentor the team's rising stars, even while carrying the pressure of expectations.

Finally, his emotional regulation was visible on and off the court. The Lakers struggled in his first season. He was injured. The media questioned everything. But LeBron stayed composed. No blame. No drama. Just consistent effort and calm leadership. By 2020, he led the Lakers to their first NBA championship in a decade, during a pandemic, inside the high-pressure NBA Bubble.

His ability to manage his own emotions, support those around him, and take calculated risks with clarity turned a controversial move into a defining leadership moment.

Emotional intelligence transforms risk-taking from a daunting challenge into an opportunity for growth. By cultivating self-awareness, empathy, and emotional regulation, you approach risks with clarity, confidence, and purpose. Risk-taking isn't just about logic, it's about leading with both your head and your heart.

APPLYING EMOTIONAL INTELLIGENCE TO YOUR NEXT RISK

Take a moment to reflect on a risk you're currently considering. Write down:

1. Your Emotions: What feelings are coming up, and why?
2. Others' Perspectives: How might your decision affect others involved?
3. Your Plan: How can you regulate your emotions to approach this risk with clarity and confidence?

Use the answers to guide your next step with emotional intelligence.

Section 4: Building Resilience for Risk-Taking

"Resilience transforms setbacks into stepping stones for success."

Every risk carries uncertainty and the potential for failure. It's natural to feel apprehensive, but resilience ensures that setbacks don't define you. Instead, they become opportunities to grow, adapt, and come back stronger.

Resilience isn't about avoiding failure; it's about how you respond to it. It's the ability to rise after falling, to reflect on what went wrong, and to use those lessons as stepping stones toward success. Cultivating resilience transforms risk-taking from a daunting challenge into a pathway for growth.

RESILIENCE IN MY RISK-TAKING JOURNEY

There was a time in my life when I faced a personal setback that shook me deeply. I had trained relentlessly for a long-distance cycling event—months of preparation, discipline, and pushing my limits. But just days before the event, an injury forced me to pull out. The frustration and disappointment were overwhelming. It felt like all my effort had been wasted.

I had two choices: dwell on what I couldn't change or focus on what I could learn. Instead of seeing the setback as a failure, I used it as fuel. I worked on recovery, focused on building strength, and restructured my training approach. A few months later, I completed an even tougher endurance challenge, one that might not have been possible if I hadn't learned patience, adaptability, and resilience from the first setback.

That experience reinforced a powerful truth: resilience isn't just about bouncing back, it's about coming back stronger, smarter, and more prepared.

THE THREE PILLARS OF RESILIENCE

1. Adopt a Growth Mindset:
    » Resilient leaders see challenges as opportunities for improvement rather than insurmountable obstacles.
    » Example in Action: After missing a project deadline, instead of focusing on the failure, analyze what caused the delay and implement changes to prevent it next time.

2. Celebrate Progress:
    » Acknowledge even small wins to maintain motivation and momentum.
    » Example in Action: If you're learning a new skill, celebrate completing a challenging module or successfully applying your knowledge in a real-world scenario.

3. Learn From Failure:
    » View setbacks as feedback, not a reflection of your worth.
    » Example in Action: If a presentation doesn't land as expected, seek feedback from your audience and adjust your approach for future talks.

Oprah Winfrey's journey to success is a powerful example of resilience. Born on January 29, 1954, in rural Mississippi, Oprah faced significant challenges early in her life—including poverty, abuse, and neglect. Despite these difficulties, she rose to become one of the most influential women in the world.

At the start of her career, Oprah faced several setbacks. In 1976, she was hired as a news anchor at WJZ-TV in Baltimore; but in 1977, she was fired from her job as a television reporter because her boss deemed her "unfit for TV." This could have easily crushed anyone's confidence, but Oprah used this rejection as fuel for her future success. Rather than giving up, she pushed forward and found a new opportunity as the host of a local talk show, *AM Chicago*, in 1984. Within months, the show's ratings skyrocketed; and Oprah's career began to take off.

However, the road to success wasn't without its challenges. She battled against societal stereotypes, personal hardships, and public scrutiny. Yet, through it all, Oprah embraced her setbacks as opportunities to learn and grow. She not only built a media empire but also became a force for positive change. In 1986, she launched *The Oprah Winfrey Show*, which ran for 25 years and became the highest-rated talk show in TV history. Throughout her career, Oprah has launched initiatives to support education, women's rights, and empowerment, such as the Oprah Winfrey Leadership Academy for Girls, which opened in 2007.

Her story illustrates that resilience isn't about avoiding failure; it's about using setbacks as stepping stones, learning from them, and ultimately rising stronger. Oprah's ability to turn her most painful experiences into a platform for growth and success shows that resilience can transform adversity into opportunity.

STRATEGIES FOR BUILDING RESILIENCE

1. Adopt a Growth Mindset:
    - » Shift your perspective by asking, What can I learn from this?
    - » Actionable Tip: After a setback, write down three lessons you can apply to future challenges.

2. Practice Self-Compassion:
    - » Treat yourself with the kindness you'd offer a friend. recognise that failure is part of growth.
    - » Actionable Tip: When self-doubt creeps in, reframe your inner dialogue with affirmations like, "I'm learning and improving with every step."

3. Reframe Setbacks as Feedback:
    - » Replace the idea of "failure" with "valuable insight."
    - » Actionable Tip: Create a "Lessons Learned" journal where you document what went wrong and what you'll do differently next time.

4. Build a Support Network:
    - » Resilience grows stronger when you're supported by people who encourage and challenge you.
    - » Actionable Tip: Share your challenges with a mentor or trusted colleague to gain perspective and guidance.

5. Celebrate Your Wins:
    - » Regularly recognise your progress, no matter how small, to stay motivated.
    - » Actionable Tip: Keep a "Win Jar" where you write down small victories on slips of paper and revisit them during tough times.

THE RIPPLE EFFECT OF RESILIENCE

When you build resilience, you not only improve your ability to handle setbacks but also inspire others to persevere. Resilient leaders set the tone for their teams, showing that challenges are part of the journey and that growth comes from pushing through adversity.

Resilience is the key to navigating risk with confidence and clarity. By adopting a growth mindset, celebrating progress, and learning from failure, you transform setbacks into stepping stones for success. Every fall is an opportunity to rise stronger and wiser.

STRENGTHENING YOUR RESILIENCE

Take 10 minutes to reflect on a recent setback. Answer the following questions:

1. What lessons did this experience teach me?
2. How can I apply those lessons moving forward?
3. What small win can I celebrate today to remind myself of my progress?

Commit to one action that turns your setback into a stepping stone for future growth.

Section 5: Broaden Your Horizons with Universal Scenarios

"Risk-taking isn't just for leaders it's for anyone seeking growth in any area of life."

Risk-taking isn't confined to boardrooms or high-stakes decisions. It's a universal skill that applies to every area of life, from personal relationships to career changes to creative pursuits. No matter the context, the principles of taking bold, calculated risks remain the same: they require courage, clarity, and the willingness to embrace uncertainty in pursuit of growth.

Whether you're starting a business, moving to a new city, or pursuing a dream you've always kept on the back burner, risk-taking is the bridge between comfort and progress. The scenarios may vary, but the lessons are universal.

WHEN I TOOK THE LEAP

One of the biggest personal risks I ever took was traveling solo to a country where I didn't know the language or anyone there. It wasn't just about stepping into a new place; it was stepping into the unknown, far outside my comfort zone. I hesitated, questioning whether I'd feel lost, unsafe, or completely out of my depth.

Despite the uncertainty, I booked the ticket. At first, it was overwhelming, navigating unfamiliar streets, ordering food with gestures, and adjusting to a different culture. But as the days passed, I adapted. I met people who became lifelong friends, learned to embrace discomfort, and discovered a confidence I didn't know I had. That trip taught me that risk isn't just about making a bold move; it's about trusting yourself to handle whatever comes next.

That experience changed how I approach life. I learned that the fear of taking a risk is often greater than the risk itself. And once you take the leap, you realise that every challenge is an opportunity to grow.

THE UNIVERSALITY OF RISK-TAKING

1. In Personal Growth:
   » Risk often takes the form of stepping out of your comfort zone to pursue something meaningful.
   » Example in Action: Taking up a new hobby, like learning an instrument or joining a fitness group, can feel intimidating. But the confidence and connections gained often far outweigh the initial discomfort.

2. In Relationships:
   » Building meaningful relationships—whether personal or professional—requires vulnerability and the willingness to take emotional risks.
   » Example in Action: Opening up to a partner about your goals and fears, or reaching out to a mentor for guidance, can lead to deeper connections and transformative growth.

3. In Career Decisions:
   » Whether it's starting a business, changing industries, or advocating for a promotion, career risks often carry the potential for significant rewards.
   » Example in Action: Indra Nooyi, former CEO of PepsiCo, demonstrated boldness by pushing for long-term sustainability initiatives despite initial resistance. Her risks reshaped PepsiCo's brand and global impact.

David Goggins, a former Navy SEAL and ultra-endurance athlete, is known for his incredible mental toughness and unwavering commitment to pushing beyond what most consider humanly possible. His story of transformation is one of profound personal risk-taking.

In his early life, Goggins struggled with obesity, a dead-end job, and deep self-doubt. At one point, he weighed over 136 kg (300 lbs.), and his physical health was deteriorating. Yet, he made a decision that would change the course of his life: he set an audacious goal to become a Navy SEAL. The challenge was massive. Not only did he need to lose more than 50 kg (110 lbs.) in under three months to qualify, but he also had no athletic background.

Goggins' journey was not smooth. He faced physical pain, exhaustion, and numerous setbacks; including breaking bones and failing his SEAL training twice. However, rather than quitting, he used these challenges as fuel to strengthen his mental resolve. Each failure pushed him harder, and each setback became an opportunity to build a stronger mindset. Ultimately, Goggins became a Navy SEAL and went on to break records in ultra-marathons, including some of the most grueling endurance events in the world.

His journey proves that the greatest risks are often the ones that challenge our limits. Goggins teaches us that embracing discomfort, failure, and uncertainty can be transformative. It's not about guaranteeing success but about the relentless pursuit of overcoming obstacles. His life exemplifies that taking risks, no matter how daunting, can lead to persona mastery and a level of strength that was once unimaginable.

STRATEGIES FOR BROADER RISK-TAKING

1. Start Small:
   » Take incremental steps toward the risks you're considering. Small actions reduce fear and build momentum.

- » Example in Action: If you're thinking about moving to a new city, start by visiting for a weekend or researching neighborhoods online.

2. Visualise Success:
   - » Picture the benefits of taking the leap and how it aligns with your goals.
   - » Example in Action: Before starting a new relationship, imagine the joy and growth it could bring rather than focusing solely on the fear of vulnerability.

3. Embrace Discomfort:
   - » Growth often requires stepping into the unknown. Use discomfort as a sign that you're moving forward.
   - » Example in Action: Joining a public speaking group may feel intimidating at first, but the confidence gained from improving your skills will make the initial discomfort worth it.

THE RIPPLE EFFECT OF UNIVERSAL RISK-TAKING

Taking risks doesn't just lead to external success it transforms you internally. Each leap you take, whether personal or professional, builds resilience, confidence, and a deeper understanding of your potential. By broadening your horizons and embracing risk in all areas of life, you create a foundation for continuous growth and fulfillment.

Risk-taking isn't confined to specific roles or situations; it's a universal principle for growth. Whether you're navigating a personal relationship, exploring a new hobby, or leading an organisational shift, the courage to embrace risk opens doors to transformation. Start small, act boldly, and trust in your ability to rise to the challenge.

UNIVERSAL RISK-TAKING

Take 10 minutes to reflect on a risk you've taken in a non-professional area of your life:

1. *What motivated you to take the leap?*
2. *What challenges did you face, and how did you overcome them?*
3. *What did you learn about yourself in the process?*

Write down one area of your life—personal or professional—where you've been avoiding risk, and brainstorm one small step you can take this week to move forward.

Section 6: Reflection Challenge: Mapping a Risk

"Reflection transforms experience into insight. By mapping a risk from all perspectives, you unlock clarity and create a path forward."

Taking risks is rarely a straightforward process; it involves emotions, uncertainties, and complex dynamics that can feel overwhelming. Reflection is a powerful tool to navigate these complexities, allowing you to learn from past risks and approach future ones with greater confidence and clarity.

By mapping a risk through multiple perspectives of your own, others involved, and a neutral observer you gain a deeper understanding of the situation and the insights needed to act decisively.

THE POWER OF REFLECTION IN RISK-TAKING

Reflection isn't about dwelling on what went wrong or what could go wrong. It's about extracting lessons, identifying patterns, and preparing for future challenges. When you take the time to reflect, you move from reaction to intention, equipping yourself to approach risks with clarity and purpose.

A client faced a significant risk in their personal life. They had strong feelings for someone but hesitated to express them: fear of rejection, uncertainty about how it might change their dynamic, and the possibility of losing an important connection kept them stuck. From their own perspective, taking that risk felt like stepping into the unknown, where they had no control over the outcome.

Through our conversations, they began to consider the other person's perspective. They realised that their feelings might not have been as obvious as they assumed, or that the other person could have been experiencing similar uncertainty. From an observer's perspective, they saw that avoiding the conversation wasn't protecting them, it was only creating more anxiety and preventing any real growth from happening.

That reflection gave them the clarity to take action. Instead of overanalysing, they had the conversation. It didn't go exactly as planned, but it provided closure, honesty, and a sense of confidence they wouldn't have gained otherwise. The experience taught them that risk in relationships—whether it's expressing feelings, setting boundaries, or making a commitment, isn't about controlling the outcome; it's about having the courage to show up with honesty and trust that whatever happens, they will handle it.

MAPPING A RISK

Take 10 minutes to map out a risk you've taken in the past or are currently considering. Use the following steps to guide your reflection:

1. Your Perspective (First Position):
    »   What are your thoughts, feelings, and motivations about this risk?
    »   Example in Action: If you're considering starting a business, reflect on your excitement about the opportunity and your fears about potential failure.

2. Others' Perspectives (Second Position):
    »   How might others involved view this situation? What are their motivations, concerns, or expectations?
    »   Example in Action: A business partner might focus on financial implications, while a mentor might view it as an opportunity for growth.

3. The Observer's Perspective (Third Position):
    »   What might a neutral observer notice about this situation? What patterns or dynamics could they point out?
    »   Example in Action: An observer might notice that your focus on "what ifs" is overshadowing the tangible steps you could take to mitigate risks.

Write down one specific action you can take based on the insights gained from these perspectives. For example: if your reflection highlights a gap in preparation, your action might be to conduct more research or seek advice from a trusted expert.

THE VALUE OF MAPPING RISKS

Mapping risks through reflection provides several benefits:

1. Enhanced Clarity: Seeing the situation from multiple angles reduces emotional bias and reveals actionable insights.
2. Informed Decision-Making: Understanding how others might perceive the risk helps you anticipate challenges and build stronger plans.
3. Empowerment Through Awareness: Reflection transforms fear into confidence by showing you the full scope of the situation.

APPLYING THE REFLECTION CHALLENGE

Imagine you're considering asking for a promotion:

1. Your Perspective: You feel ready for more responsibility but worry about being perceived as overconfident.
2. Others' Perspectives: Your manager might value your initiative and see this as a sign of leadership.
3. The Observer's Perspective: A neutral observer might suggest that preparing evidence of your contributions could strengthen your case and reduce your anxiety.

Actionable Step: Schedule a meeting with your manager to discuss your goals, backed by examples of your achievements.

Reflection is the compass that guides you through risk. By mapping a risk through multiple perspectives, you uncover hidden insights, anticipate challenges, and create a clear path forward. Every risk, when approached with thoughtful reflection, becomes an opportunity for growth.

YOUR TURN

Think about a risk you're considering or one you've taken in the past. Answer these questions:

1. What did you learn (or could you learn) from your perspective?
2. What might others involved have experienced or thought?
3. How might an observer have evaluated the situation?

Commit to Action: Write down one step you'll take based on these insights, and plan to complete it within the next week.

Section 7 Reflection:

"The biggest risk isn't failure; it's never finding out what you're actually capable of."

Risk is never comfortable, and it's not supposed to be. Growth doesn't happen in the safe zones. It happens at the edge of discomfort, just beyond the point where you usually stop.

This chapter wasn't about making reckless moves. It was about learning to move with intention when fear shows up. You've seen how to shift your mindset, expand your perspective, apply emotional intelligence, and build resilience, all in service of one thing: progress.

You're never going to feel 100% ready. That's the point. You take the risk, and then you grow into the person who can handle it.

Stop waiting for certainty. You don't need more clarity—you need motion. Shift your view. Trust your instincts. Use your setbacks. Lead with more awareness. And above all, start before you feel ready.

Reflection Questions:

SECTION 1:

What's one risk you've been avoiding because of fear or self-doubt? What small action could you take in the next 24 hours to start moving forward?

SECTION 2:

Think of a challenge you're facing. What new insights emerge when you view it through each of the three perceptual positions?

SECTION 3:

When considering your next bold move, what emotions are influencing your decision, and how are you managing them?

SECTION 4:

What recent setback could you reframe as feedback? What one lesson can you carry forward into your next challenge?

SECTION 5:

What area of your life (outside of work) have you been playing too safe in? What's one move you could make this week to stretch yourself?

SECTION 6:

What decision are you hesitating or? When you map it through all three perspectives, what's the most obvious step you should take next?

CHAPTER 10

The 5 States of Optimisation: Mastering the Journey

> *"Mastery is not about perfection, it's about progress.*
> *The leader who evolves is the leader who inspires."*

You're not chasing a finish line—you're mastering the art of continuous evolution. Every challenge, every decision, every adjustment you make refines your leadership, mindset, and potential. True optimisation isn't about doing more; it's about leading with intention, thinking strategically, and aligning your actions with what truly matters.

Having a framework that guides you—not just when things are clear, but when uncertainty, change, and opportunity collide. The 5 States of Optimisation: Planning, Productivity, People, Prospect, and

Performance, aren't just leadership principles; they're a way of life. These interconnected states help you navigate every uphill battle, every sharp turn, and every stretch of momentum.

Like gears on a bike, sometimes you need more power to push through resistance. Other times, you need to shift down and recalibrate. Mastery isn't about speed; it's about knowing when to accelerate, when to adjust, and when to recover. The leaders who embrace this rhythm, who learn to optimise rather than just operate, are the ones who don't just succeed. They outlast, outgrow, and outperform everyone else.

This chapter will give you the tools to master these five states—helping you take control of your focus, your energy, and your impact. You'll learn when to push harder, when to step back, and how to create sustainable success. Because true leadership isn't about keeping up, it's about knowing how to shift, when to adapt, and how to stay in control of your own momentum.

Section 1: Planning State– The Blueprint for Clarity

"No successful leader wakes up and wings it. Planning turns chaos into clarity."

The Planning State is where everything begins. It's the foundation that transforms overwhelming possibilities into a focused roadmap. Without a plan, you're not leading, you're reacting. Planning is about setting your sights on where you want to go and charting the steps to get there. It's intentional and adaptive, providing the clarity and structure needed to prioritise and execute with purpose.

When I began writing this book, the scope felt overwhelming. There were countless ideas and concepts I wanted to explore, and without a plan, it could have spiralec into chaos. The Planning State grounded me. By breaking the project into manageable sections, setting milestones, and creating a timeline, I turned a daunting vision into an achievable goal. Each day, I knew exactly what I needed to focus on, and that clarity fueled my progress.

THE POWER OF THE PLANNING STATE

Planning isn't about rigidity or micromanagement; it's about designing your life with intention. Leaders who thrive in the Planning State don't just map out their tasks; they align their time, energy, and focus with their goals. This is how they move from chaos to clarity, from uncertainty to action.

When we think about success, it's not just about the end result; it's about the deliberate process of planning and executing with clarity and precision. Take, for example, the career of basketball legend Kobe Bryant.

Kobe Bryant wasn't just a phenomenal player because of his raw talent; he was known for his meticulous planning and preparation. One of his most remarkable attributes was his "Mamba Mentality," a philosophy rooted in relentless dedication to improvement. Kobe often spoke about the importance of setting goals and working towards them with unwavering focus, both on and off the court.

But it wasn't just about showing up and playing—Kobe was notorious for his detailed approach to mastering every aspect of his game. Even after winning five NBA championships, he continued to break down his game and plan how to improve, year after year. During the offseason, while many players took a break, Kobe was in the gym, working on the areas of his game that needed refining. He didn't just practice his shots; he planned every movement, every routine. This level of strategic thinking is a prime example of how the Planning State works in action.

Kobe's approach was methodical. He set clear objectives for each season, focused on specific aspects he needed to improve, and developed a roadmap to make those improvements happen. When you're at the top, like Kobe, it's easy to assume you're already good enough—but he never fell into that trap. He embraced the Planning State fully, ensuring his plan was as refined as his execution on the court.

This mindset—planning with precision and working relentlessly toward those goals—was key to Kobe's legendary success. Just as Kobe planned his career with intention, the same principle applies to leadership and personal achievement. Success isn't about luck; it's about intentional planning and making steady progress toward your vision.

Kobe's commitment to constant improvement is a great reminder that planning isn't just about setting goals; it's about following through with calculated actions—just like he did throughout his 20-year career.

Consider a CEO who blocks off their mornings for deep strategic thinking and leaves afternoons for meetings. Or a leader who dedicates one day each week to personal development, recognising that investing in their own growth is just as important as delivering results. These leaders understand that if they don't manage their time, energy, and focus, the world w ll manage it for them and they won't like where that leads.

STEPS TO OPTIMISE THE PLANNING STATE

1. Define Your Priorities:
   - » Start each week by identifying your top three goals.
   - » Actionable Insight: Ask yourself, *If I could only accomplish three things this week, what would make the biggest impact?*

2. Create Time Blocks:
   - » Dedicate focused time for your most important tasks while leaving room for flexibility.
   - » Example in Action: Reserve your mornings for high-priority work and block off afternoons for collaboration or administrative tasks.

3. Review and Adjust:
   - » End each day by reflecting on what worked, what didn't, and how you'll refine your plan for tomorrow.
   - » Actionable Insight: Use a simple journaling prompt: *What did I achieve today? What needs my attention tomorrow?*

THE RIPPLE EFFECT OF THE PLANNING STATE

The Planning State doesn't just create structure—it creates momentum. When you plan with purpose, you start each day with clarity and direction, empowering you to tackle challenges and seize opportunities. By designing your life intentionally, you reduce stress, increase focus, and set yourself up for sustainable success.

YOUR PLANNING BLUEPRINT

Take 10 minutes to reflect on your current approach to planning:

1. Are your daily actions aligned with your long-term goals?
2. What's one change you can make to bring more clarity and focus to your planning process?

Identify one high-priority goal for the week ahead and map out three steps you'll take to achieve it.

Planning isn't just about getting things done—it's about making sure the things you do are moving you closer to where you want to be. It's the difference between drifting and driving your journey.

Section 2: Productivity State– Focused Action, Meaningful Results

"Productivity isn't about doing more, it's about doing what matters most."

In the Productivity State, you shift your focus from activity to impact. Productivity isn't measured by busyness; it's about aligning your actions with your goals and making meaningful progress on what truly matters. The key to mastering this state lies in self-awareness—understanding when you're at your best, recognising distractions that pull you off course, and taking deliberate action to stay aligned.

True leaders don't just manage tasks—they manage themselves. They recognise that productivity is the currency of leadership, and how they spend their energy determines the results they achieve.

At 27, working for a tech startup in London, I fell into the trap of mistaking activity for productivity. My mornings often started with clearing my inbox, a habit that felt satisfying but left me drained for the high-impact work that required creativity and focus. Over time, I realised that this pattern wasn't serving me.

By guarding my mornings for strategic work—whether brainstorming, writing, or problem-solving, I transformed my productivity. Those golden hours became my most valuable resource; and I saw immediate improvements in my results and overall energy.

Now, I approach my day with clarity: I prioritise what truly matters and leave low-value tasks for later. This shift wasn't just about changing how I worked—it was about changing how I thought about productivity.

THE POWER OF THE PRODUCTIVITY STATE

Shonda Rhimes, the visionary behind *Grey's Anatomy*, *Scandal*, and *Bridgerton*, exemplifies what it means to master the Productivity State. While many people mistake productivity for simply doing more, Rhimes proves that true productivity comes from focusing on what truly matters. She has built an entertainment empire by prioritising high-impact, meaningful work over getting bogged down by non-essential tasks.

One of her most powerful productivity strategies is her practice of "protected writing hours." During these dedicated blocks of time, she shuts out all distractions—no emails, no phone calls, no meetings. These hours are sacred and are fully reserved for the creative work that drives her business forward. This allows her to stay deeply immersed in her stories without the constant pull of everyday distractions.

Rhimes also knows how to delegate effectively. As the head of Shondaland, she empowers her team to manage the operational side of the business, freeing her to focus on what only she can do—crafting compelling narratives and building strong, culturally significant shows. She trusts her team to handle everything from production to scheduling, which lets her operate at the highest level of her capabilities.

By recognising that her time and energy are finite, Shonda Rhimes has mastered the art of focusing on the tasks that make the most significant impact, leading to some of the most successful television shows of the last two decades. Her ability to focus on what truly matters, and to trust others to take care of the rest, has allowed her to balance multiple high-profile projects without compromising her creative output.

Rhimes' approach shows that productivity isn't about being busy; it's about aligning your actions with your goals and giving your full attention to the tasks that drive success. This mindset is what's made her not only a cultural icon but also a model of leadership and creative success.

Self-awareness is the foundation of true productivity. It's about understanding:

- When You're in Flow: Recognising your peak energy hours and aligning your most important tasks with them.
- What Pulls You Off Course: Identifying distractions, self-doubt, or habits that derail your focus.

- How to Manage Yourself: Taking deliberate actions to stay on track and make your effort count.

Think about the entrepreneur who realises that responding to emails first thing in the morning kills the creativity for the day. By reserving the mornings for high-value work—such as strategy or product development, they protect their time and energy. This intentionality isn't about working harder; it's about working smarter.

STRATEGIES TO BOOST PRODUCTIVITY

1. Eliminate Distractions:
   » Identify what pulls your focus—whether it's notifications, unnecessary meetings, or multitasking—and take steps to minimise them.
   » Example in Action: Turn off notifications during focus blocks and schedule email checks at specific times.

2. Prioritise Energy:
   » Align tasks with your natural energy rhythms. Tackle creative or challenging work during your peak hours, and save routine tasks for when your energy dips.
   » Example in Action: If you're most focused in the morning, reserve that time for strategic planning or problem-solving.

3. Start Small:
   » Progress, not perfection, builds momentum. Break large tasks into manageable steps to overcome procrastination.
   » Example in Action: Instead of writing a full report in one sitting, start with a rough outline or a first paragraph.

4. Batch Similar Tasks:
    » Group related tasks together to maintain focus and efficiency.
    » Example in Action: Reserve an hour for all calls or administrative tasks, so your mind isn't constantly switching gears.

THE RIPPLE EFFECT OF PRODUCTIVITY

When you operate in the Productivity State, the benefits extend beyond your to-do list. You gain clarity, reduce stress, and free up mental bandwidth for creative thinking. Productivity isn't about hustling endlessly; it's about making your effort count and aligning your actions with your purpose.

OPTIMISE YOUR PRODUCTIVITY

Take 10 minutes to reflect on your current approach to productivity:

1. What tasks or habits drain your energy without adding value?
2. What time of day do you feel most focused and energised?
3. How can you realign your schedule to prioritise high-impact work?

Identify one low-value activity you'll eliminate this week and one high-priority task you'll protect during your peak energy hours.

Productivity is the foundation of leadership impact. The time and energy you spend on what matters most will define the legacy you leave behind.

Section 3: People State– The Heart of Connection

"Leadership is a people's game. Connection builds trust; trust builds success."

At its core, leadership is about people. The People State focuses on sharpening your social awareness and creating authentic connections that build trust, foster collaboration, and inspire action. If you don't know how to connect with and understand those you lead; you'll always be reacting instead of leading.

The ability to read people to sense what's unspoken and adapt to the dynamics in the room isn't about being a mind reader; it's about emotional attunement. Great leaders understand that influence comes not from force, but from empathy. When you master the People State, you stop pushing people toward your vision and start pulling them in with shared purpose and trust.

THE POWER OF THE PEOPLE STATE

Social awareness is your ability to walk into a room, a conversation, or a negotiation and sense what's really going on beneath the surface. It's about seeing beyond words—to understand the emotions, motivations, and fears driving others.

Melanie Perkins, the co-founder and CEO of Canva, didn't build a billion-dollar company through aggressive leadership or top-down management, she did it by prioritising people, culture, and connection.

In the early days of Canva, Perkins faced countless rejections from investors. Instead of letting those setbacks define her, she focused on building a team that believed in the vision as much as she did. She ensured that every new hire wasn't just talented, but aligned with Canva's culture of collaboration, creativity, and mutual respect.

One of her defining leadership strategies is radical transparency. She holds open company-wide meetings where employees, regardless of rank, can voice ideas, ask tough questions, and challenge assumptions. By actively listening and implementing feedback, Perkins has created an environment where employees feel heard and valued, leading to higher engagement and innovation.

This people-first leadership has paid off. Canva has not only grown into a global design platform with over 100 million users, but it has also become one of the best workplaces in tech, known for its positive, mission-driven culture.

Perkins' leadership proves that business success isn't just about products, it's about people. By fostering trust, inclusivity, and shared purpose, she turned Canva into one of the most innovative and people-centered companies in the world.

Consider the leader who notices subtle signs of burnout within their team before it's voiced. They adjust workloads, hold honest conversations, and provide support proactively. By addressing challenges early, they prevent disengagement and strengthen trust.

Or think of the CEO who senses hesitation during a high-stakes negotiation. Instead of pushing harder—they pause, ask clarifying questions, and adjust their approach to meet the other party's needs. That emotional attunement closes deals and builds lasting relationships.

I've worked with leaders who excelled technically but struggled to connect emotionally with their teams. One client, a highly skilled C-suite member, was frustrated by declining team performance. When we explored the dynamics, it became clear that the issue wasn't a lack of effort, it was a lack of trust.

By focusing on the People State, they began holding regular one-on-one conversations—not just about work—but about their team members' goals, challenges, and motivations. The transformation was remarkable. Team members who had been disengaged started contributing actively, and the manager's influence grew, not through authority, but through connection.

STRATEGIES TO MASTER THE PEOPLE STATE

1. Listen Beyond Words:
   » Pay attention to tone, body language, and unspoken cues during conversations.
   » Example in Action: If a team member says they're fine but their energy suggests otherwise, ask open-ended questions to uncover their true concerns.
2. Adapt Your Approach:
   » Recognise that different people require different leadership styles. Some thrive on autonomy, while others need frequent check-ins.
   » Example in Action: Tailor your feedback to suit individual preferences—direct for some, more conversational for others.
3. Prioritise Empathy:
   » Seek to understand before being understood. Empathy builds bridges and fosters trust.

- » Example in Action: If a colleague misses a deadline, instead of immediately reprimanding them, ask what challenges they faced and how you can support them.
4. Create a Safe Space:
   - » Encourage open communication by making it safe for others to express concerns or share ideas.
   - » Example in Action: Hold regular feedback sessions where team members can speak candidly without fear of judgment.

THE RIPPLE EFFECT OF THE PEOPLE STATE

When you operate in the People State, your influence grows organically. By developing trust and collaboration, you create a culture where people feel valued and motivated to contribute their best. This ripple effect extends beyond the workplace—enriching your relationships and strengthening your impact as a leader.

DEEPENING YOUR CONNECTION

Take 10 minutes to reflect on your current approach to social awareness and connection:

1. When was the last time you noticed and responded to an unspoken need within your team or network?
2. What's one specific action you can take this week to deepen trust and collaboration with someone you lead?

Identify a team member or colleague you'd like to connect with more deeply. Schedule a conversation to ask about their goals, challenges, and how you can support them.

Leadership isn't about telling people what to do, it's about showing them why it matters and inspiring them to believe in it as much as you do.

Section 4: Prospect State– Building Lasting Relationships

"Relationships are the foundation of opportunity. Build them with trust, not transactions."

Relationships are everything. Whether in business, life, or leadership. Success is built on the foundation of meaningful human connections. But here's the key: mastering relationships isn't about being everyone's best friend—it's about creating trust, respect, and loyalty that stand the test of time.

The Prospect State is where emotional intelligence comes into play. It's not just about networking or meeting new people; it's about creating relationships that matter. Whether you're working with employees, clients, or partners; your ability to connect authentically and align mutual goals determines the opportunities you create.

THE POWER OF THE PROSPECT STATE

Strong relationships don't just happen; they're built intentionally. The Prospect State requires you to focus on trust, transparency, and emotional intelligence. These qualities turn surface-level interactions into enduring partnerships that drive success.

Anne Boden, the founder and CEO of Starling Bank, has transformed the UK banking landscape with her digital-first approach. Her success is not just a result of her technical and strategic expertise, but also her ability to build lasting relationships with both her team and customers.

When Anne founded Starling Bank in 2014, she recognised that building meaningful, trust-based relationships would be critical to the bank's success. Unlike traditional banks, she focused on understanding the needs of customers and ensuring that the relationships she nurtured within her organisation prioritised transparency, integrity, and mutual respect.

Anne's leadership style, rooted in authenticity, transparency, and collaboration, enabled her to form strong partnerships with investors, stakeholders, and customers. She was not just building a bank; she was creating a platform where every relationship mattered—whether with her employees, customers, or other businesses.

One of the key factors in Anne's success has been her ability to foster trust with her customers. From the outset, she positioned Starling Bank as a customer-first business, aiming to provide an alternative to the legacy banking system with products and services that truly benefited the user. Her focus on customer relationships was not about pushing transactions, but about building long-term loyalty by meeting real needs.

Under her leadership, Starling Bank has seen tremendous growth, becoming one of the UK's leading digital banks, consistently innovating while maintaining a strong, transparent relationship with its clients. Anne Boden's approach demonstrates how building authentic, relationship-based business practices can lead to massive success in a digital age.

I've learned that the strength of my relationships determines the depth of my impact. A CEO of an online dating app, I worked with initially, approached our sessions with hesitation, unsure of whether coaching could truly help them. By focusing on trust, listening to their concerns, aligning my approach with their goals, and following through on every commitment, we built a partnership that not only transformed their leadership but also strengthened their confidence.

This experience reinforced a critical lesson: real relationships aren't built on transactions. They're built on understanding, empathy, and the willingness to invest in the long haul.

EMOTIONAL INTELLIGENCE IN THE PROSPECT STATE

Mastering the Prospect State requires navigating the emotional landscape of others. Leaders who do this effectively don't manipulate— they care deeply and act authentically.

- Understanding Needs: The best leaders don't assume—they ask. They take the time to understand what matters most to others.
- Transparency Over Tact: Real relationships are built on honest, sometimes tough, conversations. Leaders who avoid sugarcoating earn respect.
- Mutual Benefit: Strong partnerships are created when both parties see value in the relationship.

Think about the manager who isn't afraid to address a performance issue directly but does so with empathy and respect. Their team trusts them because they know the feedback is coming from a place of care and commitment to growth.

BUILD RELATIONSHIPS IN THE PROSPECT STATE

1. Listen Actively:
   » Focus on understanding, not just responding. Give others your full attention and acknowledge their perspectives.
   » Example in Action: During a meeting, paraphrase what someone says to confirm your understanding before responding.

2. Invest in Trust:
   » prioritise transparency and follow through on your commitments. Consistency builds credibility.
   » Example in Action: If you promise to deliver feedback or resources, make it a priority to follow through promptly.

3. Align Goals:
   » Seek mutual benefits in your partnerships. Strong relationships are built on shared purpose and outcomes.
   » Example in Action: When negotiating with a client, identify how their goals align with your organisation's long-term strategy to create a win-win outcome.

4. Be Proactive:
   » Reach out regularly, not just when you need something. Relationships thrive when nurtured over time.
   » Example in Action: Send a thoughtful note or share a resource with a colleague or partner, even if there's no immediate agenda.

THE RIPPLE EFFECT OF THE PROSPECT STATE

The Prospect State is more than a strategy—it's a mindset. When you prioritise relationships built on trust and authenticity, the opportunities you create are limitless. These relationships don't just drive results; they enrich your life, strengthen your leadership, and amplify your influence.

STRENGTHENING YOUR CONNECTIONS

Take 10 minutes to reflect on the relationships in your life:

1. Who are the people you rely on most, and how have you nurtured those relationships?
2. What's one relationship that could benefit from more attention or alignment?
3. What specific action can you take this week to deepen trust and connection in that relationship?

Commit to reaching out to one person this week to strengthen your connection—whether it's through a conversation, an offer of support, or simply expressing gratitude.

Relationships aren't built overnight, but they're the foundation of everything you achieve. Lead with empathy, invest in trust, and remember: the connections you build today shape the opportunities you create tomorrow.

Section 5: Performance State– Continuous Growth

"The best leaders don't settle; they strive for constant evolution."

The Performance State is the pinnacle of the 5 States where everything comes together. It's the relentless pursuit of growth, fueled by self-reflection, resilience, and an unwavering commitment to improvement. In the Performance State, you wake up each day asking, *"How can I grow today?"* You understand that growth is infinite and that the moment you believe you've "arrived"—you're already falling behind.

Great leaders, like elite athletes, never stop training. They embrace discomfort, challenge themselves to go further; and see setbacks not as failures, but as stepping stones to something greater. The Performance State is where you push past fear and lean into challenges; knowing that growth doesn't happen in comfort zones, it happens in the stretch.

Every major milestone in my career, from launching coaching programs to delivering a TEDx Talk came from stepping outside my comfort zone. These moments weren't easy. They were filled with self-doubt, fear, and uncertainty. But each time, I chose to push through.

The process wasn't just about building skills—it was about building confidence and perspective. For example, when I prepared for my TEDx Talk, the challenge wasn't just mastering the content, it was overcoming the fear of standing on that stage. Yet, the growth I experienced from taking that leap reshaped my understanding of what I was capable of.

The Performance State isn't about perfection, it's about progress. It's about asking: *What's next? How can I improve?*

The world's best performers share one trait: they're never satisfied with "good enough." Whether they're athletes, CEOs, or artists, they're constantly seeking that next edge, the skill, insight, or mindset that will elevate their performance.

Tim Grover, the elite trainer behind legends like Michael Jordan, Kobe Bryant, and Dwyane Wade, built his reputation on a single principle: greatness isn't a goal, it's a relentless pursuit. His entire philosophy revolves around the Performance State; where success isn't about talent alone but about the willingness to outwork, outlast, and outgrow the competition.

Grover didn't just train athletes physically—he transformed their mindset. He taught Jordan to push beyond exhaustion, to never accept "good enough," and to use failure as fuel for greater achievement. When Kobe Bryant wanted to sharpen his game, Grover designed brutal, 4 AM training sessions that tested his mental toughness as much as his physical ability. These weren't just workouts; they were lessons in commitment, resilience, and continuous growth.

Grover's methods were unconventional. He believed that true challenge was not about the physical grind, but the mental conditioning to face adversity head-on, to endure what others would quit. These lessons were not about maintaining success; they were about constantly refining, resetting, and pushing past limits. Even after winning championships, Jordan, Kobe, and Wade returned to their training with a clear focus: getting better, no matter how much they had already achieved.

In his book *Relentless*, Grover reveals what separates the elite from the rest of the world: they never stop improving. They don't settle. They recognise that growth is infinite, and the moment they believe they've "arrived," they've already lost. Grover's philosophy isn't just for athletes; it's for anyone striving for excellence in any field. His training reflects the Performance State mindset: the best never think they've arrived. They reflect, refine, and reset, constantly.

This relentless pursuit of growth, this constant fine-tuning of performance, is what keeps the world's greatest performers at the top. Whether you're an athlete, a CEO, or a leader, Grover's work proves one thing: growth isn't optional, it's essential.

Think of the leader who, even after achieving massive success, continues to invest in their personal development. Leaders who attend workshops, read voraciously, and work with coaches not because they have to, but because they know that growth is the foundation of sustained success.

The Performance State demands this same mindset from you. It requires embracing discomfort, leaning into challenges, and seeing failure not as an end but as a setup for your next leap forward.

OPTIMISE THE PERFORMANCE STATE

1. Set Stretch Goals:
   - » Push yourself beyond what feels comfortable to unlock new levels of capability.
   - » Example in Action: If public speaking terrifies you, commit to delivering a presentation to a small group. Growth happens in the stretch.
2. Reflect and Refine:
   - » After each project or milestone, take time to evaluate your performance. Ask:
     - · What did I learn?
     - · How can I improve?

» Example in Action: After completing a team project, hold a debrief to identify lessons learned and opportunities for future improvement.

3. Commit to Lifelong Learning:
   » Make personal growth a non-negotiable habit.
   » Example in Action: Dedicate time each week to reading, attending workshops, or learning new skills that challenge your thinking.

4. Embrace Failure:
   » Reframe setbacks as learning opportunities.
   » Example in Action: If a project doesn't succeed, analyze what went wrong, and use those insights to refine your approach for the next one.

THE RIPPLE EFFECT OF THE PERFORMANCE STATE

The Performance State isn't just about personal growth—it creates a ripple effect. When you embrace growth, you inspire those around you to do the same. Your courage to push boundaries encourages your team, peers, and loved ones to lean into their own potential.

EMBRACING YOUR PERFORMANCE STATE

Take 10 minutes to reflect on your approach to growth:

- When was the last time you set a goal that scared you?
- What's one area of your life or leadership where you're holding back?
- What's a stretch goal you can commit to this month to challenge your limits?

Write down your stretch goal and identify the first step you'll take toward it. Share it with someone who will hold you accountable.

The Performance State reminds us that leadership is about evolution. The more you challenge yourself, the more capable, confident, and impactful you become. Growth isn't a destination; it's a journey.

Section 6: Mapping the 5 States

"Growth begins with awareness. The more you reflect, the further you go."

The 5 States of Optimisation are your roadmap for continuous growth and leadership excellence. But like any roadmap, their power lies in how you use them. Reflection is the key. By taking the time to evaluate where you are and where you need to focus, you unlock the clarity and direction to move forward with intention.

This isn't a one-time exercise. The 5 States are cyclical, evolving with you at every stage of your journey. Sometimes you'll need to revisit the Planning State to recalibrate your goals. Other times, you'll need to lean into the People State to navigate a team challenge or double down on the Performance State to embrace growth. The beauty of this model is its flexibility: it meets you exactly where you are and evolves with you as you grow.

THE CYCLE OF INFINITE GROWTH

The 5 States aren't linear; they're cyclical and interdependent. They feed into one another, creating an endless loop of growth and optimisation.

1. Planning feeds Productivity: Clear plans empower focused action.
2. Productivity drives People: Purposeful output builds trust and collaboration.
3. People inform Prospect: Strong relationships unlock new opportunities.
4. Prospect enhances Performance: Deep connections fuel innovation and success.
5. Performance refines Planning: Insights from growth shape better strategies.

This cycle is infinite. There's no final destination, no summit where you "arrive." The leaders who truly excel understand this—they embrace the idea that every time they conquer one peak, another one emerges. That's where the magic lies: in the relentless pursuit of the next level.

REFLECTION AND ACTION

1. Assess Your Current State:
   » Evaluate how each state is currently serving you. Use a simple scale (e.g., 1–5) to rate each state's strength in your life.
   » Example in Action: If your Planning State feels strong (5), but your Performance State feels weak (2), focus on setting a stretch goal to elevate your growth.

2. Identify One Focus Area:

   » Choose one state that needs immediate attention and
     commit to improving it.
   » Example in Action: If your Prospect State needs work,
     reach out to one person this week to strengthen or build
     a connection.

3. Revisit and Refine Weekly:

   » Growth is iterative. Revisit your reflection weekly to
     track progress and adjust your focus as needed.

THE RIPPLE EFFECT OF REFLECTION

Reflection isn't just about identifying where you are, it's about deciding where you want to go. By pausing to assess and recalibrate, you ensure that every step you take aligns with your vision and values. This process not only fuels your personal growth but also strengthens your leadership impact—inspiring those around you to embrace their own potential.

WHERE ARE YOU NOW?

Take 10 minutes to reflect on the 5 States of Optimisation. Answer these questions honestly:

1. Which state feels strongest for you right now?
2. Which state needs the most attention?
3. What's one specific action you'll take today to strengthen
   that state?

EXAMPLE IN ACTION:

If the Productivity State feels strong because you're focused and organised but the People State needs attention, commit to having one meaningful conversation with a colleague or team member this week. Small, intentional actions compound into significant growth.

The 5 States of Optimisation are a living, breathing framework. They grow with you, evolve with you, and adapt to the challenges and opportunities you face. Embrace the cycle of infinite growth, and remember: the journey itself is the destination.

Section 7: Reflection

"The leaders who outperform aren't the ones who hustle hardest, they're the ones who optimise with purpose, every single day."

So, as you step out into the world, book in hand. Here's what I want you to remember: You are never done. Mastery is an ongoing journey. You don't get to check the box and say: "I've made it." No—you're in this for the long haul.

The leader you are today is just the beginning. Who you become tomorrow, next year, or in the next decade will be determined by how relentlessly you pursue these five states.

There will be days when the climb feels impossible; when you doubt yourself, when you wonder if it's all worth it. And that's when you lean into these states. You come back to the core principles that have brought you here and will take you further.

The 5 States of Optimisation—Planning, Productivity, People, Prospect, and Performance—aren't just concepts; they're a framework for living and leading with clarity and purpose. These states offer a guide to continuously improving yourself and your leadership—no matter where you are on your journey.

When you embrace these states, you equip yourself to:

- Adapt to challenges with resilience.
- Lead authentically, inspiring trust, and collaboration.
- Pursue growth with intention and curiosity.

But mastery is not a finish line. It's a cycle of growth, reflection, and action. The more you integrate these states into your life, the more they'll shape who you are and the impact you have on those around you.

Reflection Questions:

SECTION 1:

Where are you planning reactively instead of intentionally? What's one adjustment you can make this week to align your plan with what actually matters?

SECTION 2:

What's one habit or task that drains your energy but adds little value? How can you shift your focus toward high-impact work during your most productive hours?

SECTION 3:

When did you last pause to understand what your team or peers really need—beyond what they're saying? What can you do this week to lead with more empathy and presence?

SECTION 4:

Which relationship in your life or work feels transactional or neglected? What's one way you can reconnect or rebuild trust through meaningful action?

SECTION 5:

What's one area where you've settled for "good enough"? What would it look like to challenge yourself there and pursue your next level of growth?

SECTION 6:

Which of the 5 States is currently underdeveloped for you—and why? What's one action you'll take this week to intentionally strengthen that area?

The game is infinite. The journey doesn't end. The only question is: how far are you willing to take it?

Leading From Within Is a Choice, Make It Yours

From the moment you opened this book, you were challenged to rethink leadership—not as a title, not as a position, but as a way of being. You've read about breaking free from expectations, navigating uncertainty, and stepping into your own power. You've explored what it means to burn the rules and replace them with something better: your own framework for success, energy, and resilience.

We started with a simple but uncomfortable truth: most people live by rules they never questioned. They follow a script that tells them how success should look, how leaders should behave, and what paths are acceptable. Yet, real leadership—the kind that transforms both individuals and organisation—begins when you stop following and start leading from within.

WHAT HAVE YOU LEARNED?

Throughout this book, you've seen the power of shifting gears when the road ahead demands it. You've been pushed to step beyond comfort, confront fear, and take control of the one thing that truly determines success, your mindset.

- You discovered that stepping out of your comfort zone is not just about risk, it's about growth. Whether it was a 180-mile bike ride or taking on a challenge you felt unprepared for, every moment of discomfort revealed new strengths.

- You saw that fear is not your enemy; it's a signal. The question is, will you let it stop you, or will you use it as fuel to move forward?

- You learned that failure is not the opposite of success; it's part of it. Leadership, business, and life itself are not straight paths. Every setback is an opportunity to reflect, adjust, and come back stronger.

- You confronted the biggest obstacle to change: your own doubt. If you've made it this far, you know that doubt doesn't need to define you; it's simply a choice to hesitate or to act.

THE 5 STATES OF OPTIMISATION—
AND EVERYTHING BEYOND THEM

Yes, the 5 States of Optimisation gave you a structured way to assess and elevate how you think, operate, and lead. But this book was never just about a framework. It was about a mentality shift.

- Planning taught you to stop reacting and start designing your life and leadership with intent.

- Productivity reminds you that being busy isn't the same as being effective. You must focus on what truly moves the needle.
- People showed you that relationships, both personal and professional, are at the heart of every major breakthrough.
- Prospect forces you to stop waiting for opportunities and start creating them.
- Performance reinforced that growth is not about perfection, but about progress, consistency, and resilience.

But what makes the difference is not the framework itself; it's your willingness to use it. Knowing the 5 States is meaningless if you don't apply them. The same is true for every lesson you've absorbed in this book.

WHAT HAPPENS NOW?

This book isn't the end of your journey. It's the starting line.

You will face moments of fear, doubt, and resistance. You will be tempted to revert to old patterns. But now, you know better.

The question is: will you choose to lead from within?

Here's your challenge:

- Act. Pick one concept from this book and apply it immediately; today, not tomorrow. Whether it's taking control of your schedule, having a difficult conversation, or finally committing to that next big step. Do it.
- Own your lane. Stop comparing yourself to others. Stop waiting for permission. Success is not about following someone else's formula; it's about creating your own.

- Burn the rules. If something isn't working, change it. If you've been holding onto outdated beliefs about success; let them go. If you've been waiting for confidence, understand that action creates confidence, not the other way around.

The greatest leaders are not the ones who had everything figured out. They are the ones who kept moving despite uncertainty.

They didn't wait. They decided. They acted.

Now, it's your turn.

Burn the rules. Lead from within. And don't look back.

Acknowledgments

Writing this book has been a journey of reflection, growth, and gratitude. It wouldn't have been possible without the people who shaped, supported, and inspired me along the way.

TO MY WIFE, ROMI

You are my partner, my challenger, and my mirror. Your love and support have carried me through my toughest moments, and your honesty has pushed me to become better in every way. This book is as much yours as it is mine—and I couldn't have done it without you.

TO MY DAUGHTER, LANA

You've shown me the beauty of curiosity, and the importance of seeing the world through fresh eyes. Your energy and perspective have been a gift that keeps me grounded and inspired.

TO MY PARENTS, MANJI AND JAYA

You laid the foundation of everything I stand for. Dad, your kindness and wisdom taught me the true meaning of compassion in leadership. Mom, your resilience and unwavering discipline continue to remind me that strength is built from within. Your values are woven into every page of this book.

TO MY SISTER, RUPA
Your encouragement and belief in me have been a constant source of strength. You've always been my sounding board and my biggest cheerleader; and for that, I am deeply grateful.

TO MY MENTORS AND COACHES
You've guided me with your wisdom; challenged me to think bigger, and encouraged me to step into my purpose. Thank you for sharing your knowledge and reminding me that leadership is a lifelong journey.

TO MY CLIENTS
Your trust, stories, and resilience have been the greatest teachers. You've shown me the power of transformation and the limitless potential of leading from within. It has been an honor to walk alongside you on your journeys.

TO MY TEAM AND COLLABORATORS
Thank you for your hard work, insights, and dedication to bringing this book to life. Your efforts have made this vision a reality, and I'm grateful for every late night and brainstorming session that brought us here.

TO MY FRIENDS AND COMMUNITY
Thank you for cheering me on, sharing your wisdom, and reminding me of the power of connection. Your encouragement has meant the world to me.

AND FINALLY, TO YOU, THE READER

Thank you for choosing this book and for investing in yourself. Writing it was a labor of love, and my hope is that it will inspire you to step into your potential, lead with authenticity, and create a life that reflects who you truly are.

This book stands as a testament to the belief that none of us walks alone. It reflects every conversation, lesson, and moment that has shaped me.

To everyone who has been part of this journey—thank you. Your impact is immeasurable, and I carry it with me always.

Chet

ABOUT THE AUTHOR

Chet Hirani

Chet Hirani is a renowned Executive High Performance Business Coach, TEDx speaker, and the founder of NYOC (Not Your Ordinary Coach), a platform dedicated to empowering leaders to unlock their full potential by aligning their internal energy with external impact. Known for his straight-talking, results-driven approach, Chet specialises in helping individuals and organisations break through limitations, achieve 10x results, and thrive in the face of challenges.

Chet's journey into coaching and leadership development is deeply personal. From navigating a health scare to overcoming professional redundancy, his experiences taught him the importance of resilience, self-awareness, and authenticity. Drawing on these lessons, he has shaped a career dedicated to guiding others through their own transformational journeys.

As a former corporate leader, martial arts instructor, and endurance athlete, Chet brings a unique perspective to his work. Whether teaching discipline and focus through martial arts, building emotional intelligence in boardrooms, or inspiring action from the TEDx stage, his message remains consistent: true leadership begins within.

Through his proprietary framework, the 5 States of Optimisation, Chet equips leaders with the tools to master their energy, align their actions with their values, and create a lasting impact in both their personal and professional lives. His coaching methodology combines practical strategies, powerful insights, and actionable steps, making his work accessible and transformational for leaders at every stage.

Chet's ability to connect deeply with his clients, challenge them to think bigger, and inspire meaningful change has earned him recognition as a trusted advisor to executives, entrepreneurs, and professionals across industries globally.

Beyond coaching, Chet's passion for personal growth extends into his own life. Whether cycling 180 miles for charity, mentoring emerging leaders, or sharing stories with his wife, Romi, and daughter, Lana, he lives the principles he teaches: leading from within every step of the way.

> *"Leadership isn't about commanding results; it's about inspiring transformation. The greatest leaders don't just create success they create a legacy."*

SCAN HERE TO
LEARN MORE ABOUT

www.ingramcontent.com/pod-product-compliance
Lightning Source LLC
Chambersburg PA
CBHW061134120626
46546CB00005B/1781